What People Are Saying About *The Underground Church*...

If you want to better understand the move of God inside China, *The Underground Church* is a great read.

—*David L. Meyer*
CEO, Hand of Hope
Joyce Meyer Ministries

Author Eugene Bach takes us inside the church movement that sparked the largest revival the earth has ever seen. What's more, he does not write as an outsider. Instead, he explains from firsthand experience details about the house churches, much of which has never before been published.

—*Billy Humphrey*
Director, International House of Prayer Atlanta

On my first visit to the underground church in China, I was struck by the raw courage of its members. I remember being ready to teach when the Holy Spirit came and called many of the young men and women to martyrdom; those not called were disappointed! It is their courage, their passionate commitment to Jesus, and their total sacrifice of self that sets them apart, and it is our privilege to partner with them. If you take it to heart, this book will transform your life.

—*Lieutenant Colonel (Retired) Jan Ransom MBE*
Director, Flame International

The Underground Church gives an unparalleled perspective into the revival and the emergence of the House Church movement. I have had the privilege of being able to travel and minister in China for the last thirty years and have been able to experience the growth of this enormous revival firsthand. I was deeply touched by this book and can give it my warmest recommendation. *The Underground Church* will inspire you and challenge you. As a Chinese pastor said to me recently, "If God can send a revival like this to China, He can send one anywhere."

—*Eivind Froen*
Missions Strategist
Founder of YWAM Norway

In the West, we have problems grasping what is really going on in the most populated country in the world. Eugene gives us a unique insight into the things God is doing in China. We learn how the church has been organized, and we get to know about many of the underground networks. We get to hear about the miracles in Bible printing, evangelism, and church planting. At the same time, the book is not hiding the human weaknesses and challenges. In spite of difficulties, these churches are all consumed with one thing: "How can we fulfill the Great Commission and bring the gospel of Jesus Christ to every people group?"

—*Noralv Askeland*
Director, Ministries Without Borders Philippines

The Underground Church is written by someone in the field who has years of experience with the House Church movement in China. For the first time, we get an inside view and a little grasp of this great work God has developed under severe circumstances. Having traveled multiple times within this network of churches and seen firsthand the work of God, and having personal friendship with the authors, I can verify the trustworthiness of this book. Enjoy your reading.

—*Erik Jensen*
AsiaLink Norway
National leader, Foursquare Norway

After working in China for more than thirty years with the underground House Church, I enthusiastically recommend this book to anybody and everybody who is truly interested in what God is doing in China. Eugene Bach reveals for the first time some of the most miraculous things that God has done in China, and I can verify their authenticity.

—*Rev. Rauno Jalavisto*
China Coordinator, Keymedia, Finland

THE UNDER GROUND CHURCH

EUGENE**BACH** & BROTHER**ZHU**

WHITAKER
HOUSE

Original manuscript edited by Minna.

THE UNDERGROUND CHURCH

Back to Jerusalem, Inc.
277 Lower Airport Rd.
Lumberton, MS 39455
update@backtojersualem.com
www.backtojerusalem.com
www.facebook.com/pages/Back-to-Jerusalem/117360681628804

ISBN: 978-1-62911-157-5
eBook ISBN: 978-1-62911-158-2
Printed in the United States of America
© 2012, 2014 by Back to Jerusalem, Inc.

Whitaker House
1030 Hunt Valley Circle
New Kensington, PA 15068
www.whitakerhouse.com

Library of Congress Cataloging-in-Publication Data

Bach, Eugene, 1976–
The underground church / Eugene Bach and Brother Zhu.
    pages cm
Includes bibliographical references and index.
    ISBN 978-1-62911-157-5 (trade pbk. : alk. paper) — ISBN 978-1-62911-158-2 (ebook : alk. paper) 1. China—Church history—20th century. 2. China—Church history—21st century. I. Title.
    BR1288.B33 2014
    275.1'082—dc23

                            2014032716

3 4 5 6 7 8 9 10 11 12 **UJ** 23 22 21 20 19 18 17 16

Contents

Foreword

God wants to take you on a path that you could never imagine!

Greetings from "the Heavenly Man." As a follower of Jesus, I am your partner in patiently enduring the suffering that comes to those who belong to His kingdom. The Bible tells us, *"Jesus Christ is the same yesterday and today and forever"* (Hebrews 13:8). And Jesus Himself tells us the following truth: *"I am the way, and the truth, and the life. No one comes to the Father except through me"* (John 14:6).

Before the God who loves us, I sincerely recommend to you this great book, *The Underground Church*. I can assure you that if you truly surrender yourself to God's purposes, this book will not only convert your old, wrong concept about being a missionary but will also guide you onto a radical mission path. Thanks be to God!

As you read this work, you will be amazed at so many wonderful acts that God is doing in the Chinese church today. The Back to Jerusalem vision is not merely a call to the Chinese church; Western believers of this age should also share a part in it. Perhaps your specific plan or commitment differs from mine. But, remember, Jesus' Great Commission is for everyone who follows Him: "Preach this good news about the kingdom through the world for a witness to all nations."

O Lord! May Your kingdom come down upon China, the Middle East, and Jerusalem! Surely, God's time to move has come near! Through our Lord Jesus' death on the cross and the power that raised Him from the dead, the Holy Spirit will take us step-by-step into the very destiny to which God has called us in the last days—to go and spread Jesus' great love among the nations that are full of atheism, Buddhism, and Hinduism, and those that are in the Middle East.

With God's truthful words, we can say with full conviction that the good news about Jesus Christ is going to save all who believe. Descendants of Ishmael and Isaac alike can be saved by believing in Jesus' name! Will you accept and respond to God's call for your life, and then start to work together with Him?

—*Brother Yun*
Author, *The Heavenly Man*

Introduction:
A Miracle of Bibles for China

I was finally able to sit down with the mysterious Brother Ren. He was seated across from me at a small wooden table and seemed to be deep in thought as he began to tell me about the things that he had seen in China over the past thirty years.

It is not easy to arrange a meeting with Brother Ren. Some would say that it is next to impossible. Brother Ren, also known as the "Flying Finn," can meet with you for dinner one evening, preach a message on the opposite side of the globe before you even wake up the following morning, and be back in time to greet you for lunch. It had taken a lot of planning, and nothing short of an act of God, to "trap" him long enough to talk with him about his vast experiences with the underground House Church in China.

Brother Ren has been the pastor of Brother Yun—more widely known as "the Heavenly Man"—for many years. He is also the official translator for Brother Yun, because he is one of the few Mandarin speakers in the West who can understand Yun's strong rural dialect.

Like most people, you've probably never heard of Brother Ren. Keep in mind that in secret organizations, such as the CIA, the Chinese PSB (Public Security Bureau), or the KGB in the former Soviet Union, recognition and fame are synonymous with failure. This reality is also true for Brother Ren. Any fame or advertisement of his achievements would be a major failure, as they would most likely lead to the shutting down of projects and missionary work in many closed countries around the world.

So, Brother Ren and I were sitting on a remote island in Northern Europe. The island, only about one kilometer across with no signs of human life, had no running water or electricity. It was truly a remarkable place, the complete opposite of the crowded and dusty streets of rural China that Brother Ren has called home for over three decades.

Brother Ren has been responsible for printing and delivering more than eleven million Bibles in China; organizing the training of over two hundred thousand Chinese Sunday School teachers; arranging for the training of thousands of pastors, evangelists, and missionaries; funneling tens of millions of dollars directly to the mission field; and participating in what may quite possibly be the largest missionary movement in the history of mankind.

I started off the interview with this question: "I know that you have been one of the few people able to print and distribute the Bible in China. How did that happen? How did that start?" He leaned back in his chair and paused for a moment to think, then sat up and excitedly moved to the edge of his seat as he began to tell the story in vivid detail.

What follows is a true account as told by Brother Ren. The facts have been cross-checked and confirmed with other participants in the events mentioned. Never before has this true tale of Christian boldness been written down or told in any formal manner.

"It was not easy to get Bibles into China after Deng Xiaoping opened up the nation for international trade in the 1980s. The Bibles were trickling in one by one, and it was considered a huge success if one believer in a thousand could get their hands on a Bible. This carried on even in the 1990s. One of the growing trends at the time was bringing Bibles into China in suitcases. Many missionaries and students from around the world began to travel to Hong Kong and cross the border to China to carry in Bibles and drop them off at predesignated collection points. In those days, most Bibles came into Hong Kong from Japan, because Japan was one of the few places in Asia where the high-quality paper needed for Bible printing could be purchased.

"During the 1980s, I was living in Taiwan and preaching the gospel there. The Lord had placed a heavy burden on my heart for China, and in the 1990s, my family and I moved to Hong Kong. I had taken tour groups from the West into China and was familiar with Hong Kong and southern China. The needs of the church in those days were even greater than today, because, in many ways, it was still in the beginning stages. With so many needs, it was hard to decide where to begin, but the need for Bibles throughout China was so huge that I decided to start there. I became a 'donkey' for Jesus and began to carry Bibles into China. I often took the Bibles into the southern area and dropped them off in places like Guilin.

"After carrying Bibles into China for several months, I began to feel challenged by the expense involved. Being a donkey for Jesus was not cheap. I sat down and figured out the actual cost of taking Bibles into China. If you calculated the cost of printing the Bibles in Japan, shipping them to Hong Kong, paying travel expenses for the courier (such as airfare, food, and lodging), and losing some Bibles to confiscation, it was a very expensive operation. I figured it out to be more than U.S.$50 per Bible—and that was in the 1990s.

"God gave me the idea of printing Bibles inside China, but I was a courier, not a printer. Who was I to begin a printing operation? I went to people from several missions organizations that I knew had a history of doing these kinds of projects. I asked them what they thought about the idea of partnering with me to print Bibles in China. Every time I mentioned the idea, I got one of two responses. They either said that they had tried before and it didn't work, or they hadn't tried before and didn't want to. The Bible League said that they had just made a large financial investment in an expensive printing press in Japan, so printing in China would make that investment obsolete. Many organizations had 'burned their hands' in China and didn't want to try again.

"I was disappointed at the results of trying to find a partner who knew what they were doing. I had no clue what to do next, but the Lord would not take the burden from my mind. On one occasion in 1994, I was able to have a meeting with a well-known businessman from Taiwan who owned one of the major skyscrapers in prestigious Causeway Bay, Hong Kong. We met and discussed the idea of printing inside China. The business owner was a Christian and wanted to use his resources to help the church in China. He would later be one of the people who helped get Brother Yun out of China.

"The Taiwanese Christian businessman liked the idea of printing Bibles in China and agreed with me that there must be a better way than carrying the Bibles across the border in suitcases. He arranged for his secretary to meet me at the Hong Kong airport, and she gave me the money to begin the process of searching for a way to print Bibles inside China.

"From Hong Kong, I traveled to Guilin and contacted a professor at one of the local universities who was a good friend of Brother Yun. This is the same professor who spent time living with Brother Yun and who painstakingly handwrote Yun's entire testimony on a pad of paper. That pad of paper eventually led to a book known around the world today as *The Heavenly Man*.

"'I have someone I would like you to meet,' the professor said to me when I saw him in Guilin. In China, you don't just look up potential partners in the yellow pages; you are either introduced to them or you don't get any partners at all. With most things in China, it is not about what you know but *who* you know.

"The professor thought that it would be beneficial for me to meet his friend. He knew what I was up to and knew the risks involved with printing Bibles in China, so he connected me with someone who he thought would be experienced enough to help me tackle the dangerous task. I needed someone who could help me navigate the underground world of illegal activity in China.

"When I met with the professor's friend for the first time, he looked like he was straight out of a movie. The man looked like a CIA agent. Just by looking at him, you could tell that he was used to living on the other side of authority. There was something that was very shady about him. He was wearing a hunting vest, his thick black hair was pulled back into a ponytail, and he just looked like someone who seemed to be fully aware of everything going on around him. When he walked into the room, I thought that I had been compromised. I thought that the professor had told the wrong person, and now China's Public Security Bureau had assigned this man to take me down.

"'This is my friend Simon [not his real name],' the professor said as I reached out to shake his hand. Even though I had my suspicions, I quickly found myself falling victim to Simon's quick wit and charm. However, I remained very cautious the first time that I met him and chose not to share with him the idea for printing Bibles.

"I soon went back to Hong Kong but often traveled to Guilin. Many foreigners liked to take Bibles to Guangzhou, and their favorite place to stay was The Garden Hotel. Because of this fact, it was heavily watched, and most of the rooms were wired. The hotel was a gold mine for the Chinese authorities, because many foreign guests would talk about their ideas and projects, carelessly mentioning names of coworkers. All of this information was thus made available for the Chinese authorities to collect and exploit. This was one of the reasons I chose Guilin for my meetings instead of more traditional places like Guangzhou or Shenzhen. Guilin was frequented by tourists and government officials, rather than by conspicuous missionaries.

"On one of my trips to Guilin, the phone in my hotel room rang soon after I had arrived. I answered the phone, and it was Simon. I wondered how he knew I was in town, because I hadn't told anyone that I was going to Guilin. No one should have known which hotel I was staying at, let alone the very room I was in! Immediately, I was suspicious.

"'*Ni hao*,' I said as a general greeting. Simon invited me to come to his home for dinner, a huge honor in China. I was still suspicious. He seemed to know too much. I thought that dinner might just be a ruse to trap me, but there was another part of me that said to trust him. My policy was to follow the old Ronald Reagan strategy of 'Trust, but verify.' I accepted the invitation.

"I took a taxi to the location he had told me to go to, but I didn't go directly to the address. Instead, I asked the driver to keep driving. We drove a few blocks down the road, and then I walked around the area, looking for anything suspicious and for possible escape routes if I needed to leave in a hurry.

"Simon would later tell me that he had contacts in the hotel I was staying in who had been instructed to look out for me and alert him if they saw me. I didn't know it then, but Simon would soon play a huge part in my life, and we would grow to be very close friends.

"When I went into the home, the house was filled with some of the most amazing aromas I have ever smelled in my life. Simon was an amazing, world-class chef! He warmly welcomed me into his home and showed me around. It is not easy to explain, but we had an immediate connection. Simon was a new friend, but it felt as if I had known him for years.

"I had never eaten such good food in all my life! Simon was able to work magic with food and put together flavors that danced across your tongue. After dinner, Simon showed me his photography awards and shared stories with me about his family's grand and royal history. As the evening came to a close, Simon invited me to return and spend time with his family.

"I later went and spent time with his parents and grandparents. I am usually very secretive about my vision and projects for China, but with Simon's family I shared exactly what God had called me to do. I shared with them about my ideas regarding the movement of God in the world and what I felt God had told me regarding the future of China and the Chinese underground House Church. Upon hearing my story, Simon's grandmother took me by the hand, looked intensely in my eyes, and asked me one of the strangest questions I had ever been asked: 'Would you like to be adopted by our family?'

"I heard the words that she said but immediately thought that I must not be able to understand her Chinese. She asked again, 'Would you like to be adopted by our family?' As she said it again, I realized that I did in fact understand the words coming out of her mouth; they just didn't make sense to me. Why would I want to be adopted? I was more than forty years old. The time to adopt me was over. Besides, I had my own mother, father, and grandparents.

"I began to tell myself that maybe the family needed money or some 'golden goose' to help their family with financial problems and saw that this foreigner might provide them with a way out of poverty. I took that opportunity to reiterate that I was only a missionary who was financially poor and had nothing to offer. The grandmother looked at me. You could tell from the expression on her face that my financial status had never even crossed her mind.

"The grandmother was persistent. She felt that God was telling her to bring me into her family. I also felt the presence of the Lord and humbly accepted their great honor. Together, we went through the entire official process. I filled out all of the paperwork, and, upon completion, we had an official ceremony marking the time when I became an adopted member of Simon's family.

"From that day on, Simon and I became inseparable ministry partners. Whenever people saw us and asked who we were, I jokingly replied that we were brothers. This was funny to everyone who witnessed it, because it was obvious that this Chinese man and a Western European were not brothers. We would always tell people that we had different mothers but the same Father.

"Simon became my partner in crime to print the Bible in China. He turned out to be an amazingly resourceful man.

"Once we decided to print the Bible in China, we quickly arrived at the same conclusion: It couldn't be done. But we just continued to believe in God. I began to bring the Chinese Bible to Simon in pieces. Simon had been a photography instructor and had many students who had graduated and started their own businesses. Many of those businesses were major photo shops. Piece by piece, we desired to build an archive of photographic negatives of the Bible for printers.

"Simon's former students were everywhere, and they all welcomed us with warm and open arms. Everywhere we went, Simon would joke with them as he introduced me as his brother. After the formalities of meeting with the photography shop owners, we began to talk about our objectives. Eventually, we were able to find a place to make the film for the Bible printing. After some time, I received a phone call letting me know that the film was complete. The film was rolled up in newspaper when I picked it up.

"Once we had the film in our hands, we began to meet with each of the students again to see if we could get the Bible printed. When the students saw us coming, they were excited, I think for two reasons. One, they loved Simon. He really knew how to make a grand entrance and make his presence known. He didn't have much money, but no one knew that. Simon was able to present himself in a way that impressed people and made them think that he had a lot of money. He knew only two English words, and he used them all the time, which made a big impression on the rural Chinese who thought Simon must have been really cultured to be able to speak English. Little did they know that the only two phrases Simon knew were 'No problem' and 'Sit down, please.' He used those two phrases all the time and was really good at pronouncing them well. The other reason I think they were excited to see us is that they saw a foreigner, i.e., an opportunity to make money. One by one, we shared with them our desire to print the Bible. Each time we told one of them, their heart would sink and they would hang their head in disappointment. 'Dear honorable teacher, you are always welcome in our place. We would do anything to please you and assist you, but we are unable to help you on this project,' they would often say in reply.

"I understood their challenge. If they agreed to help us, their livelihood would be in danger. At that time, a law had just come out that said that anyone caught printing a Bible would be arrested, their business confiscated, and they would be given a minimum of seven years in prison. We visited twelve to fifteen different photography shops, all of which were owned by Simon's former students, but every one of them was reluctant to help us. Even though I understood, I still found the fact that they wouldn't print the Bible a bit perplexing. I mean, we were traveling in the kinds of places that I had never been to before in the interior of China. These printers said they were not able to print Bibles illegally because the risk was too high, but most of them printed many illegal things that I considered to be much more dangerous than printing the Bible. They were printing pornography and antigovernment and anti-Communist materials. Personally, I thought that those materials were more damning for the government than a mere religious book.

"More time passed, and we visited all potential printing places Simon could think of. We traveled to places far from the city center and met with people who really knew the underground printing world well. We searched high and low and came up empty-handed. We felt that this vision was directly from the Lord and were really confused. If God wanted us to do this, then why were all of the doors closing on us? If God truly had given us the vision to print these Bibles in China, then why did every road lead to a dead end?

[One day,] "Simon had returned to the city. We were standing in the town square, and a sense of depression descended upon me. I looked at him and said, 'Simon, we have done all that we can do. There is nothing more than can be done.'

"'We haven't done *all* that we can do,' he replied.

"'Of course we have. Is there a place that we have not tried? Do you know someone else that we haven't talked to yet? It seems that everyone has turned us away because it is just too dangerous to print Bibles in China.'

"'No. We have not tried *that* place.'

"I turned to look at the place he was pointing to. I saw a massive building within walking distance with a big red banner draped across the front. As I began to make sense of the bold Chinese characters on the banner, I realized what Simon was proposing was suicide!

"'We can't go there!' I said quickly. 'No way!'

"'Why not?' he replied.

"I looked at his face, expecting there to be a smirk or a laugh; maybe he was trying to lighten the mood from all of our disappointments. But as I studied him, I realized that he had a look of seriousness in his eyes. He wasn't joking.

"I looked back up at the banner. The sign indicated that the building in front of us was the official printing headquarters for the Chinese government.

"'How can we honestly tell the Lord that we have done all that we could if we have not?' he said indignantly. 'I cannot go to the Lord and tell Him in good conscience that I have done everything in my power to do what I believe He has called us to do. There is a printing press right there in front of us; all we have to do is try.'

"He was serious and had to be stopped. 'Simon! Look at that building. It is the official printing press. Take a good long look at those guards. If we go over there with our request, it is possible they will shoot us. This is not funny. We are talking about a serious situation here.'

"Simon had made up his mind. He believed strongly that a believer who has been given a task from the Lord such as this one must put all of his or her trust in the Lord. Only walking by faith will allow us to see the glory of the Lord.

"I tried to reason with him, but he compelled me to trust in the Lord. I was encouraged by his faith but grounded by reason. As I looked at Simon, I knew that this was something he felt strongly about, and he would go into that building with or without me. On the other hand, I felt that it was not only hopeless to try, but we were needlessly endangering our lives and work.

"It was at that moment that I wondered what kind of family I had been adopted into. I was reluctant to go, but as I looked back at Simon, he looked at me with a smirk on his face, patted me on the back, and said his famous phrase: 'No problem.'

"Together we walked to the main gate. We didn't have an appointment with anyone (you don't just walk up to one of these places unannounced). Simon boldly approached one of the guards—acting as if he had every right to walk into any top-security area in China—and said, 'Hello, I need to speak with the director. Can you please let him know that I am here?'

"The guards did exactly as they were told without missing a beat. They called the director on his direct line. 'Sir, there are two gentlemen here who have arrived without an appointment and would like to see you,' the guard said. I could hear the voice on the other end of the phone reply, 'Send them up to the fourth floor. I am waiting for them.' I stood still. The guard motioned for us to go on up. I looked over at Simon in disbelief, but he didn't look back. He was acting like things were going along just as he had envisioned.

"We arrived on the fourth floor and walked into the director's office. The office looked as large as a full-sized basketball court. It was decorated in hand-carved rosewood and made a very imposing impression on everyone who entered that office door. I could tell right away that this was a guy with enough power to have us arrested on the spot. I didn't know exactly how to start the conversation. I mean, how do you begin? *Hello sir, I know that you are employed by the government to print its most important propaganda in this country of more than one billion people, but would it also be possible for you to print this here Bible that has been outlawed?* What we were doing was absurd in every way.

"'Hello, hello,' he said warmly. 'Please come in and sit. How may I help you?'

"'We have come to see about having this book printed,' Simon explained to him. Coming from behind, I slowly unwrapped the Bible that I had been carefully concealing. This was the point of no return. Once I handed him the Bible and he saw what we were doing, there would be no explaining our way out of this.

"I slowly reached across to give him the Bible. He took it, looked at the cover, and ran his hands over the surface. He opened the Bible and flipped through the pages quickly, as if to examine the quality of the binding and to gauge the paper thickness. He then turned to a certain passage in Genesis. He flipped through the chapters in Genesis deliberately, as if he knew exactly what he was looking for. I stood there in shock as he began to read a story from the book of Genesis! He read aloud the story of Ishmael. After he read the passage, he asked us, 'Are you Christians?'

"The room was silent. His question echoed in the room as well as in our minds. It took only a few seconds to answer, but the silence seemed to linger for an eternity.

"'Yes,' we said, refusing to deny the name of Christ, but still confused as to what would happen next.

"'Well then, doesn't that make you sons of Abraham?' he asked as a matter of fact. We nodded our heads in agreement. 'So am I. I, too, am a son of Abraham,' he said as he handed back the Bible, indicating that he was actually a Muslim. Immediately, he asked, 'How many books do you want me to print?' I was not able to answer. I was in a state of shock. 'No matter, I will call you when I have the sample ready.' We shook hands, turned, and walked out the door—just like that!

"God is amazing, but the miracles were not done yet. Two weeks later, I received a call telling me that my package was finished. I met Simon, and we traveled there together. I arranged to get a small fold-up bag to carry the book or books in and also had stuffed my pockets with the needed cash because I had made it clear that we were not paying for the samples until the product was complete. I didn't want a situation where I paid for a project that was later reported to the authorities so the printer could take my money while I was detained by the police.

"When we arrived at the printing headquarters, we met with the Muslim fellow, and he led us down to a storage area. He walked up to these two massive doors and opened them. I almost fell over—the room was filled with Bibles! The stacks were higher than I have ever seen in my entire life. There were thousands of them.

"I dropped the small bag that I brought to carry them in; it was useless now. I couldn't fit twenty thousand Bibles in my pitiful duffel bag. We now had a huge load of Bibles in China, sitting in the warehouse of the Communist printing headquarters! There was no way on earth we could get these Bibles out of the building undetected. I looked over at Simon and asked, 'Great! What in the world are we going to do now?' Simon just smiled and replied, 'No problem.'

"Simon had a friend during elementary school who had sat next to him in class. As I said earlier, in China, it's not about what you know but *who* you know—referred to in Chinese as *guanxi*. Simon pulled out a phone and called his old classmate. I didn't know it then, but his old school chum was the commanding officer of the entire southern China armed forces. I could hear Simon using very polite language when talking with him over the phone. The commanding officer talked with him and, after some time, asked Simon, 'Simon, what is it I can do for you?'

"'Well, we happen to have a very sensitive document of a secure nature here at the Communist printing headquarters, and we would like some assistance in getting it to another location.'

"I could not hear the reply, but they talked for a little longer, and then Simon hung up the phone. I asked him what his friend said, and Simon smiled at me and said, 'He said, "No problem."'"

"Within minutes, a huge military truck came barreling our way. There were three men sitting in the truck and two men hanging on both sides. They backed the truck up to the warehouse and began to load all of the 'sensitive, top-secret' documents. We didn't even lift a finger; the soldiers loaded it all on the truck in no time. Simon told the driver that we needed the 'sensitive' materials to be taken to the airport. The distance from the printing headquarters to the airport was thirty to forty miles [thirty-eight to sixty-four kilometers]. During that time in China, there were many road-blocks on the way to the airport to check documentation. Though there were several roadblocks between us and the airport, we were never stopped once. As we drove up to the checkpoints, the police and soldiers saluted us and allowed us to pass without ever check-ing the cargo.

"When we arrived at the airport, we had another problem: There was no way to fly this cargo to Beijing on any of the shipping routes. We had looked into all the different options, and noth-ing was working out at the airport. Simon looked at me when I was at the peak of my frustration and said in perfect English, 'No problem.'

"While he was in school—something I believe God had planned all along—on one side of him sat the future commanding officer of the southern armed forces in China, and on the other side sat a boy who would become the director of China's largest cargo company. Simon called his other friend and told him he had 'top-secret' military cargo that he needed to be flown to Beijing. His friend said that he would arrange it right away. Within min-utes, we had the military truck pull onto the tarmac of the heavily guarded airport.

"I was standing below the plane just in awe. I had never seen the nose of a plane open up like that. The truck pulled up to the plane, and the soldiers worked together with the crew to load up every single box of Bibles. I was not allowed to fly with the cargo, so I walked inside the airport and got on the next flight to Beijing.

"I called Brother Yun and our other friends who still live in China today to come and help us at the Beijing airport. There were thirteen people in Beijing waiting for the plane to land. I wish I had brought my camera! These Chinese brothers were hiding behind trees and watching the planes intently as they came in, trying to see if the plane with the Bibles was landing. It was late in the evening, and Brother Yun and the rest of the team had brought several vehicles to help with transportation. To get into the cargo area, they had to register their names. They all registered with fake names.

"Small vehicles came, pulling a train of carts loaded with the Bibles. Sitting next to the driver of one small vehicle was Simon. He was just smiling and laughing as if we were all having the best time of our lives. I opened the back door of one of the carts loaded with Bibles. As I opened the door, I noticed that the big red Chinese characters for 'Bible' had been written on the box. I looked at the other boxes, and they, too, had been written on. All of the boxes had the words *Shengjing* written on them in enormous bright red ink. Immediately, I thought we had been compromised.

"'Simon! Look! Someone has written the word "Bible" on all of these boxes.'

Simon began laughing. This guy was really having the best time of his entire life.

"'I did that,' Simon said. 'As the soldiers were loading and unloading God's Word, I took out a red marker and put the word "Bible" on every box.'

"'Why? Why would you do something like that?'

"'Because,' he explained, 'I wanted to see if God was truly with us.'

"'Please do not ever do that again.'

"Before morning came, we had loaded all of the Bibles into privately owned vehicles and were able to ship them out all over China to Christians who were hungry to have the Word of God. Not one Bible was lost from that operation.

"The miracles, of course, did not stop there. They happen every time we do a Bible printing. A few months after that miraculous airlift, the situation changed when one of the delivery company workers was loading Bibles and a box broke open, revealing the illegal contents. Once again, Simon called his friend and asked for a temporary shelter for our 'sensitive items.' The army trucks came and picked up all of the cargo and took it to an ammunition depot guarded by around fifteen thousand troops. I have often wondered if the government will ever know what critical role they play in the domestic Bible printing we continue to do to this day."

In the chapters that follow, you will learn much more about how God is moving in the Chinese underground House Church.

—*Eugene Bach*

*This book is dedicated to all those
who will join God in what He is doing
through the Chinese House Church.*

Part 1:
Uncovering the Mystery

A Bible delivery van in the 1990s

Brother Ren with Peter Xu and his sister

Enoch Wang, Zhang Rongliang, and Brother Yun

1
The Crimson Cross

Brother Yun and others representing the Chinese House Church travel the globe to share what God is doing in China. As they do, people ask many questions, such as "What is the 'House Church'?" "What is its origin?" "What is it like?" "Where is it headed?"

At the same time, there is a great deal of misinformation about the Chinese church being disseminated in many nations around the globe, and it is causing people confusion. Some individuals spread this misinformation maliciously for personal gain. Yet most of it is spread ignorantly by unwitting foreigners or overseas Chinese who have had the wool pulled over their eyes by the Chinese government.

Some would have us believe that there is no House Church in China! Others would have us imagine that Chinese believers are just a ragtag group of unorganized country bumpkins making bumbling and misguided attempts at preaching the gospel. (These stories tend to come from groups that value the number of advanced theological degrees a pastor has more than they do his calling from God.) Still others will go as far as to say that the House Church is an outdated, irrelevant nuisance to Christianity in mainland China because there is now complete freedom of religion there. (This is the official party line fed to many unsuspecting foreigners.)

A main purpose of this book is to dispel such rumors—hopefully, once and for all—as well as to share with you the "Back to Jerusalem" vision embraced by the Chinese House Church. This vision is to preach the gospel to the unreached peoples in the eastern provinces of China and in all the countries between the border of China and the city of Jerusalem. My coworkers and I at Back to Jerusalem International are partnering with the church in China as it seeks to fulfill this vision.

We invite you now to join us as we open the Bamboo Curtain and step into the hearts and lives of the millions of believers who make up the Chinese House Church.

THE "RISING RED STAR"

China is a place of mystery and fascinating discoveries. In the minds of people the world over, the very name of this country invokes images of dragon dances, clanging gongs, the Forbidden City, and rich culture. The Chinese are a proud people with a long history that has left fingerprints all over the development of humankind.

Not only is the history of the Chinese people rich and vibrant, but the future of the Chinese people has never looked better. Today, China is considered to be the "rising red star" in the East that is beginning to challenge the world's largest superpower. Children across the world, from India to the United States, are starting to learn Mandarin Chinese as their second language, and previously scoffed-at traditional Chinese medicine is being embraced worldwide.

China's rapid growth can be seen almost everywhere in the nation. Those who travel to China end up finding cities that are developing faster than the travel guidebooks can keep up with. The nation's expansion is a major issue in news stories and political debates around the world.

AN "EXPLODING" MOVEMENT OF GOD

However, behind China's rapid economic growth is a movement that cannot be seen on a guided tour of Beijing's ancient streets and monuments. You will not learn about it while studying Chinese at the Beijing Language and Cultural University, nor will it be addressed in Western political debates. Yet the movement is one of the largest in the world and is shaping every facet of China today.

The underground house churches of China (collectively referred to as the Chinese House Church) are exploding at a phenomenal rate. The Chinese church is one of the greatest miracles in modern history. Never before have so many people in such a short time left one belief system for another without a hostile takeover. Lives are being completely transformed every day by nothing more than the gospel of Jesus Christ and the display of His miraculous power. Many experts claim that there are about thirty thousand people coming to Christ in China daily. That is a shockingly large number of people, coming from every age group, ethnic group, and income level.

As China rises in global economic prowess, the Chinese are making increasingly more money and enjoying more freedoms than ever before, but true happiness and fulfillment are managing to evade them. The expectation of finding happiness in riches, mixed with atheistic materialism, is leaving many people feeling empty and without purpose. China has indeed become a world superpower, but her fast-paced economic development has led many of its citizens to search for a joy and purpose that cannot be purchased in the local market nor copied and sold beside Rolex knockoffs in the back streets of Shenzhen.

Chinese parents are scraping together money to put their children through the very best schools in China or abroad so they will have a chance at grabbing some of the new money in China's burgeoning business world. The better schools allow children to have special opportunities not available by any other means in China, so doting parents are more than willing to do anything to get them into those schools. The parents often go into debt, work twelve-hour days every day of the week, and pour all they have into their one child so that he or she may take advantage of every opportunity for career advancement. It is thus a serious blow to the entire family when their little emperor or empress becomes a

Christian, leaves the competitive rat race, and forsakes all to serve Jesus Christ as Lord and Savior.

Amy (not her real name) is a prime example. She is an only child and was the first in her family to attend a university. Both of her parents worked for the Communist government. Her mother was an auditor and her father a family planning official who enforced China's infamous one-child policy. They used all of their combined resources to put their daughter through one of the best schools in Jiangxi Province, and Amy eventually received a degree in international business. However, during her time at the university, she was introduced to Jesus Christ and ultimately became a Christian— and a radical one, at that.

Amy left the big cities—ripe with opportunities for a girl with her prestigious background—and instead went to work for a small hotel in the rural area of Guangxi Province. She did so in order to preach the gospel to the ethnic minorities living in that area. Her reputation began to grow as she preached the gospel to everyone she came in contact with. Soon, her passion for the gospel grabbed the attention of some underground House Church leaders who wanted to meet with her. Two representatives visited her at the rural hotel where she was working and heard about her vision to preach the gospel. They were surprised to find that Amy did not even know it was illegal to preach Christ in China. Even as a Chinese, she had never heard of the underground house churches. Amy quit working at the hotel that very day and dedicated her life to serving beside underground Chinese Christians. In only a couple of days, she found herself in Sichuan Province helping the earthquake victims through the efforts of the underground House Church networks.

Amy later traveled to another city to help the underground House Church and moved in with a foreign missionary family. Soon after her arrival, in love with Jesus but completely unaware of what was or was not illegal in her own country, she began to go out into the streets and proclaim the message of salvation. She then made evangelistic tracts and handed them out throughout the city.

Thinking it would be helpful for people who got saved through the tracts and needed more information, she wrote the exact contact information of the Western missionary family on the back of every tract. Needless to say, the Western missionary was alarmed and told Amy to act wisely in a country where it is illegal to proselytize.

Clearly, the underground House Church movement is therefore not only mysterious to people outside China, but even to those like Amy who live there. A singer named Zhao Ming (also called Benjamin), who is very well-known inside China, became famous when he and his family won the Chinese version of *American Idol* by singing a Christian song about loving one's family. He went on tour in Finland with Brother Yun, a well-known Chinese evangelist whose life has been documented in the popular book *The Heavenly Man*. During that time, Zhao Ming read Brother Yun's book and was blown away by learning of the torture and sacrifice that he had endured in China for being a follower of Christ. "I have never heard before of those things happening to Christian believers in China," Ming said.

The fact is, every single day, thousands of people are coming to Christ in China, and the vast majority are doing it illegally. The best estimate we have that accurately depicts the current situation is that there are 130 to 150 million believers in China, and the majority of them belong to the illegal underground churches.

DEMYSTIFYING THE **CHINESE HOUSE CHURCH**

As I wrote earlier, people all over the world are asking questions about the underground church in China. They want to know the answers to questions such as the following: "What is the Chinese House Church?" "Why is that term even used?" "How did it start?" "How can you prove it exists?" "Who does it consist of?" "Where is it?" "How does it continue to grow at such an astronomical rate?" "Why are the Chinese experiencing a revival when other countries on their borders are not?"

My coauthor, Brother Zhu, and I will attempt to answer each of these questions while demystifying the Chinese House Church. We hope that anyone who reads this book will be able to gain a basic understanding of what exactly the underground House Church of China is.

As the story unfolds, we include examples and personal testimonies from underground Chinese Christians whenever possible to help better explain certain ideas and concepts. It is important that the Chinese themselves be able to describe in their own words what they have witnessed in their nation. None of these stories has been shared in a book before, and many of them had never left the borders of China. Although these stories are factual, the names of people and places have often been changed to protect the safety of individuals who are still living and/or serving in China.

Many of the laws and restrictions on Christians in China are not easy to explain and can be controversial. There are not many official laws restricting Christians that are specifically spelled out in the same way that they are enforced. In addition, the reader must keep in mind that China is a huge country where certain laws are enforced to differing degrees from province to province and even from city to city. A believer living in Beijing may tell you that the laws are such and such, but a believer living in Chengdu may argue that the laws are different, while a Christian in Lhasa, Tibet, will say something about Chinese law that is entirely distinct from the other two.

Chinese politics are simply not easily understood by outsiders. The average tourist quickly discovers this fact when he or she tries to go between Hong Kong and the mainland. What country is Hong Kong a part of? China. Then why can an American or a European go to Hong Kong for three months without a visa but need to pay an exorbitant price for a mere thirty-day visa to cross the border into China proper? What kind of unified country has customs and immigration offices between two of its own regions?

Another example is the issue of international driver's licenses. It is no problem for most foreigners to drive in Hong Kong; they just need to use their foreign driver's license. However, just across the border in Shenzhen, foreigners are not allowed to drive until they go through the complicated and expensive process of getting a Chinese driver's license. On paper, Hong Kong is indeed a part of China, yet the laws, banking system, currencies, and, to a large degree, government systems, are all completely different. China is officially referred to as one country with two systems, but the difference between the two sides of the border is quite remarkable. Macau is another part of China that has completely different laws and policies from those of either Hong Kong or the rest of China.

Even more baffling is China's relationship with Taiwan. China says that Taiwan belongs to China, and the United Nations also takes that stance. In fact, the vast majority of the world—the United States included—affirms that claim. Yet Chinese officials cannot set foot on Taiwan's soil without permission from the independent democratic Taiwanese government.

Taiwan also has its own laws, banks, and currency. It even has its own military, which is primarily set up to defend itself against the very country that claims to own it. Much to China's outrage, America even provides Taiwan with highly secretive military equipment and training, and also frequently conducts joint military exercises with the Taiwanese.

If all those issues seem complicated and confusing, so, too, is the situation of Christians in mainland China. As stated earlier, the laws, practices, and degrees of enforcement are different from province to province, and they also change from year to year. There will be people familiar with China who will undoubtedly try to challenge the authenticity of some of this book's content, even citing their own experiences as validation, but let the reader beware of anyone who is considered to be a "China expert." The country is so complex that the term is an oxymoron.

THE FRUIT OF AN **UNDERGROUND SEED**

What China's underground house churches are experiencing at present is a combination of many different factors. One significant factor is that today's Chinese Christians are standing on the shoulders of those who sacrificed their lives in China many years ago. The current spiritual explosion is the fruit of a seed that sat underground, unseen by the outside world, for many years. This seed fought to survive through the cold, harsh winter, was watered by the blood of a myriad of martyrs, and today has grown into a mighty tree bearing so much fruit that the branches are bent and almost breaking under the weight.

At the same time, it is interesting to note that the very people who brought the gospel to China and sacrificed so much were also the very people who needed to leave before the seed could fully sprout. Foreign missionaries provided much of the support and strength for the Chinese believers in the early days. The same strength and faith that contributed to the revivals of today were a hindrance to the spiritual growth of the Chinese church in that time.

Missionaries brought with them doctrinal and cultural systems that crippled the growth of the indigenous Chinese church. Control of the church through monetary means is rarely talked about in the Bible, but because of flawed human nature, even the saintliest missionaries often wielded the power of money over the power of the Holy Spirit.

The early church in China was fascinated by the ingenuity, education, and wealth of the foreign missionaries. Since the majority of the missionaries were highly skilled in trades like medicine, they were considered by many to be superior. Even some missionaries considered themselves superior to the poor heathens they came to proselytize. However, the Chinese Christians didn't realize that these seemingly superior qualities like knowledge and wealth were not due to nationality or ethnicity but rather were the by-products of cultures massively influenced by the gospel and teachings of Jesus Christ.

There were no differences between the missionaries and the Chinese in the human sense. The missionaries were just as vulnerable to disease, needed daily nourishment, and were subject to the same temptations as any human being. The missionaries and Chinese were both initially lost sinners in need of a Savior. The difference was in their cultural backgrounds. By and large, the Western missionary had been raised in a society formed by biblical ethics and morality. The Judeo-Christian understanding of the fear of the Lord as the beginning of wisdom had helped to create a society that greatly benefited all its members. On the other hand, Chinese culture had been covered in darkness for generations under the influence of Buddhism, Taoism, and animism. This was the antithesis of light and biblical truth, and it created a dog-eat-dog society of degradation and brokenness where people were constantly oppressed.

Today, institutions of higher learning around the world often propound these ignorant and godless teachings under the auspicious title "wisdom of the East," attempting to mask their religious nature as mere ancient wisdom. Far from it, the religions of the East are responsible for a great deal of the suffering that continues to this day, not only in China but throughout Asia. As international test scores in recent years have proved, the Chinese are in no way intellectually inferior to their Western counterparts. Rather, it is the errors of these dark religions that have counteracted their extremely resourceful and productive natures. It was the Light of the World that the Chinese saw in the missionaries of yesterday, and that same Light is now piercing through the darkness of China today.

THE "**10/40 WINDOW**"

China's Christian population is currently growing, along with the nation's economic influence, medical capabilities, educational development, technological breakthroughs, and even the refinement of its leisure activities. And, alongside the growth of everything else in the country, China is becoming increasingly engaged in world missions. The Chinese church is beginning to send out missionary teams to the most dangerous regions of Southeast and Central Asia, the Middle East, and Africa. They feel called to carry out the Great Commission in areas that Christians in the Western world have largely neglected or could not even go to if they wanted to. Chinese Christians are specifically targeting the "10/40 Window," which refers to that part of the eastern hemisphere north of the equator between the ten- and forty-degree latitudes.

This vision is not unique to the Chinese but stems from the Great Commission as given to the first-century church. What makes this vision sound so novel today is that many churches in the West have lost sight of it. In many ways, the current Western missionary effort is feeding on itself, with many missions organizations becoming massive self-feeding mechanisms constantly trying to create a new fad movement. Like much of the Western church itself, missions has become a big industry that is stuck doing the same things over and over again but marketing them differently each time. The hottest new missions strategy becomes obsolete soon after it makes it to a PowerPoint presentation, but then it is just chopped up and reworked into something that sounds fresher for the next missions conference.

Once a "big name" walks out on stage with a new idea, a catchy slogan, or a clever missions idiom, we all want to buy his book, and organizations the world over basically copy and repackage it with their own logo prominently displayed. This practice may raise some financial support, but it often does very little to actually make an impact for the advancement of God's kingdom. Missions seminars quickly turn into something akin to a high school pep rally, and money raised on "Missions Sunday" ends up going more to the domestic side of comfort enhancement than for true international outreach to the lost.

This harsh evaluation of the current common procedure among Western missionary efforts may seem sacrilegious, but after one has read a plethora of new books, attended numerous meetings, and read years of e-mails in relation to Western missions, it becomes apparent that most Westerners are focused on the *thought* of doing something good rather than actually doing it. The sad truth is that the only thing tangible about many of the Western missions organizations today is the money that they raise and the shiny new offices they spend it on.

All that being said, China still has many things to learn from Western missionaries. For generations, the West has been sending its young men and women to live, serve, and die in the most unforgiving foreign lands imaginable. The Western church has done and is still doing many wonderful things for missions that shouldn't be drowned out by the circus of strategists trying to market the newest missions trend. The Chinese need all the tools Westerners can give them in order to tackle the daunting task God has placed before them.

A Christian missions strategist now living in Dallas, Texas, who is helping with the placement of Chinese missionaries, sat with me in a restaurant one evening in 2011 and reflected on his own missionary experience: "I remember going to a missions conference in the 1980s where a famous missionary had come to recruit missionaries. The missionary stood up and began to talk about being seriously alarmed about the church in the West and the growing lack of interest for missionary work. He implored us to pray for the church in the West, because there was a growing trend of young people rejecting a life of missions, and, in his mind, if the West did not send the missionaries, the world would be lost."

He paused as he remembered the anxiety of that time and how ignorant people were of the sovereign God. "Little did that missionary know," he continued, "that God was raising up a church in a country that the rest of the world had written off as a completely lost mission field, thinking it would have to be restarted in the future when the country reopened. Little did he know that God had plans to raise up a church in China and send more missionaries to the Middle East, Southeast, Central Asia, and Africa than had ever been sent in the history of mankind."

BEHIND THE **BAMBOO CURTAIN**

China's budding missionary movement was born out of a church that is largely unknown to people around the world. There is still great confusion about what God is doing behind the Bamboo Curtain, but it isn't drastically different from other movements of God in history. Not unlike the past missionary movements of the West, China's surge of missionary activity has been born out of revival fires. There are many similarities between the revivals in China and those that have taken place around the world in recent history, one of them being an intense passion for global evangelism that has sparked multiple missionary endeavors.

There are also many characteristics that are unique to the Chinese church. As will be seen, many pearls distinct to the House Church were formed under intense pressure from conflict, suffering, and persecution. Chinese Christians like to say that the history of China runs red, like the crimson blood that was shed on the cross for man's sin. China's cross is crimson—as if stained by the blood of the countless saints who died so that her church could rise. This book is the story of that rise.

May your faith be challenged and may your heart be set aflame for Christ as you read about God's tremendous work in the Chinese House Church.

2

Roots of Chinese Christianity

Our goal is to lift the veil of the underground House Church movement in China so that the world can look inside and see some of the characteristics that are unique to the Chinese church and that have contributed to the world's largest revival and missions movement. We want to help you understand the House Church and what God is currently doing in the Middle Kingdom.[1] Thus, it is important to know the history that shaped the Chinese people and their churches into what they are today.

The following overview of Christianity in China makes no attempt to be exhaustive. It would be impossible to give a comprehensive account of China's long and rich history, and there are already many great books that go into detail on this subject. Those interested in more thorough accounts of Chinese church history may refer to the endnotes for further references. However, the next three chapters will give a brief summary of the development of Christianity in China and provide the historical backdrop for the Chinese House Church movement.

THE **GOD OF HEAVEN**

One of Beijing's most popular tourist attractions, the image of which has ironically become a symbol of the Communist nation's capital, is the Temple of Heaven (*Tiantan*, literally, "Altar of Heaven"). Foreign Christians who tour the sight are often surprised to learn that the purpose of the temple was to offer sacrificial worship to *Shangdi* (the God of Heaven) in prayer for a good harvest. This temple was completed in A.D. 1420 as part of the Ming Dynasty's attempt to reinstate long-lost *Shangdi* worship practices. Once a year, at the winter solstice, China's emperor would come to the temple to offer prayers and animal sacrifices to the God of Heaven. After fasting for three days, he would take a tablet inscribed with the phrase "Heavenly Sovereign *Shangdi*" and place it on a throne in the Hall of Prayer for Good Harvests. While bulls were being sacrificed outside the hall, he would intercede on behalf of his nation. This ritual was known as the "Great Sacrifice" and was even referred to by Confucius, who recognized that its true meaning had been lost generations before his time.[2] Although it had turned into nothing more than an empty ritual early on in Chinese history, the practice continued even through China's last imperial dynasty.

This means that thousands of years before Confucianism, Taoism, Buddhism, or Communism even existed, the ancient Chinese knew of a merciful God who heard their prayers. Monotheistic faith was not brought to China by Western imperialists, as is taught today in China, but had existed in China's ancient past.[3] The wave of Chinese coming to faith in the one true God in our time is really a return to the nation's most ancient spiritual roots.

The oldest existing Chinese records date from the Shang Dynasty (1600–1046 B.C.). These first archeologically verifiable records of Chinese history, known as oracle bones, were written on tortoise shells and cow bones. They mention *Shangdi* as the one Supreme God who ruled over all other spirits and had control over the weather, the harvests, and the outcome of battles. The Chinese characters on the oracle bones are interesting in themselves, because they contain references to pre-flood biblical history and theological concepts. One of the clearest examples is the ancient character for "boat," which combines the pictographs for "eight," "mouth" (referring to people), and "ship," or "vessel." There were exactly eight persons on board Noah's ark. Though the interpretation is debated by some, it seems quite clear that this character makes a reference to Noah's ark.[4]

船 = 舟 VESSEL
BOAT   几 EIGHT
        口 MOUTH

A LOST KNOWLEDGE OF GOD

These facts beg the obvious question, "What happened to the faith of the Chinese people?" When Protestant missionaries first landed on Chinese soil, they found a people totally lost in darkness. When had they forgotten about *Shangdi*? At the outset of the Zhou Dynasty (1045–256 B.C.), it was decided that knowledge of *Shangdi* was too high for commoners, and anyone other than the emperor was forbidden from worshipping Him. It was from this point onward that sacrifices to *Shangdi* were limited to once a year and could be carried out only by the emperor, who was given the new title "Son of Heaven." Although this was most likely a political move to solidify allegiance to the new dynasty, the end result was a vast nation looking for something to worship. That void would be filled a few hundred years later by Confucian ancestor worship, Taoism, and an idolatrous form of Buddhism unlike what first came out of India.[5]

THE ARRIVAL OF FOREIGN MISSIONARIES

Evidence of any belief in God doesn't appear again in Chinese history until the Han Dynasty (206 B.C.–A.D. 226). In recent years, stone carvings on Han tombs dating from A.D. 86 were discovered in Xuzhou.[6] These artifacts depict what appear to be stories from both the Old and New Testaments. One carving looks very much like a nativity scene, complete with angels flying over the baby in a manger. Although it can't be proven without a doubt, these carvings could very well be evidence that someone from the first-generation church made it all the way to China.

Speculation turns to solid fact by the time of the seventh century after Christ. Today in the city of Xi'an stands the remains of a stele (stone tablet) from the Tang Dynasty (A.D. 618–907) that gives an official account of a Christian presence in China. The Nestorian tablet, inscribed with the date A.D. 781, records the first arrival of the "Religion of Light of the West" as taking place in A.D. 635 via the Silk Road. Alopen, a leader from the Nestorian church, came from Persia with a syncretistic version of the gospel tailored to please the Taoist Chinese. Nestorianism was a heretical form of Christianity that denied that Christ's human and divine nature could coexist in one entity, so the gospel these missionaries presented was questionable. Nevertheless, the tablet states their belief in a Creator God, the fall in Eden, the virgin birth, and the crucifixion of Jesus. In some form, at least, the name of Christ was finally proclaimed within China's borders and was even well received by Tang royalty. Perhaps the Nestorians' biggest contribution to the gospel in China was the first Chinese translation of the New Testament, completed in the ninth century. Although there were times when Nestorian converts numbered in the tens of thousands, by and large, their growth was severely hampered by their monastic way of life, which brooded suspicion among the locals. Their success as a mission ebbed and flowed until the arrival of Roman Catholic missionaries in the thirteenth century.[7]

The Franciscan friar John of Monte Corvino (1247–1328) was the first Catholic missionary to set foot on Chinese soil. During his thirty-year ministry in Beijing, he baptized over six thousand converts and translated the New Testament and the book of Psalms into Mongolian, the language of the Mongols ruling China at the time. With the fall of the Mongolian Yuan Dynasty in 1368, Christianity again vanished from the scene.

The founding of the Jesuits—sometimes referred to as Roman Catholic "shock troops"—brought on a global wave of Catholic evangelism. These men set sail with European explorers and proselytized in many previously uncharted areas. The most famous Catholic missionary to China, Matteo Ricci, came from their ranks and served there from 1583 to his death in 1610. In accordance with Rome's official policy of focusing on creating political influence with national governments before evangelizing commoners, Ricci served in the imperial court. Garbed in flowing silk robes like a Confucian scholar, Ricci avoided teaching Christian doctrines that would be offensive in Chinese culture and even allowed converts to continue practicing ancestor worship, considering the observance to be more cultural than religious.

This toleration for idolatry would later come back to harm the Catholic cause when the pope issued a decree in 1704 that expressly forbade ancestor worship. Feeling betrayed, the Chinese emperor was enraged at what looked like an attempt to step on his sovereignty. He responded by severely persecuting Christians throughout China and later passing the "Edict of Expulsion and Confiscation," which forced all missionaries to either work in secular government positions or to live in the foreign area of Guangzhou. From that point on, Catholicism went underground in China.

In God's sovereignty, the forced gathering of Catholic missionary exiles in Guangzhou led to the first Catholic translation of the New Testament into Chinese. This manuscript was given to the British Museum and was later discovered by Dr. William Moseley, who spoke to many missions organizations about making a Chinese Bible.[8] After being rejected by one missions society after another, he was finally put together with Robert Morrison, the missionary who would one day complete the first Chinese Bible. The New Testament made by refugees in Guangzhou became a major source text for this Protestant translation. How amazing it is that God would use exiled Catholic ministers to prepare the way for the ministry of the first Protestant missionary to China almost a century later. This pattern of persecution eventually leading to great spiritual fruit is a hallmark of the Chinese church to this day.

Robert Morrison taught himself Hebrew, Greek, and Latin while working in his father's workshop. In 1806, he began learning Chinese with nothing more than the British Museum's Chinese New Testament, a Chinese-Latin dictionary, and a Chinese roommate he lived with in London. Just a year later, he left for China, stopping in the U.S. on the way. Due to the laws strictly forbidding foreigners from entering the Chinese mainland at the time, Morrison lived for a short time in Guangzhou's foreign enclave and spent most of his life in Macau. Once in the field, he wasted no time and was able to complete a 1,100-page Chinese-English dictionary within nine months. It was a capital crime for Chinese to teach their native tongue to foreigners, but several of them risked their lives to teach Morrison and to help him translate the Bible.

Morrison's Chinese New Testament was completed in 1813 and relied heavily on the old Catholic translation. A year later, he baptized the first recorded Chinese Protestant convert, Cai Fu. With the help of William Milne, Morrison went on to complete the Chinese Bible in 1819. After a very fruitful twenty-seven years of service to the Lord, this father of Chinese missions died in Guangzhou in 1834.

If there were a Chinese missionary hall of fame, it would be full of names, but space limits us to mentioning just one more missionary to China, perhaps the most famous of them all. Like Morrison, J. Hudson Taylor hailed from England and devoted his entire life to bringing the gospel to the Chinese. Several years before his arrival, the First Opium War (1839–1842) had forcibly pried open China's gates to foreigners, bringing many more opportunities for mainland ministry than in Morrison's day. Taylor arrived in China at the peak of the Taiping Rebellion, a long and bloody revolt led by a man who claimed to be the brother of Jesus sent to usher in God's kingdom on earth. Taylor's writings recount the artillery bombardments of his neighborhood and the horror of watching prisoners of war brutally beheaded before his eyes.[9] All these experiences made him long even more to see China come to Christ.

What quickly set Taylor apart from the other Western missionaries was his insistence on living among the Chinese and adopting native dress. This outraged many of the missionaries hiding within the walls of their mission compound. They considered his methods to be radical and even savage, forgetting that Christ, too, had adopted the culture of those He had come to serve. Hudson Taylor's novel approach to missions, traveling upriver in junks while sporting his dyed black hair in a Chinese queue, gave him unsurpassed access to parts of inner China where no foreigner had ever trod. As the work expanded, in 1865, Taylor founded the China Inland Mission with the express purpose of sending like-minded missionaries deep into China to raise up local churches.

As the imperial government lost more ground to Western powers, the empire increasingly opened up to foreign missionaries. Hospitals, orphanages, schools, and the first universities were all built by Western missionaries seeking to share Christ's love through both word and deed. Many of the universities famous in China today were founded by such missionaries.

Needless to say, not everyone was happy with the increasing foreign influence. With the tacit support of the Empress Dowager, the Boxer Rebellion erupted in 1898 and wreaked havoc across the nation until it was quelled by foreign armies in 1901. It was a terrifying time for missionaries as riotous hordes ransacked cities in search of foreigners and those sympathetic to them.

The Boxer Rebellion was a last-ditch effort by the Chinese to rid their crumbling nation of the influence of foreigners—including the foreigners' God. There are numerous tales from that era of missionary families huddled under farmhouses in silence for days before narrowly escaping with their lives. Many of those who attempted to flee south to foreign-occupied safe areas were mercilessly cut down on the roads.

Missionaries suddenly found themselves in a crucible, and the China Inland Mission suffered the most. More than thirty thousand Chinese Christians and over two hundred foreign missionaries—men, women, and children—were slaughtered in the rebellion, many of them brutally hacked to death with swords and farm implements. Rightly had Morrison said many years before, "It is not possible but that this land must be watered with the blood of many martyrs before the gospel prevails generally." Much blood had been shed, but a great harvest was soon to come.

To the imperial palace's dismay, the defeat of the rebels actually increased the Western military presence in China. Foreign powers marched through Beijing and into the Forbidden City, many of them demanding war reparations. The Qing Dynasty was all but broken and would eventually fade into history with the child emperor's forced abdication in 1911.

Meanwhile, the first decade of the twentieth century became the most fruitful for missionaries in China. By 1910, there were 5,144 Protestant missionaries in China discipling 15,500 potential native church leaders and over two hundred thousand converts.[10] The foreign missionary enterprise in China was reaching its peak.

Along with this sudden church growth came the problems frequently linked to success. Many missionary organizations felt like they needed to become more "professional" and began focusing on medical and educational reforms rather than preaching the gospel. China's physical health and prosperity became more important than her spiritual condition. In many missionary-run schools and universities, the gospel became something extra, taught only outside class. As A. J. Broomhall noted sadly, "The means of presenting the gospel was replacing the gospel itself."[11] Today's gospel-less "social gospel" is definitely nothing new to the mission field.

Another problem was the virtual stranglehold that Western missionaries had on their Chinese congregants. Fledgling Chinese churches were divided along Western-made denominational lines, and Chinese ministers were often totally dependent on their foreign mentors. The 1907 General Inter-Mission Conference clearly portrayed this Western dominance. Out of the five hundred delegates who met to discuss the future of Protestant Christianity in China, only six or seven were actually Chinese. It became clear that as long as the Chinese church was connected to Westerners, it wouldn't keep growing and become a truly organic church.

On January 1, 1912, Sun Yat-sen, a professing Christian who had married a pastor's daughter, declared the founding of the Republic of China. Many leaders in the new government were influenced by Christianity and even made April 27, 1913, a Day of Prayer for China, requesting churches around the world to intercede on the nation's behalf. The era ended soon after Sun's death in 1924, and the republic quickly crumbled into chaos, with warlords and bandits ravaging the country.

THE EXPULSION OF **FOREIGN MISSIONARIES**

The unpredictable nature of widespread civil war made missionary work quite perilous, but those who toughed it out witnessed immense fruit in many places. Some warlords even invited them to preach to their troops, and great numbers of soldiers were saved. During those violent times, many Bible institutes were established all over the country where missionaries trained future Chinese church leaders. It was also during those days that Christians began to worship in homes—the first Chinese house churches. Despite the growing anti-Christian sentiment that was being propagated by the newly formed Chinese Communist Party, there were 8,235 Protestant missionaries on the ground in 1926.

As Communism spread, violence against Christians also increased. Communists frequently captured and executed foreign missionaries. After the Japanese invaded China in 1937, missionaries were forced to leave Japanese-occupied areas or be interned in squalid prison camps. The hostile environment created an ever-increasing stream of missionaries returning to their homelands—either by choice or by compulsion. Leadership of the Chinese church was gradually falling into native hands.

With the rise to power of Mao Zedong (Tse-tung) and the Communist takeover in 1949, the curtains finally closed on the foreign missionary effort in China. Most missionaries had been forced to leave by 1952, but in 1959, Helen Willis was the last Protestant missionary to depart. As the Bamboo Curtain fell, to the outside world, it looked as if Christianity was going to once again disappear from the Middle Kingdom. God, however, had other plans.

THE EMERGENCE OF AN INDIGENOUS **CHINESE CHURCH**

The closing of all China's churches and the imprisonment of their leaders didn't happen overnight. While Mao and his cronies tightened their grip on the people, faithful Chinese evangelists worked feverishly to bring in a harvest of souls before nightfall. Throughout the early 1950s, men like Watchman Nee planted house churches like there was no tomorrow. By 1949, Nee's "Little Flock" had grown to around 70,000 members meeting in over 700 churches. Though he died in prison after his arrest in 1952, his writings have been influential to Chinese Christians ever since.

In 1954, the "Three-Self Patriotic Movement" (TSPM) became the official government entity for handling church affairs. The organization got its name from its emphasis on "self-governance, self-support, and self-propagation," which, interestingly, were all ideals originally espoused by the China Missionary Society and Hudson Taylor's China Inland Mission. During the formation of the TSPM, well-known Chinese pastors were asked—and then coerced—to join the movement. Those who refused were usually imprisoned for decades, and many died in Chinese prison labor camps. Their primary reason for refusing to join the TSPM was their understanding that the Three-Self was ultimately under the authority of the Communist Party, not Christ. Many of them were also opposed to partnering with the leaders of the organization because they seemed to be wolves in sheep's clothing, claiming to be Christians but so theologically liberal that the unregistered church pastors doubted their salvation. Thus, the underground Chinese House Church was born.

The government's extreme crackdown on all who refused to register their churches with the Three-Self put a bad taste in the mouths of many Christians that continues to this day. Although there are regions of China where Three-Self churches and house churches work together, in most areas, there is a clear divide that is sometimes antagonistic.

A cloud of intense persecution formed on the horizon as Beijing tightened the noose around those refusing to go along with its religious "reforms." In the decades ahead, countless Christians would lose their homes, their possessions, their dignity, and even their lives because they remained faithful to their Lord and Savior.

Though tragic at the time, it was in this furnace of affliction that the Lord refined the Chinese church to form it into the unstoppable force it is today. God used an evil Communist dictator to take the foreign crutches off Chinese Christianity so that it could become an indigenous faith. With its "training wheels" removed, Christianity in China exploded in ways not seen since the church of the first century. In the flames of persecution, the dross of denominationalism brought by Westerners also burned away, and the Chinese church became unified in suffering. With nothing more than a few hidden Bibles, the Holy Spirit, and faith in an almighty God, the Chinese church was being forged into a powerful weapon for God's purposes.

3

Clearing Up the Confusion

Those who are unfamiliar with China may think that house churches are part of a mysterious society, meeting by candlelight like some Druid sect. In actuality, the Chinese House Church refers to a movement of unregistered Christian gatherings that operate independently of governmental authority. Far from being mysterious, these gatherings are probably more like church meetings described in the book of Acts than anything else.

As mentioned in the previous chapter, the Chinese House Church as it exists today officially developed after Mao Zedong and the Communists came to power in 1949. Again, China set up a government-sanctioned church called the Three-Self Patriotic Movement. The TSPM is overseen by the China Christian Council (CCC). The underground, unregistered churches in China are often called house churches because they are not allowed to con-gregate in official worship places like church buildings and must meet secretly in private homes and businesses.

During the days of intense persecution, leaders of unregistered church meetings were constantly on the run from the police. These traveling "convicts and vagabonds" began to gather followings and to plant house churches. These churches were forming literally in the homes of believers and were meeting without the knowledge or permission of the local government. Being forced to hide together created an intense and close bond among the believers within a short period of time. This was the beginning of the House Church networks.

House churches in places like Henan Province became linked by those who traveled around preaching the gospel. Soon they became secret, but well-organized, national networks with centralized leadership and local cells. The organizational structure began to be formed in the 1980s and 90s under the tutelage of the founding leaders.

At first, the underground Christians were just fighting to survive, but by the 90s, funding and training from abroad began to come in and assist the Chinese to reach larger crowds with effective training. Bible printing, distribution, Bible schools, seminars, and even baptisms became essential parts of this underground society. This type of House Church movement became especially strong in the Henan and Anhui provinces.

One of the key components of this movement has been women. Anyone who has had exposure to the underground Chinese House Church will immediately notice that women are at the heart of it. They are often preaching, teaching, leading, administering, and providing places to hold meetings.

THE GOALS OF THE **THREE-SELF CHURCH**

Competing with this underground movement is the official church of China. After taking over the nation, the leadership within the Communist Party quickly realized that their future political success depended on their ability to control and manipulate the thoughts of the entire population, including Christians.

Though the official church in China has changed over the years, in the beginning, it was implemented as a tool to register, control, and eventually eliminate Chinese Christianity. The Communist Party of China spawned the TSPM, which was sold to the people as a way to remain loyal to the country and still maintain a form of godliness. The TSPM often substituted the propaganda of the party for the Word of God. Teaching from the Bible that encouraged sacrifice and devotion to the Messiah was redirected to brainwash congregants into unquestionable loyalty to the party, diluting the power of the cross and the promise of Christ's return.

In its initial stages, TSPM church leaders didn't plan to assist in the destruction of Christianity in China. They were sincere and saw themselves as patriots who were standing up against enslavement and exploitation by foreign imperialists. Communist ideology was very new at the time and seemed to agree with the teachings of Jesus Christ. Communism appeared to promote equality for all, equal distribution of wealth, and community responsibility for the poor—all things that seemed to align with Jesus' teachings.

Little did those leaders know that the atheists had planned their systematic destruction. The Christians were promised autonomy and more freedom than ever if they would join the cause of Red China. Many believers even applauded having the chains of foreign missionary control broken off. Many of them didn't protest when the laws of an atheistic government began to make rules regulating the church. Some of them started to wake up when their leaders and clergy began to be sent to labor camps for not adopting the control mechanisms of the government at a faster pace. By the time the church realized what was going on and began to resist, it was too late.

The TSPM was created not only as a control mechanism to register, monitor, and redirect the teachings of the Christian church, but it was also meant to wean the church off the Truth—Jesus Christ. According to *China News and Church Report*, there are seven very strict rules to be followed in Three-Self churches:

1. Christian believers must fervently love the People's Republic of China, support the leadership of the Chinese Communist Party and the Peoples' Government, uphold the unification of the motherland and the harmony among ethnic groups, and work steadfastly on the road of socialism.

2. Christian believers must strictly abide by all the laws, regulations, and policies of the Communist Party and the State and strive to be patriotic and law-abiding citizens.

3. Christian believers must actively work to increase the material wealth and cultivate the spiritual morals of the socialist civilization. They must comply with the government's labor codes and strive to contribute to the development of the "Four Modernizations" established by the Communist Party. When scheduled religious activities are in conflict with production and work schedules, the economic activities must take priority.

4. A permit must be obtained from the county State Administration for Religious Affairs in order to establish religious meeting points. No unauthorized meeting points are allowed.

5. Christian believers must actively cooperate with the government to thoroughly carry out the party's religious policies to the letter. They shall not persuade and force others to believe in Christianity. They shall not brainwash teenagers under 18 with religious beliefs. They shall not bring children under 18 to religious activities.

6. One should see a doctor for medication when sick. Christian believers must not resort to prayer alone for healing so as not to endanger people's health and lives.

7. Christian believers shall not preach their religion outside the church building and specific places which have been designated for religious activities. They shall not preach itinerantly. They shall not receive self-proclaimed evangelists into their homes, churches or meeting points.[12]

In addition to these seven rules are codes that are enforced but not necessarily written in legislation, which is a common practice in China. These codes prevent evangelism, children's ministry, preaching by visiting pastors, unauthorized baptism, unauthorized independent Bible training, multinational cooperation, printing teaching materials, handing out Bibles, and teaching about the virgin birth, the resurrection, and the second coming.

Anyone who has ever had to go through immigration, start a business, or watch a court procedure in China quickly learns that there are few written rules that are actually practiced in China. Most of the rules are widely understood but rarely captured on paper.

In China, there is a lot of bureaucracy, and the various names and titles can be confusing to people in the West who are unfamiliar with them. The Communist Party is at the top of the chain, and, by definition, one must be a professed atheist to be a part of the Communist Party. The atheists in the Communist Party dictate the religious policy, which is then written up by the United Front Work Department. The laws that are written on the books by the United Front are then carried out by the State Administration for Religious Affairs. This Bureau also writes the rules regarding religion and foreigners.

The China Christian Council and the Three-Self Patriotic Movement both fall under the State Administration for Religious Affairs. These two bodies have the impossible task of keeping the church members under control, compliant with policy, and spiritually satisfied. At the same time, they must always put forth the best possible presentation for foreigners.

This system is similar in many ways to what King Jeroboam set up in the Old Testament in the final days of the nation of Israel before the exile. After Israel (the ten northern tribes) and Judah (the two southern tribes) were divided, many Israelites in the northern tribes were brokenhearted because they were separated from the city of Jerusalem, which was in the territory of Judah, ruled by King Rehoboam. The pain of the loss was eased for many during the annual pilgrimages to the temple in Jerusalem.

Jerusalem was rich in history and held deep meaning for the Jews, and those who traveled from the land of Israel were emotionally attached to the capital city. To curb this challenge to patriotism toward the northern kingdom, King Jeroboam built new places of worship in the territory of Israel. He fired all the priests of the Lord and installed new priests. (See 1 Kings 12:20–33.)

In like manner, to curb the challenge to Chinese patriotism, the Chinese government formed its own church and chose its own leaders. Many of the unauthorized Christian leaders were hunted down, publicly humiliated, beaten, and jailed. Their families were stripped of everything and were ostracized in the community. Many of them were given the opportunity to deny Christ, swear their allegiance to the Communist Party, and avoid all the hardships and pain. There were many reports of those who denied Christ being rewarded with leadership in the official TSPM church.

Therefore, those who denied Christ were placed in high positions in the official church, and those who didn't deny Christ went on the run from the authorities, becoming leaders in the underground movement. In addition, many official church members were used by the government to secretly infiltrate underground House Church meetings; identify the locations, leaders, and networks; record details; and then turn them in. This practice, of course, led to distrust and deeply buried animosity. A huge divide was created between the underground church and the official church in China. As mentioned earlier, it is a divide that exists to this day.

Because many believers felt betrayed by the first leaders of the official church in China, there remains a deep scar that is still raw and sensitive. Although the situation between the House Church and the Three-Self has improved in many parts of China, that scar in particular continues to keep the House Church from registering with the government.

COMPARING THE THREE-SELF CHURCH WITH THE **HOUSE CHURCH**

What is the main difference between the Three-Self church and the House Church in China today? It would be best to obtain the answer to this question directly from Chinese who are still living in their homeland. For one of my previous books, *The Heavenly People*, we conducted interviews with senior members of the underground House Church networks in Henan and Anhui provinces. The following is one of those interviews:

This interview was with a senior leader who is from a House Church network in Henan Province and has been charged with caring for churches in Guangdong, Guangxi, Yunnan, Guizhou, and overseeing missionaries sent to South East Asia. It took place in a car driving from parking place to parking place in Humen, China, on April 14, 2009.

In America and Europe, there are many people claiming that there is growing religious freedom in China. Is this true?

Yes and no. China is a big country, and there have been many changes, but some of those changes have only been new ways of expressing old habits.

Can you elaborate? Many people in West feel that there is free-dom for Christians in China, and they cannot understand why the house churches will not register with the government.

This topic is very important to me. I have never discussed this with any foreigner before. We believe that Christians should not get political. We don't want to argue with anyone; we don't want to get involved in politics. We don't want to be for China what the Roman Catholic Church was in Western history, but we also do not want to have the politicians run-ning the church, setting the doctrine, and leading us away from Christ.

The government in China controls the Three-Self church and has led many people away from the truth. In 1983, when

I was living in my hometown in southern Henan Province, there was a surge of persecution of Christians in China. The government was not able to destroy the church under Mao Zedong, so they tried a different tactic under Deng Xiaoping: control. Many pastors were arrested. During that time, my older sister, who was a well-known leader in our hometown, was arrested and told to deny Christ. If she would deny Jesus Christ, they promised she would be released from prison and be given a post in the official church. The first leaders of the Three-Self church in my area were all people who had denied Jesus Christ. My sister served three years in prison for refusing to deny the name of Jesus Christ.

Many pastors in the Three-Self church in China are paid by the government. They are salaried employees. This is not true everywhere, of course, but it is true in my hometown (Henan). If pastors are paid by an atheistic government, who is their real boss?

For those who do not believe what we are saying, let them see for themselves. They can look into it and find that the government decides who is ordained. The government decides who a church's pastor is. The government dictates the number of baptisms allowed per month or year. The government dictates how many Bibles can be distributed. The government dictates what can be taught or not taught in the churches. The government dictates where a pastor can preach and not preach. These are all facts that can be proven. They cannot be denied.

The Bible clearly says that we are one body. We are the body of Christ. How can we be separated? How can the government tell us that churches in Guiyang cannot fellowship with churches in Kashgar? How can the government tell us that Westerners cannot fellowship with believers in Nanyang? How can the government tell us that Chinese cannot attend international services in Kunming without a foreign passport? The body of Christ is one body. It cannot be separated.

You mentioned before that the government controls what is taught in the Three-Self churches of China. How do you know this? You are a part of the underground House Church movement. Do you have any proof of these teachings?

Yes. Have you ever been to a Three-Self church?

No. I have attempted a few times in Kunming a couple of years ago, but because I was a foreigner, I was denied entrance every time.

Inside the official government churches there are red banners stretched from one side of the room to the other. They are one of the most prominent displays in the churches and are put up by the *Ai Guo*, or "love country," movement, also known as the patriotic movement, which reminds all believers that country comes before God. Under those banners is a posting of laws. There are eighteen sections or parts on these postings. Some postings have fewer sections, and some churches have taken them down altogether, but they are still very much a part of the government church of China. Among those postings, the patrons are told that they cannot baptize people under the age of eighteen, they cannot teach about the resurrection of Jesus Christ, and they can't teach about the second coming.

Are these still posted at the front of the churches today in 2009, though?

Oh yes, they are, and I can take a picture of them for you and get it to you if you want.

An interview with another leader from a different network in Anhui Province is provided here in order to give a different opinion and broader perspective. This interview was done with the head pastor of a network of about one million believers in Anhui on April 9, 2009.

In America and Europe, there are many people claiming that there is growing religious freedom in China. Is this true?

I would agree that there is more religious freedom today than before in most areas.

Are there restrictions on Christians in China? If so, what are they?

Yes. There are many freedoms that we still do not have in China. I know that this is hard for the church in the West to understand. We [the house churches in Anhui] do not have, nor are we allowed to have, an outlet to let the world know the things that we face on a daily basis. The basic tenets of our faith, such as fellowship, evangelism, teaching children about Christian values—these are all forbidden in China.

There have been Christian leaders and pastors from America and Europe who have been asked to come and see the practice of Christianity in China. They have seen the difference and have even been asked to come and speak at many venues (including churches). During these speaking engagements, they have not been told what to speak about or what not to speak about. The number of people present during these events has been amazing. After they return back to their home countries, they tell others about the freedoms in China. What is your response to this?

Oh, this is a common practice of the Chinese government. Of course these foreigners see these things. It is a show that has been arranged by the government. If they believe what they see during this time, then they are believing a lie.

Do you want proof? Tell those leaders who say this after a trip to China that they should arrange another trip to China, but this time, they can tell the government that they do not need their help. They can arrange their own trip, their own speaking engagements, and they can kindly decline the involvement of the government. Then we will see how things go. Only those who want the truth will do this. Others who continue to repeat what the government has given them are willfully believing a lie.

There are many well-known workers in China who are trying to unite the house churches with the government in China in an

*arrangement similar to the Three-Self church in China. How do
you feel about this?*

With the work that we do, it is not possible for me to
register.

Why?

You see, one of the big problems is that the head of any
government church in China would be run by an atheist.
Someone who does not believe in what the Word of God says
would be telling us how to practice it. Maybe this is something
that others can compromise, but I believe that the Word of
God is clear: I must preach the Word, I must reach the lost,
I must pray for the sick—these are the things that I must do.

Even if I were to register—where would I register? Any
city where I register would be on my license, and I would not
be able to conduct the work that I do today. I would not be
able to travel to other areas and evangelize as I do today all
over China. I have been called to preach the Word in many
areas of China. How can I agree to stay in just one city?

*Many leaders and experts in the West claim that there are enough
Bibles in China. What is your response to them?*

There are not enough Bibles in China.

*Why is that? Is it because the government makes it hard to get
them, or because the areas that are in need are too poor to purchase their own Bibles?*

Both. Right now, almost all our work is in the villages.
The people who live in these areas are not able to afford Bibles,
but this is not the only reason. We are not able to get access to
the number of Bibles that we need.

*Many people in the West quote from Amity Press that there are
more than enough Bibles made in China. Do you know that more
Bibles are made in China than anywhere else in the world?*

Listen, when I go to the Three-Self church in Hefei to
purchase Bibles, I can buy maybe five or ten without any problem. However, if I purchase large numbers of Bibles or put in

a request for numbers exceeding a thousand or so, I am asked why I need so many, where they are going, whom they are going to, and so forth. My information is logged and kept on record for large purchases. This is not safe for me, so I get my Bibles from an underground press.

But do you know—even with the ability to purchase Bibles—there are not enough. Even through the official channels.

Are you saying that there are not enough Bibles available through the Three-Self church?

Yes, I am saying that there are not enough Bibles through the official churches. There have been many times when I went to Hefei Three-Self church to buy only between five and ten Bibles and was turned away because they didn't have any. When the meetings take place to distribute Bibles from the printing office to the Three-Self churches, many negotiations take place. For instance, one church leader might say, "We need one million Bibles." The response from the government official in return might be, "Why do you need so many? You don't need that many. You will get only 200,000." And that is that. End of story.[13]

In the next chapter, we will learn more about the origins of the Chinese House Church.

4

Tested by Fire

At Los Angeles' Cottonwood Christian Center in 2010, Brother Ren—the man partially responsible for that intrepid airlift of Bibles mentioned earlier—introduced his dear friend Brother Yun to a packed house. The crowd had gathered to hear from this man who had endured great persecution and miraculously escaped from a Chinese maximum-security prison. It was a special privilege that night to also have Peter Xu, the founder of China's Born Again Movement, on stage, as well. Before giving the floor to Yun, Ren gave some background on China's spiritual situation after the Communist takeover.

"In 1949, the Communist Party came to power in China," he began. "As a first order of business, the Communist Party began to wipe the country clean of any visible signs of Christianity. Pastors and evangelists were tortured, killed, or sent to labor camps where they would suffer, rot, and die. Bibles and hymnals were piled up in public squares and burned. Missionaries were kicked out of the country. Churches were closed, never to be opened up again. The world watched as China purged itself of Christians and all signs of Christianity."

David Aikman, the former Beijing bureau chief for Time magazine and respected authority on China, wrote in his landmark book, *Jesus in Beijing,*

> Many former missionaries from the West cried when they saw all of their dedication and sacrifice washed away. The world waited for the first glimpse back into the country to see if there were any Christians left. When the

doors to China finally did open, Mao Zedong's wife Jiang Qing was quoted as boasting to the foreign delegation that "Christianity in China has been confined to the history section of the museum. It is dead and buried."[14]

Mao Zedong stood in front of the Tiananmen Square audience on October 1, 1949, and announced a new era for China. The first order of business was to ensure a one-way exit for all foreign missionaries. Next, he would work on eradicating the faith from the native population. However, we will see that the impact of his actions could not have been more counterproductive to his purposes. Romans 8:28 really rings true when we see how God worked out the foolish schemes of evil men to expand His church. By effectively removing the foreign community from China, the Communist government was paving the way for a more powerful revival than had ever been recorded in Chinese history. Although the 1950s and 60s saw many pastors and Christian leaders sent to gulags where they were indoctrinated, tortured, or killed, a great spiritual harvest would follow.

THE "GREAT LEAP FORWARD"

One of the largest efforts at eradicating Christianity from the borders of China was attempted during the Great Leap Forward (1958–1961). Perhaps it is more than a coincidence that the worst famine, poverty, and anguish ever recorded in Chinese history all took place during this intense time of Christian persecution. Just as under the Romans in the first century, believers were scattered to the winds because of the persecution. As in the past, when those believers were scattered, they took their zeal and faith in Jesus with them and shared the good news in areas that might never have heard it otherwise.

In order to purge China of Christianity, it was important to proceed in phases, because many Chinese Christians believed they, also, were doing what was best for their country. The government gathered well-known Christian leaders and tried to get them to follow the Party line, knowing full well that if the shepherds were on board, the sheep would soon follow. Once all the believers were registered and put in controlled areas, mass indoctrination programs could be implemented, and the leadership could be disposed of. This would ensure the further consolidation of the Party's power.

Mao held the same view as Marx and Lenin—quite fitting, considering that Russia paid to put him in power and saved him from annihilation by the Nationalists on numerous occasions. He believed that religion was the "opiate of the masses" and should be eliminated by internal struggle. Y. T. Wu (Wu Yaozong) published the "Christian Manifesto" at the prompting of the Communist Party, and, by 1952, more than four hundred thousand Chinese Christians had signed it. The manifesto stated that Christianity was essentially a mechanism of Western imperialism and that Chinese Christians should be self-reliant and separate themselves from all Western instruction. Wu unwittingly helped to disassemble the Chinese church, and the Communist government that he assisted eventually turned on him, as well, and sent him to labor camp for "reeducation" during the Cultural Revolution.

"ENEMIES OF **THE STATE**"

In those days, enthusiastic students went throughout China seeking out "class enemies," a term not specifically defined but understood to mean anyone who did not agree with everything taught by the Communist Party. Christians were considered some of the foremost class enemies. Those who did not immediately renounce their faith were dragged out to be tried in makeshift courts, publicly humiliated, and persecuted. They were often forced to wear dunce caps or to carry signs that advertised their alleged crimes against the state. A common phrase on the dunce cap of a Christian was "Down with the foul intellectual," because many Christians in China at that time had been exposed to Western education and were considered to be worthless "intellectuals." As the "enemies of the state" (including women and children) were paraded down the street wearing these dunce caps, it was the civic duty of locals to verbally and physically abuse them.

The book *Project Pearl* tells the amazing story of a former U.S. Marine who led a daring operation in 1981 to smuggle one million Bibles into Shantou, China. In 2012, I was in Shantou, meeting with House Church leaders to discuss the need for Chinese believers to put their lives on the line in the same way in order to get God's Word into North Korea. On the same beach where that massive Bible delivery had taken place, a man in his eighties came up to me and spoke to me in perfect English. When I asked if he had ever heard about the one million Bibles dropped on those shores in 1981, he smiled and replied, "Heard about it? Son, I was there!" and began to explain how he had buried Bibles in the sand to hide them from the authorities and then dug them up days later to pack them onto delivery vehicles.

This man, Mai Fu Ren, was a Christian living in Shantou when Mao came to power. His mother and father were also Christians and wanted him to be a missionary. He remembered when the Communists took over in 1949. His family became enemies of the state overnight because his father was a pastor and worked closely with foreign missionaries. His family members were soon arrested and scattered throughout Guangdong Province to serve in intense reeducation camps. Both of his parents were sent to labor camps where they were forced to work until they succumbed to premature death. Many of Mai Fu Ren's twelve brothers and sisters died in those camps, as well.

For delivering Bibles in China, Mai Fu Ren spent a total of thirty years in prison. He recounted, "The police pointed at me and yelled, 'You are an antirevolutionary!' They announced over the loud speakers, 'Mai Fu Ren is an antirevolutionary!'"

Though his suffering and loss were extreme, they were not unique for the Chinese in those days. Christians throughout China were experiencing the same kinds of difficult challenges, torture, and even death for refusing to deny the name of Jesus Christ. The Chinese government employed a united front against not only the Christian faithful but anyone Mao's regime was suspicious of.

In her book *Mao: The Unknown Story*, Jung Chang and her historian husband, Jon Halliday, record the results of a decade of research on Mao. They begin the biography by writing, "Mao Tse-Tung, who for decades held absolute power over the lives of one-quarter of the world's population, was responsible for well over 70 million deaths in peacetime, more than any other twentieth-century leader."[15] Seventy million is not an easy number to fathom. Put into perspective, it is almost the same as killing the entire populations of Sweden, Finland, Norway, Denmark, and the Netherlands—twice. There aren't any museums, federal holidays, or even a simple monument to remember these millions of poor souls.

MAO'S **PERSONALITY CULT**

Soon after the rise of the Communist Party in China, Mao's personality cult swept the nation. Implementing the personality cult of Chairman Mao was vital to consolidating the power that was being wielded against the personal lives of so many citizens.

Below is a poster from 1954 that says, "Chairman Mao gives us a happy life." Every home was required to have a picture of Mao, usually an oil painting, and it was to remain clean enough to be ready for inspection.

As noted earlier, Zhao Ming, or Benjamin, is a well-known Christian singer in China. During a meeting in Malaysia, he shared his memories of being a small boy during that time. He vividly recalled the personality cult that was put into place shortly after Mao had come to power.

"I can remember when a member of our family was cleaning the portrait of Mao. He wanted to honor the picture of Mao by keeping it perfectly clean, even though the rest of his home was dirty and poor. He didn't have any proper cleaning detergent, so he heated up water and used it to clean his portrait. However, the water and his rag were so hot that the steam ruined the paint on Mao's cheek. The paint came right off of the portrait!

IISH / Stefan R. Landsberger Collections, chineseposters.net

The man panicked. He did not have the money to buy a new one and could not afford to have the town see what he had done. It was a horrible mistake. Other relatives quickly came and publicly condemned him. Destroying a picture of Mao Zedong was a punishable offense."

Personality cults in totalitarian regimes that attempt to radically transform society are not uncommon, but there were characteristics unique to the worship of Mao. China, by its very nature, is more paternal than most countries. Mao was the face of the struggles of the revolution.

History books would have us believe that Mao and his army forced the country to bow to his power, but that is not exactly true. At that time, China had just been humiliated by the Japanese. A group of islands off the east coast of China had been able to subjugate a large portion of the most populated country in the world with a handful of disciplined troops.

Japanese occupation was just the culmination of decades of foreign domination in China. As we have noted, places like Shanghai, Beijing, Qingdao, and Hong Kong had long been under Western control before the Japanese took them. The Chinese felt helpless against these powers and demoralized that such small armies could infringe on their soil with little effort. They were looking for a hero who could restore honor and dignity to the nation. Consequently, rather than rejecting Chairman Mao, many actually welcomed him. They were infatuated by him, praised his name, and deified everything he did. Army leaders and spiritual leaders followed the energy of the mobs.

Even the Dalai Lama played into this mania. There is a hand-written letter from the Dalai Lama in a Buddhist temple in Beijing that "Free Tibet" activists and the Dalai Lama would like to forget. In it, he wrote words of praise that come close to deifying Mao. A portion of it reads:

> O! Chairman Mao! Your brilliance and deeds are like those of Brahma and Mahasammata, creators of the world,
> Only from an infinite number of good deeds can such a leader be born, who is like the sun shining over the world.
> Your writings are precious as pearls, abundant and powerful as the high tide of ocean reaching the edges of the sky.
> O! most honourable Chairman Mao, may you long live!
> All people look to you as to a kind protecting mother, they paint pictures of you with hearts full of emotion,
> May you live in the world forever and point out to us the peaceful road!
> Our vast land was burdened with pain, with shackles and darkness.
> You liberated all with your brilliance. People now are happy, full of blessings![16]

This hymn shows that, at one time, even the leader of Buddhists worldwide bowed to Mao. Such infatuation was enrapturing everyone in China. Everyone, that is, except the Christians. A determination to worship God over man was the reason why Christians like Mai Fu Ren and his family were such a threat to the government and its Maoist cult. They held on to the truth of Jesus Christ and did not bow to the newly proclaimed savior of China.

The Dalai Lama was not the only one to compare Chairman Mao to the sun, nor was he the first, but he was one of the top religious leaders in China who gave his endorsement to the personality cult mania.

Below is a poster that could be found in China during Mao's day that makes him out to be the sun, shining light on all the

IISH / Stefan R. Landsberger Collections, chineseposters.net

people. Even today in China, it's not uncommon to see shiny gold cards with Chairman Mao's image on them hanging from the rearview mirrors of taxis. The shiny gold material is designed to symbolize sun-like radiance.

One day, while traveling by taxi from Shenzhen to Guangzhou, I saw a picture of Chairman Mao hanging from the rearview mirror.

The image of the beloved, half-balding, long-dead leader staring at the passengers was quite creepy. A conversation between the taxi driver and me ensued. When I asked facetiously who it was a picture of, the driver replied with complete surprise, "You don't know who that is? That is Chairman Mao, the founder of our country. How do you not know who that is?"

"I am from America. We never learned about Chairman Mao in American school. Why do you have a picture of him in your car?"

His eyes glanced back at the strange foreign passenger. "He was a great leader of China, and even now he is able to provide my car with protection from disasters and bring me good luck."

"Well, don't you think he should be turned around so that he can see the road? I think he would be able to help us avoid disaster if he actually watched where he was going." Such humor was totally lost on the driver.

During the Cultural Revolution, the cult of Mao not only had its savior, but, like Christianity, it even had a holy book.

All over China, posters like the one below showed every citizen carrying a copy of *Quotations from Chairman Mao Tse-Tung*, a book known diminutively in the West as "The Little Red Book." Everywhere the Chinese traveled, they were to have this book in hand. Except for the Holy Bible, Mao's "Little Red Book" is the most printed book in history. It also holds the world record for being the most printed book in less than four years, with 720 million copies in print by the end of 1967. The personality cult, with its red booklet and constant brainwashing, eventually led to complete governmental control of everything and certain destruction for anyone who was willing to oppose worship of the chairman.

HOW MAO HELPED TO SPREAD **CHRISTIANITY IN CHINA**

At the same time, Mao implemented many practical improvements that greatly assisted the spreading of the gospel. Even in his days of intense hatred for the Christian community, he unwittingly helped proselytization in ways that were never even imaginable before his time. He united in one country a diverse land that included Tibet and Xinjiang—areas that had previously been independent nations—which effectively eliminated the need for passports and other travel documents in order for secret missionaries to serve in those areas. He connected the entire country with railways and road systems that helped make the hardest-to-reach places much more accessible to Christ's ambassadors.

Another huge work he accomplished was uniting the entire country under a single language. Before it became compulsory in China to learn Mandarin Chinese, people spoke hundreds of minority languages, making it impossible for someone to preach in many different areas without learning each region's language. Thanks to Mao, it became possible to share the gospel, conduct training, and implement mass Bible printing in one language for all of China. If that wasn't enough, he even ordered the Chinese characters to be simplified so that more people could learn to read and write, effectively opening the door for millions of people to read the Bible.

Even police pursuit of preachers served to extend the kingdom of God. Being on the run forced the evangelists to travel great distances around the country as itinerant preachers, resulting in even more areas hearing about Christ than if the police hadn't been making them flee. Ironically, Mao's pragmatic approach to making his country more mobile, literate, and competitive would defeat his other goal of destroying Christianity in China. It is safe to say that few people in the history of China did more for facilitating the spread of the good news than Chairman Mao.

DIE-HARD **CHRISTIAN FAITH**

One of several men well-known for not bowing to Chairman Mao was Lin Xianggao, or Samuel Lamb. Although his attacks on Brother Yun (whom Lamb has never met) and Yun's testimony, told in *The Heavenly Man* (which Lamb has never read), have caused some controversy, he remains an example of die-hard Christian faith against all odds. While he has some disagreements with many believers in the Back to Jerusalem movement, he is undoubtedly a true man of God who has dedicated his life to serving the Lord.

Samuel Lamb was born among the Portuguese in Macau and was raised among the British in Hong Kong. After Mao came to power, more than 100,000 Chinese fled to Hong Kong every month. By 1955, there were more than 2.2 million people living in Hong Kong, turning it into one of the most densely populated cities in the world. Most Christians who had the chance to leave China in the 1950s, 60s, and 70s did, but not Samuel Lamb. He easily could have resided in Hong Kong and ministered to the mass influx of Chinese refugees, started a nice church, and even settled down with his family. Instead, Lamb answered God's call and served inside China during the most terrifying days of her history.

He refused to bow to the new god of China and was labeled a counterrevolutionary, arrested, and thrown into prison. After being incarcerated for more than a year, he was released and told that he should never teach the Word of God again. However, it was not long before he was pastoring a church again in Guangzhou. In 1958, when he was arrested a second time, he was given a twenty-year sentence and put to work on a farm—out of sight and mind. Things changed when he was caught making a handwritten copy of the Bible. The authorities realized they had found a man who could not be beaten down, so they sent him to a coal mine for twenty years of hard labor.

Lamb endured many winters without proper clothing and many summers without air-conditioning. People were dying all around him from beatings, work accidents, and frostbite, but, by God's grace, he survived. The suffering didn't end when he was finally released after twenty years. He returned home to be greeted with the news of the deaths of his wife and his father. His mother was also very ill and died soon after his return.

Instead of finding a way to escape from China to find a better life in Hong Kong or abroad, he began to preach the gospel again. His church grew larger than it had been before his imprisonment. The Chinese government was not able to stop the Word from going forth.

Samuel Lamb's humble church of five thousand now meets in small rooms in Guangzhou, where everyone crowds together to hear him preach through a series of closed-circuit television cameras and monitors. Though he is constantly being harassed and is even detained from time to time, the authorities have left him alone, for the most part, probably because they have bigger problems in the north. His church is but a small sampling of the tens of millions of believers scattered throughout China's House Church networks.

PREACHING THE GOSPEL "**ON THE GO**"

The persecution in China that led many believers to preach the good news "on the go" created a huge logistical problem for the Public Security Bureau (PSB). Instead of a church like Pastor

Lamb's, where the congregation meets regularly in the same location, churches began blossoming in the rural areas all over Henan, Anhui, and Shandong. The PSB used to think that pastors like Lamb posed huge threats to their vision for a new China, but now, in their minds, churches like the one led by Pastor Lamb are from the "good old days." Such stationary churches took few resources to monitor, and the pastor could easily be summoned to the local police station for questioning at any time. In contrast, this new breed of pastors was running throughout the countryside, escaping the police and infecting every location they traveled to with their teachings about Christ. Instead of a few thousand people in a contained environment, now the police had to deal with several million spread over a vast area.

5

From Goose Feces to Gulags:
The Founding of China
Gospel Fellowship

To keep this book from turning into a collection of mere facts and historical data, great efforts have been made to include firsthand accounts of Chinese House Church believers whenever possible. There is no better way to understand the experiences of Chinese Christians than to see them in the mind's eye through the testimonies of eyewitnesses. There is also no more fitting testimony to further one's understanding of the Chinese House Church than that of a founding member of the largest House Church network in China. The next two chapters contain Pastor Shen Xiaoming's personal account of growing up under Mao, witnessing massive revival in Henan Province, and seeing the formation of the China Gospel Fellowship, also known as Tanghe Network.[17]

"On December 10, 1957, I was born in a southern village of Henan Province. Those were times when government reports of agricultural abundance were empty and false. According to the Communist Party, each acre of land could yield many thousands of pounds of crops, even tens of thousands, but, in reality, the land yielded nothing, and the people of China were starving. Everyone showed signs of malnutrition.

"Tens of thousands of people died in the Mao-made disaster. In the village where I lived, all the tree bark had been consumed. One day, my mother used all our money to buy a few pounds of tree bark so she could make soup for us to stay alive. Unfortunately, we were poisoned from that tree bark, and it made everyone extremely sick. My mother wept throughout the night, certain that she would die and leave her children behind. My father and grandparents had already passed away, and there was no one to take care of us.

"I was only three or four years old and remember very little, but one thing I cannot forget is the taste of goose excrement. We would have to search around the areas where the geese defecated so that we could have something to eat.

"Those years were hard for everyone. I was called the 'cat with nine lives' because most of the children in my village had already died, but I somehow managed to survive. My mother and I were the only ones who remained alive in our family. As a result, I became very close to her.

"During those days, everyone was required to go out and work in food distribution. My mother had to go and work, as well. She would leave early in the morning and return late at night. She would lock me up in the house to prevent me from leaving. I missed her so much during that time that I would often fall asleep crying at the door waiting for her.

"My mother soon remarried, and, as the family grew, I found myself as more of an outsider. I had a horrible relationship with my stepfather. From that relationship with my stepfather and stepfamily, I began to develop hatred toward everyone around me.

"Not long after I started primary school, the Cultural Revolution began. Every day, we witnessed criticism sessions where peers would condemn counterrevolutionaries. I remember an occasion when a group of people who believed in Jesus was paraded through the streets wearing tall hats with paper labels stuck to their clothes. A huge crowd followed behind cursing and swearing at them. I, too, followed but did not dare make a sound, because my uncle's family was Christian. When I was young, my maternal grandmother named me 'Victor,' because her hope was that I would grow up to be a victorious Christian. Even though I had many years of education in atheism and evolution, my deep feelings for Christians like my grandmother and uncle never faded.

"In 1975, toward the end of the Cultural Revolution, as I was graduating from high school, I contracted rheumatoid arthritis, which was difficult to treat and caused me great pain. Our family was very poor, and we were unable to seek medical treatment. I often wrestled with thoughts of killing myself. Each day was filled with tears, as I bitterly hated myself for having been dealt such a bitter fate. My days were soon occupied with questions about what methods I could use to commit suicide.

"Soon things turned even worse. In 1978, my mother suddenly fell ill. The doctors diagnosed her with cancer. We tried to borrow money from everyone we knew for her medical treatment. By August 1979, we had spent everything. Eventually, she couldn't walk or even swallow food. All she could do was wait for death. Mother told me that her last wish was to visit my uncle, so that she might bid her final farewell to her relatives there. She asked me if I would accompany her. Thinking that Mother would die very soon, and knowing that I, too, had no desire to live any longer, I agreed to join her in saying our last good-byes.

"As my mother and I rode on a rickshaw and then both had to be carried into my uncle's house, we were a pitiful sight. At once, my uncle's family began to cry and immediately shared the gospel with us. After they finished sharing the gospel with us, my mother accepted Jesus. I was hesitant and skeptical but had nothing to lose.

"Suddenly, something miraculous took place. I can't explain it, but my mother was able to eat again. At that time, I thought it was just a momentary reaction out of her excitement or maybe a mere psychological phenomenon. However, the second day passed, and then the third, and it was confirmed that my mother was completely healed! After that day, my mother never again took her medication. She was completely healed, and I had seen it with my own eyes. It was clear that this was real, but no one was able to explain it to me.

"One day, I was able to borrow a radio from my aunt's house, and I listened to a Christian radio broadcast from Hong Kong called 'Good Friend Station' that told stories about Jesus. I began to listen every night from six in the evening until after midnight, and I kept notes on everything that they taught. In this way, I was able to learn that Jesus is the Son of God and how He was crucified for our sins, was resurrected, and gave us new life. At that time, I truly received Jesus as my Lord and Savior.

"After receiving Jesus, I was given a new life, a life without fear and hurt. Many of the villagers heard about my conversion, and they also rejoiced. They brought their unbelieving sons and daughters to my house and asked me to share the gospel with them. The Holy Spirit began to move mightily, and people were added to the church every day.

"In the summer of 1980, the House Church in our village was formally established. Initially, we had only a few people, who were teenagers, but by 1982, we had close to two hundred people. There were many questions for me to answer but no way for me to learn more until, one day, an older lady came by my house when I was praying in the garden. The lady told me that she was a Christian teacher from Xi'an. She told me that I could write to a group in Hong Kong and ask for a Bible. I knew that it was risky, but I did it anyway. A few months later, they sent me one!

"Tears rolled down my face as I held that copy of the Bible in my hands. Christians from all around heard that I had a Bible and traveled for miles to come and see it. From then on, we kept on copying every chapter and verse by hand and distributing the copies. The gospel began to spread like wildfire. Revival broke out, the sick were healed, and even the dead were raised. The social impact from the spreading of the gospel was also great. Children respected their parents, parents loved their children, crime rates went down, and so forth, but things took a dramatic turn in the spring of 1982 when the party officials came to our church and declared our Christian meetings illegal. We were given a stack of papers from the government to study carefully. The contents of those documents shocked us when we read about the 'Fifteen Prohibitions.' These fifteen statutes were contrary to the Word of God and impossible for us to follow.

"On Christmas Day 1982, there were more than three hundred of us celebrating and praying when, all of a sudden, the county officials arrived and surrounded us. I was arrested and was their prime target. I had to endure a barrage of verbal attacks for about two to three hours. I began to cry out to the Lord, 'Oh Lord, how can You allow these men to take Your name in vain?' Suddenly, the leader of the interrogation calmed down. He said nothing else and left the room.

"After that arrest, it was clear that we would have to meet in secret. Even when we took our meetings underground, the church grew faster than ever before.

"On July 9, 1983, there was a nationwide crackdown on the House Church, and I was one of their number one targets. The police went to my house looking for me. They interrogated my stepfather, who was not a Christian and told the police about all the possible places I might be. I remained on the run. Life on the run was challenging but full of miracles.

"At the end of 1984, we had established more than two hundred host families. Each time we had a meeting, we saw gatherings of people in the hundreds. Everywhere we went, entire villages would swarm the meeting places. From those meetings, evangelists were sent out to preach the gospel in the surrounding cities and towns. Within two years, we saw more than thirty thousand people come to the Lord. Consequently, my name was also in the hands of the Security Bureau. I was traveling all the time and preaching. One time, I arrived in a village and there were many believers, so I asked them, 'Who preached the gospel to you?' and they replied, 'You did.' I told them that they must be kidding, I was sure I had never been to their village before, but they assured me that this was indeed the case and that they had the tape recordings to prove it. They told me that one month after I had preached to them, they saw twenty-five churches established.

"As evangelists, we constantly reminded each other that we must always be ready to go to jail. I even kept my hair short so that the police would not have anything to grab on to when I ran. I would also loosen all the buttons on my shirt before starting a meeting. I did this for the first ten years of ministry. Many of us evangelists would go many days without a shower. Our clothes became our blankets at night. We often slept in open fields or cow-sheds. Many of us had gnats on our bodies, and when we would get bored, we would pick them off of each other.

"One day, while we were conducting a meeting, Public Security Bureau officials came and sealed off all exits to the house that I was preaching in. I and more than ninety members who were at the meeting were promptly taken away to the local police station. I was locked up for a night in a cell with a floor area of four square meters. The next day, they interrogated and tortured me, and were ready to transfer another brother and myself to the county prison. The rest of our members were fined and then released.

"There was a chief of the Public Security Bureau who learned of my arrest and could not control his elation. He personally drove to see me and to escort me to prison. On the way, he told me with delight, 'It took me so many years to find you. This time, there will be no turning back. You will surely die in Xidagang [the detention prison].'

"As I entered the prison, I saw a large group of men who were jaundiced and scrawny-looking prisoners, each bare-bodied and wearing only a pair of shorts. Their shorts were often worn out, and you could see their bottoms through the holes. The whole scene was a scary sight.

"In prison, I didn't have a Bible. All I could do was to meditate on the verses I remembered and silently pray to God for strength to overcome amid suffering. God answered my prayer for strength. I never desired an early release from prison. When such thoughts surfaced, I immediately prayed for God to strengthen me and give me resolve. After only three months, I was released. The police chief's prediction that I would die in prison went unfulfilled.

"As I began to minister again, I could see the body of Christ growing. House meetings developed into local churches. Brothers and sisters who were forced to leave their homes repeatedly formed alliances with one another. We began to refer to these alliances as 'united missions.' At that time, I remember a brother saying, 'All of us walk the same path. We are a gospel fellowship.' Thus, our network gradually gained the label 'Gospel Fellowship' or 'China Gospel Fellowship.' This became a widely used term.

"The area that we are from in Henan is called Tanghe. Tanghe is the largest county in Henan Province and later became synonymous with the China Gospel Fellowship. One of the highly respected founders of Tanghe Fellowship from the earliest years is a man named Uncle Feng.

"In the spring of 1994, we saw a true increase in our evangelistic mission. We gathered in Tanghe and prayed over seventy evangelists who were sent out to more than twenty different provinces. A year later, the results were astounding! The gospel had been preached, churches had been established, our network had expanded, and our understanding had grown. For instance, there were two young sisters whose names were Xile and Xiazhe who went to Inner Mongolia. Their combined age was barely forty years. They had planted churches containing thousands of families in only a year. When they were preparing to return home, many of the converts did not want them to leave, so they followed them for several thousand miles on their journey home to Tanghe.

"I left my home in 1983 and was out preaching the gospel until 1994, never even entertaining thoughts about marriage. One day, I stopped to pray to the Lord about a future wife. I asked Him to prepare a wife for me according to His will. I prayed for a wife who was in the faith, virtuous, loving, intelligent, wise, and considerate, so that she might assist me in better serving the Lord. In the summer of 1994, at a meeting in Xinyang, I met my wife for the first time at a coworkers meeting. She was at the meeting preparing the food for everyone. I didn't see her again until I was hospitalized in Xinyang in the winter of 1995.

"As I prayed to the Lord, it became clear to me that she would be my future wife. I knew that my body was not healthy like other men's, and it was not easy for me to articulate my feelings, but I finally built up the courage to tell her, 'Based on the standards of this world, I have no credentials. I have neither a permanent roof over my head nor land to till. My body is full of infirmities, and I have no money. Furthermore, I am constantly being persecuted. I have nothing really to offer you.' She was amazing. She didn't care about my inadequacies. She used her savings to help support my ministry. She even did some odd jobs to get more money to help support me.

"In the spring of 1996, we were married. It was a very simple ceremony, and we had nowhere to stay, so we stayed in the church for two nights. On the third night, I was off to work again. We were very poor and didn't have money to buy food. Over time, due to the lack of food and malnutrition, my wife became very ill. We moved to Xinyang until she was better.

"In 1997, she became pregnant. The timing could not have been worse. All of our brothers and sisters were being rounded up by the police, our closest partners were put in prison, and the police were looking for me and my wife.

"We were also the target of the Eastern Lightning. The Eastern Lightning is a cult in Henan Province that teaches that God returned as a Chinese woman. They would capture our members and try to force them to believe in the female Christ. When our members refused, they were severely beaten. Often, their legs were broken, their ears were cut off, and their mouths were slit. I went to visit a few of our members in the hospital. It was not even possible to report these atrocities to the local police, because the police were after us, too.

"On November 7, 1997, only five days after my daughter was born, I went to preach to a church in Xinyang about the evils of the Eastern Lightning cult. Outside the house was a secret van being used by the Public Security Bureau. They had been monitoring me from across the street. We were arrested and taken to the regional headquarters, where they immediately began to beat us and ask us questions. The beatings went on all night long without stopping. The next day, they took us to the local prison.

"The PSB found information about some of our partners and contacted them and told them that I had been involved in a horrible automobile accident and was at the hospital. Everyone who arrived at the hospital to see me was captured, arrested, robbed of all their money, and interrogated.

"From these interrogations, the PSB was able to learn about many different secret meeting places, and they immediately began their raids. More than one hundred of my coworkers were subsequently arrested.

"I was placed in one of the most horrible and crude detention facilities in the country. I didn't have any warm clothes, blankets, or a bed to sleep on. The prison cell was cold in the month of November and had no heat. I had to use my hand when emptying my bowels, but there was nothing to clean up with. Many of my coworkers were in the cells close to mine. I could hear them scream out other coworkers' names when they were being interrogated. It was a horrible feeling not being able to provide comfort to them or know how they were doing. Eventually, one of my dear coworkers, Brother Wang, was transferred to my cell. I learned from him how the others were doing.

"Brother Wang told me that he had been stripped naked in the cold concrete cell, and the fan was turned on full-speed until the cold penetrated his bones, causing unbearable suffering. After talking with him, it was evident that they were saving me for last.

The PSB was interrogating everyone else to get information, and they were saving me for the end because I was the leader. I knew that they would be looking to give me the death sentence.

"After twenty days, the interrogation began. It was more brutal than I could ever have imagined. They questioned me for three days straight without taking a break. For two nights, without stopping, the interrogators took turns beating me, torturing me, and asking me questions. They stripped me naked and put me outside in the cold to make me talk more. 'Your group has been branded as a cult,' they would shout.

"I responded back, 'You say we are cult, but have you any evidence of our illegal activity? Have we ever done anything to subvert national interests? What are your bases for labeling us as a cult? We are orthodox Christians. We serve God based on the Bible. You say that the Gospel Fellowship is an illegal organization, but the church is by nature an organization, one that is based on biblical models.'

"After more than forty days of imprisonment, they escorted more than ten of us from the Xinyang County Pingqiao Detention Prison onto a huge truck surrounded by a few Public Security vehicles with sirens blaring. The truck we were on had labels pasted on all sides with the slogan 'Absolute Ban on Cults.' We were paraded through the streets and then brought to the town hall for public sentencing. All fourteen of us, including two sisters, were chained together in a row as we stood in front of the chairman's podium.

"The town hall was filled to capacity, mainly consisting of university students. The chairman read out our 'crimes' and announced the time span of corrective labor allocated to each one of us. Four of us were sentenced to two years. The rest were given three years. There were some in the audience who cheered when they heard our sentence. As for us, we proudly stood with our chests up and heads held high, because our consciences were clear.

"From that day onward, we began a new phase of life in the corrective facility. In the beginning, none of the Christians was allowed to have visitors, a rule that applied only to Christians.

"The guards at the prison would question some of the inmates during mealtime, 'Do you believe in Jesus? If you do not believe, then you may eat. If you believe in Jesus, then don't eat. Let Jesus help you!'

"This was especially tough because we were given jobs to do during the day. Failure to finish one's work would incur beatings. The work day started at five in the morning and ended at nine in the evening. This kind of punishment and work on an empty stomach made life much more difficult. When I began to look at this challenge and realized that it might go on for two or three years, I was certain that I would not survive.

"In order to keep Jesus' name from shame, all of us struggled to finish our assignments. At the work site, there was no room for relaxation or casual talk. Only at night, after working hours, could we secretly gather in small groups to encourage one another with God's Word. It was also during such sessions that the brothers would share with me the dumplings they had saved up. Since I was disabled, I could not join them at the work site, so I remained within the 'Strict Scrutiny Team,' where we were never allowed to have a full meal.

"Not long after we had all arrived at the prison, the attitude toward us Christians had begun to change. They witnessed how we would faithfully complete our tasks, use integrity in dealing with others, and treat our enemies with courtesy. Even the supervising guards began to like us. We used every opportunity to share the gospel of Jesus Christ. I was given an early release on January 4, 1998.

"I went right back to the field and began working. After my release, I had seen that the church had continued to experience revival and growth. It was important that we begin to train workers. We adopted three textbooks for training workers: *Lessons* on the Christian Faith, Lessons on Christian Living, and Lessons on Christian Ministry. We also used Questions and Answers on Christian Ethics and Morals. Using these simple materials, as well as the Bible, we conducted training sessions. We designated between twenty and thirty different training schools in different locations.

"In 1999, the Chinese government rallied the nation to develop the western region of China. The church, too, saw the ministerial needs in the western parts of the country, which were further from the central plains and had lower standards of living. Although we had preached the gospel there and established a few churches, we found it difficult to stabilize our ministries due to distance, insufficient funds, lack of pastors, heretical disturbances, and so on.

"We were able to raise up thirty young couples who were willing to go and preach the gospel in western China. We were also able to identify thirty supporters who would provide the support for those missionaries.

"These thirty missionaries were among the first to preach the gospel in the areas where they migrated to. They went to the minority tribes in Tibet, Qinghai, Xinjiang, Yunnan, Guizhou, Guangxi, Sichuan, Guangdong, Hainan, Fujian, Jiangxi, and Hunan.

"This kicked off a vibrant era of missions and missionary training. The churches that these missionaries started also began to send out missionaries! Although our immediate focus was on the minority tribes, we also began to make plans to take the gospel into bordering nations like Burma, India, North Korea, and so forth.

"Of all the persecution that I have experienced in China, April 16, 2002, is one of the days that I will never forget. Thirty-four coworkers and I were invited to attend a training center in Singapore called the Haggai Institute. We were told that our studies would be sponsored, but we would have to be interviewed and evaluated. We couldn't think of a feasible way of bringing the number of leaders requested by the Institute away from the field simultaneously, for such a long time period, but eventually we agreed to meet with one of their representatives in Shanghai. I arrived in Shanghai from Zhengzhou by train on April 16. Once we arrived at the meeting location, we were told that, because of security reasons, we would have to immediately disperse. We were taken in groups of two to seventeen different locations. I was with one of my coworkers, and we were soon placed with two coworkers whom I had never met.

"The next day, April 17, an indoctrination program began. My coworker and I were students in a classroom of four. We were told that because of the security situation with persecution in China, instructors from the Haggai Institute had flown in and were willing to teach a class of four students. We didn't know it then, but this was an Eastern Lightning trap. The other two students were not real students but had been placed in the classroom to help the instructor and to pretend to be students.

"An instructor walked into the room and began to teach. He was one of six teachers. His name was Chen. As Chen spoke, I could hear the words of the Eastern Lightning teachings, so I said, 'What you are talking about sounds like the Eastern Lightning teachings.' He explained, 'The Eastern Lightning teaches from the Bible, so of course there will be material that seems similar.'

"The instructors were so loving and friendly that I didn't suspect anything. One day, in the lavatory, my coworker Brother Shen came up to me and told me that he did not feel good about these instructors. He felt that the females were too friendly. In our network, we have strict rules about maintaining a safe distance between unmarried men and women that is socially acceptable. The females in this house were constantly coming to us when we were alone and asking for advice, comfort, and counsel.

"I was asked to write a letter to all the other coworkers telling them to listen to their teachers, do as they say, and try to learn as much as possible. I wrote the letter, and it was sent out to all the other coworkers.

"However, on May 4, after hearing an increasing amount of heresy and teaching contrary to the Bible, I stood up and openly rebutted their teaching. Everything changed. I was locked in my room and, for two or three days, was not given any food. Finally, they openly declared that they were representatives of the Eastern Lightning, not from the Haggai Institute. I yelled, 'You guys are a group of gangsters, robbers of the church, false Christs, antichrists, serpents draped in human skin, the filth of society! I will never forgo my beliefs in Jesus Christ and follow your ridiculous teachings! I won't listen, I won't watch, I won't think, I won't debate, and I won't believe!'

"There was no way of getting out, and I had no idea how they were going to deal with me. I knew all too well how they dealt with people who do not convert. I was prepared to be a Christian martyr.

"One night, two men came and dragged me into a vehicle and told me that they were going to take me home. Instead, they took me to a two-story building and locked me in a room. Guards were posted inside and outside my room. Each day, the guards would preach to me, but I would not listen to them. I refused to eat or drink for fear that they would try to drug me.

"They changed tactics. The male guards soon left, and they sent in a female who immediately tried to seduce me. She kept grabbing me, hanging on me, and using shameless words. I refused her, yelling at the top of my lungs, 'I am a Christian and a married man.'

"Soon, she left. After some time, I smashed the windows and began to yell outside. They gave up. On June 3, I was driven to the train station in Shanghai and dropped off. Physically, I was more emaciated than I had been when released from prison. One of my coworkers at another location was able to escape and reported the incident to the police. Within three days, the police were able to mobilize and hunt down the different locations of the Eastern Lightning cult and force the release of our colleagues.

"We organized an open forum on June 20. Each and every one of those who had been kidnapped shared their experiences. We mentioned how the Eastern Lightning used despicable tactics, such as deceit, financial enticement, sexual temptation, sexual stimulants, drugs, dreams, visions, rage, intimidation, isolation, mind control, and disruption of family life. Through this forum, everyone realized that our previous understanding of the Eastern Lightning had been insufficient. Still, the attacks of the enemy accomplished God's good purposes. God's power is revealed through human weakness. Through this series of trials, each and every one of us had been severely tested in regard to our knowledge of our Lord Jesus Christ, our steadfastness with respect to biblical truth, our trust in God, and also our moral integrity. Through this fiery trial, we had matured and realized our inadequacies before the Lord."

6

The Growth of China Gospel Fellowship

The following is a continuation of Shen Xiaoming's testimony:

"From the fall of 2002 until now, our church has begun to emphasize helping the poor as well as preaching the gospel. This is something that Christians must essentially pursue with fervency. However, since the church is often under persecution, Christians tend to lose heart in this regard. I thought about the church during the time of the biblical apostles. They, too, were being persecuted. They, too, underwent severe and cruel treatment. The apostle Paul encouraged the churches in Galatia by saying, *'And let us not grow weary of doing good, for in due season we will reap, if we do not give up. So then, as we have opportunity, let us do good to everyone, and especially to those who are of the household of faith'* (Galatians 6:9–10). In addition, the apostle Peter once wrote to the suffering church, *'For this is the will of God, that by doing good you should put to silence the ignorance of foolish people'* (1 Peter 2:15).

"In many churches, specific people have been designated to take charge of good works, such as repairing public roads, caring for the poor, sheltering homeless children, and so forth. Christians must show concern for anything that has been neglected. Christians must step up and show love to the social outcasts that no one wants to care for, even though it may not seem beneficial.

"We sent out workers from our church who organized seminars that taught villagers better techniques of raising livestock, planting edible fungi, and other agricultural skills. By helping the poor, we are able to glorify the name of the Lord.

"I was born during the era of Mao Zedong, an era marked by combative struggles. These struggles were targeted at landowners, wealthy farmers, antirevolutionaries, rightists, and all Christians. Several million people were labeled as 'evil' and forced to squat in cowsheds, put on tall hats, and be liable to beatings and scoldings.

"The era of Deng Xiaoping, on the other hand, was marked by reform and openness. Deng disliked struggles and used slogans like 'No Disputes,' 'White Cat, Black Cat,' 'One Country, Two Systems,' 'Development Is Solid Truth,' and so on. He thereby did away with many unreasonable political policies, such as 'Huge Pot of Rice,' 'Ideology of Equal Distribution,' 'Slice with One Knife,' and the like. We moved from a planned economy toward a market economy. Such reforms were a giant step forward for China. Countless people left their hometowns and migrated to the cities to do business or seek employment. There was tremendous freedom of mobility. It was amid this change in climate that the church began to turn from looking inward to focusing outward.

"The era of Jiang Zemin has been hailed as the third generation of leadership in Communist China. Jiang advocated the theory of 'Three Representations,' which immediately became so important that it swarmed the daily newspapers, airwaves, and TV stations. When political leaders hosted foreign emissaries, this was a mandatory topic of discussion. This 'Three Representations' theory became widely credited with every sort of progress, be it the development of a small region, the prosperity of a certain market, the advancement of new scientific methodologies, the screening of a new movie, the visit of a government official, or the rescue operations of the police force. The Chinese

Communist Party began to proclaim the slogan, 'Keep Up with the Times; Reform and Renew.'

"We trust that history will not go into reverse. It is only a matter of time before we see a civilized, free, and open China where the disruption and persecution of Christian meetings will be a thing of the past. These questions arise: 'How will today's "House Church" face these new circumstances?' 'What form will she take?' 'If the situation does indeed slacken in terms of governmental control, will she have to register?' 'Will she register according to geographical location or as parachurch groups?' 'What will her responsibility toward society be?'

"These are questions that demand serious consideration. Church and state are separate, but Christians cannot ignore politics, because the two are intimately intertwined. For all these years, Christians have been hesitant in commenting too extensively on this sensitive issue of politics, for fear of being swept into this complicated whirlpool. With each wave of political upheaval, Chinese Christians have tended to adopt an attitude of withdrawal. What results over time are house churches that exist passively in the world. I think that, if the government assumes an open attitude, it will recognize the legality of the house churches. Christians must be ready to reciprocate. It is not impossible to envision the house churches and the Chinese government as equal partners in dialogue. We know what our stance and responsibility are: Christians are to be salt and light in the world, ready to purify the world through the Lord's love, justice, and holiness. We are to be law-abiding, reprimanding sinful behavior while opposing corruption and decadence. However, we must also remember that we must not get entangled in political matters unless we are certain it is God's will. We need to maintain our allegiance to biblical principles while gradually engaging our immediate circumstances with flexibility, wisdom, and prudence.

"China is a major agricultural nation. Thus, it is little surprise that the house churches of China have their roots in the farming communities. When we first started evangelizing, most people walked, while those who were better off would ride bicycles, weaving through nearby counties and cities within a radius of two to three hundred miles. As the good news spread and more people came to Christ, more and more local churches were established. Out of their love for the evangelists, brothers and sisters in the Lord started making financial gifts to help support them.

"Before 1990, church offerings did not amount to much. Due to the political situation, no one really taught on giving. If we even got close to a message on giving, it most likely occurred in the context of someone making a meager thanksgiving offering out of gratitude for a miraculous healing of some sort in answer to his or her prayers. Living standards tended to be poor in the villages. When even daily sustenance is a problem to be solved, the topic of giving hardly seemed relevant.

"After 1990, our ministries in neighboring provinces began to make progress. Since traveling expenses were naturally higher for longer journeys, stipends for evangelists also increased. This, however, put the church in a difficult position. Most of our evangelists were single and therefore without family commitments. Even those with families could not do much to support their spouses or children apart from helping out a little with farming duties. The church was never in the habit of financially supporting our evangelists due to reasons such as: (1) the poverty level of churches in farming communities; (2) the tendency to avoid slanderous labels of 'profiting under the guise of religion' amid a political environment marked by constant persecution; (3) the nature of the church as a 'citizens' army' and 'laity movement' whereby all ministerial positions were considered equal and professional pastors were unheard of; and (4) the lack of teaching that *those who proclaim the gospel should get their living by the gospel* (1 Corinthians 9:14).

"A crisis arose with regard to church ministry and the propagation of the gospel. How will single evangelists cope once they get married? Middle-aged full-time workers in local churches face the following problems: education for their children, medical bills of relatives, repair expenses for broken-down houses, and so on.

"There was the case of one family who loved the Lord, received others, and opened up their home for church meetings. When brothers and sisters gathered, the husband would preach, while the wife would serve the guests. Since the house was on the verge of collapse, they had to borrow money to make the necessary repairs. Due to their unpaid debts, creditors often came knocking. Failure to pay their dues would shame the Lord's name. Paying on time would mean giving up their ministries and moving elsewhere to find jobs. This couple was caught in the unenviable dilemma of leaving or staying, which eventually led to many domestic squabbles between them. Such cases are definitely not isolated examples among the house churches in China. It would be a tremendous shame for such unfortunate tragedies to continue, where God's workers are lost to worldly pursuits.

"This is an hour of critical need. When certain foreign missionaries enter China to carry out gospel ministries, they witness with their own eyes the poverty level of the Chinese house churches, and so they willingly make financial gifts to them. Some help with the daily expenses of evangelists, some express concern for needs of missionaries, while others focus on theological education. In this manner, such foreign aid has given both invaluable support and a great impetus to the Chinese churches. On the one hand, this generosity has become a huge blessing to churches, one that allowed for propagation of the gospel, establishment of ministry teams, migratory missions, and theological training. On the other hand, it has also resulted in the parasitic dependence of church coworkers on foreign aid.

"After the year 2000, the church faced crises on all sides. Funds were insufficient, and many ministries already under way were unable to continue, which left the Lord's work half-finished. Numerous visions and plans were conceived but were stillborn. Due to cultural disparities, there even arose sentiments of mutual suspicion. At the present time, we see a decline in assistance from foreign missionaries. Possible reasons for this include: (1) the impression that the Chinese economy has already taken great strides forward; (2) supporters themselves encounter financial difficulties; (3) monetary aid has resulted in negative impact in certain situations; (4) givers harbor ulterior motives of furthering their own careers in China; and (5) God Himself wishes for the churches in China to mature amid these trials.

"Chinese churches must seriously consider moving toward the goal of self-sustenance. It is a biblical teaching that churches be self-sustaining as a sign that they are spiritually healthy. Thus, church leaders should not lose sight of the fact that all members in Christ's body are mutually dependent. They can thereby better lead their members to make offerings for the sake of unity and a common vision for the Lord's ministry. Ministers would then be free of possible restrictions arising from financial dependence on outsiders; the church could avoid turmoil due to financial disputes; the government would loosen its foothold in accusing the churches on monetary grounds; and church leaders would not lose their self-esteem because of money. We trust that God will open the door to this major breakthrough.

"In the beginning, evangelism amid the farming communities began with one-on-one engagement. Those who were born again and saved gladly shared the gospel message with those around them. God also manifested Himself through healings, exorcisms, miraculous signs, wonders, and the transformed lives of believers. The villages were unique in that governmental scrutiny was relatively loose, such that neighbors loved to interact with one another. During less intensive phases of the agricultural season, villagers would visit neighbors or relatives. In the early days in China, the gospel gradually spread, to the extent that entire families were coming to the Lord simultaneously, and believing parents gladly dedicated their children to the Lord's ministry. After some simple form of instruction and training, they became vibrant members of the evangelistic army. In the three months before and after the Spring Festival, villages located in the Central Plains face a harsh winter, when all agricultural activities cease. This is the lightest part of the farming season, but the busiest for Christian believers. Brothers and sisters would gather together for the commencement of 'Gospel Month' events. When it first started, preachers would talk about evangelistic strategies and give out some gospel tracts.

"Compared to ministry in the villages, evangelization in the cities is much more difficult. There are many differences that distinguish cities from villages: (1) time is of the essence; (2) there are higher cultural standards; (3) the people have a sense of superiority; (4) the people are reluctant to interact with others; (5) residents live in confined places of dwelling; and (6) there is stricter legislation on nonresidents. All these factors contribute in hindering a breakthrough in our city ministries. Initially, some brothers and sisters could minister only in the suburbs. Once they had established their suburban ministries, they then hoped to make use of their relatives residing in the cities as stepping-stones to minister within the city limits. Some would do business with their hometown acquaintances. Through eating, living, and working together, Christian meetings were organized.

"Others would begin as independent entrepreneurs. With legitimate status, not only could meetings be held at their offices, but they could also be self-sustaining. Still others would enroll as students on university campuses with the help of connections and evangelize while they studied. As entrance requirements were lowered, more high school graduates became eligible for university studies. Based on the current state of affairs, the house churches need a batch of younger brethren to further their education in universities and thereby improve the quality of church coworkers.

"As for our work among the minority tribes, since commencing in 1994, progress has been less than ideal. Despite the obstacles of working in the minority regions of China, we have managed to establish a few churches among the minority tribes. We strongly believe that saving the nations is God's desire. If even Western missionaries can preach the gospel to the minority tribespeople, it ought to be much easier for Chinese Christians. However, such ministry has a long learning curve where personal experiences and strategies must be constantly evaluated and revised. Various avenues of consideration are both possible and necessary for our missionaries. We continue to pray for revival in those parts of China.

"In the China Gospel Fellowship, we try to focus on the unity of the Christian believers in China. Church unity is God's will. Before Jesus left His disciples, He prayed,

> *Holy Father, keep them in your name, which you have given me, that they may be one, even as we are one....I do not ask for these only, but also for those who will believe in me through their word, that they may all be one, just as you, Father, are in me, and I in you, that they also may be in us, so that the world may believe that you have sent me. The glory that you have given me I have given to them, that they may be one even as we are one, I in them and you in me, that they may become perfectly one, so that the world may know that you sent me and loved them even as you loved me.*
>
> (John 17:11, 20–23)

The truth concerning ecclesiastic unity is familiar to every preacher and is continually preached, but it is also very difficult to see in reality.

"The house churches are not without problems in this area. Lack of communication and of collective consensus on biblical truth led to the increasing independence of individual groups as each labored feverishly to spread the good news. In the mid-1990s, some coworkers who loved the Lord took note of the disunity and traveled all over China in a bid to gather the more influential House Church leaders for fellowship and discussion on church unity. Everyone realized the importance of unity and also agreed to maintain contact in the future. After a meeting with the most influential House Church leaders, we enacted a few important measures that would help with unity.

"In recent years, we have had numerous similar gatherings for interaction but have yet to see any major results, because everyone has a different understanding of unity. They consider denominations to be historical artifacts that arose under special circumstances in the past. To try to do away with denominations altogether is hardly a viable option, but neither is exalting one's own brand of Christianity while belittling brothers and sisters who do not believe exactly the same. It is both unloving and irresponsible to reject members of Christ's body who truly love the Lord. The churches in China all distinctly realize that many extremists and heretics have been shaped by a lack of fellowship and mutual correction. With regard to issues of mergers and organizational structures, we have all agreed upon three doctrinal foundations that are crucial to accomplishing true unity. Our churches are committed to being: (1) centered on Christ, (2) established in love, and (3) united in truth.

"To stand firm in the truth, the church must build itself upon the foundation of the apostles and prophets, exalt the Bible as the absolute measure of truth, consult theological works of the past, and avoid private or twisted interpretations of the Word. Scripture should normally interpret itself in conformity to context. Personal insights and experiences cannot ultimately replace God's truth. We must be approved and unashamed workmen of God who correctly handle the word of truth. (See 2 Timothy 2:15.)

"In twenty years of development, the House Church of China has endured much suffering. Under God's protection, she has spouted roots, blossomed, and borne abundant fruit. On this journey of growth filled with both successes and failures, she has had moments of brilliance, as well as numerous blemishes. Facing the twenty-first century, we in the Chinese house churches need to reassess and transform ourselves, affirming strengths and identifying weaknesses. Armed with lessons from the past, we will hopefully be able to better plan for the future as we face even greater pressures and challenges.

"The Chinese church has withstood wave upon wave of attacks. The Cultural Revolution in particular sought to eradicate all forms of religion and mercilessly persecuted Christians. Yet, not only did the church in China survive eradication, the house churches started taking baby steps on the road to maturity as she gradually gained strength. As of today, the gospel has taken root, blossomed, and borne fruit on Chinese soil. Not only have God's children not been silenced, they have grown up into the vibrant house churches of China that have gotten the world's attention.

"House churches from all over China have responded to the Great Commission by fanning the fires of unprecedented missionary fervor. Today, they are taking on a larger burden and shouldering a greater responsibility as they prepare to enter the harvest fields of world evangelization. This is no longer a pipe dream. It is an actual missionary movement. God has placed the Chinese church in the midst of suffering and trial. This must somehow be part of His wonderful purpose.

"The church in China must prepare for action. The harvest field ought to be the Arab world. This is a hard and tough piece of land to till. All the financial resources of the churches in Western nations will not accomplish this task. Only Jesus Christ's love can transform hearts and dissolve enmity.

"China has close ties with Islamic countries. For generations, these countries have had a tradition of forging intimate friendships with China. As China increasingly moves toward openness, and Chinese churches gradually mature and unite under the banner of a common vision for global missions, the dream of past generations of missions-minded Christians in bringing the gospel back to Jerusalem may very well be fulfilled by this generation of House Church believers.

"As far as I am aware, many Chinese churches are now running schools on world evangelization and studying English, Arabic, computer skills, medicine, business, and Arabic culture—all in preparation to better understand and enter Arabic countries as a powerful missionary force. May we in China fight the good fight and win many souls for the Lord. Amen."

Part 2:

Inside the Henan House Church Networks

Chinese House Church evangelists training in the Cave

Worship in Sister Han's secret cave

Historic meeting in Burma where representatives from almost all of the major Henan networks were present

7

A Brief Introduction to the Networks

Another aspect of the Chinese church that has mystified many foreigners is how the churches are organized. There are several different types of churches in China, which makes it hard to identify who is being talked about in any given story. As we indicated earlier, some people who have lived or worked in China, even as missionaries, will often make the mistake of thinking they are "China experts."

It is easy to see small, contained areas of China and come to the conclusion that all of China is represented in that one sample. In reality, this is simply not the case. For instance, just because someone has lived in Kunming for ten years and has met members of underground churches does not necessarily mean that he or she understands the inner workings of the super-secret House Church.

Even if someone had lived in Nanyang, a city in Henan Province that has become the incubator of today's revival in China, that person would not necessarily have had the exposure necessary to become familiar with Christianity in all of China.

There are several types of churches in China, because, as we have noted, the laws that govern China and Chinese territories are not universal. In this book, to avoid confusion, we have narrowed down the types of churches to seven of the most common native churches found in the nation today, excluding fellowships like the Russian Orthodox, Korean Protestants, and other foreign registered churches:

1. *The official Three-Self Patriotic Movement church:* This is the state-controlled church that has rules, clergy, and operations that are overseen, led, and implemented by the Communist Party. TSPM churches can be found in most major cities in China and are usually identified by marked buildings.

2. *Official non-TSPM churches:* These are churches that are registered with the Chinese government but do not necessarily qualify as TSPM churches. The clergy are not selected by the government, the rules are more relaxed, and the government has much less oversight in these churches. They are common in places like Wenzhou. We will explore the nature of the church in Wenzhou in chapter 17.

3. *Official "unofficial" churches:* China is made up mostly of ethnic minority areas, and many of these areas are setting up churches that are officially recognized by the local government but are neither registered nor controlled by the TSPM. These churches are often found in minority areas like Yi or Miao minority villages.

4. *Unregistered independent house churches (urban):* This term specifically refers to urban areas where well-educated and well-respected members of the community meet for fellowship and unified worship of Christ. These churches are usually not connected with any other church or network and are not typically involved with outreach programs or missionary work. The majority are inwardly focused small fellowships held in private homes where members share from the Word and worship together. These are some of the fastest-growing churches in China, but they still make up a small number of the percentage of Christians there. These churches are more common in metropolitan areas like Beijing, Shanghai, Guangzhou, and Shenzhen.

5. *Underground independent house churches (rural/migrant):* These unregistered churches are all over China today in the rural areas where the traditional networks do not have a huge presence. These independent churches are also strong in the migrant communities where people work in factories.

6. *Underground urban house churches:* These underground house churches in the urban areas differ from the unregistered independent house churches in that they are connected in networks and emphasize evangelism. Often, they are not registered because they either have not attempted it or have tried it and been rejected. These churches often have a single leader with several churches networked together, but not always. Sometimes, they are an independent coalition of several churches with several leaders. These churches are very strong in places like Beijing, Shanghai, Guangzhou, and Shandong Province.

7. *Underground House Church networks:* The underground House Church networks are groups that have formed over time as the result of revival and intense persecution. These are well-organized churches that cover most of China. They have a single patriarch type of leadership. Even though there are only a handful of large, well-known networks, they can be found in every province and every major city throughout China.

Space does not permit us to be exhaustive in covering each of these different types of churches in China. Therefore, the following chapters will focus mainly on the last category—the underground House Church networks. Most books and articles about the Chinese church focus on Henan Province and the massive networks that have come out of that area, but the frequently overlooked networks of Anhui are as big as their Henan counterparts and are in some ways even more effective on the mission field.

As mentioned earlier, it is estimated that there are 130 to 150 million believers in China today. Of these numbers, it is thought that more than fifty million are a part of the underground house churches discussed in this book. More underground House Church networks exist in China than can be covered in this volume, but we will identify and explore the main well-known churches, as well as some others that are not as famous.

For easier reference, we will organize the Chinese house churches under the following sections. In coming chapters, we will discuss several of them in detail and others more generally. Traditionally, the five most famous House Church networks have been three that originated in Henan Province—Tanghe, Fangcheng, and the Born Again Movement—and two from Anhui Province—Truth and Blessing.

Henan Province House Church Networks (with alternate names)
- Tanghe (China Gospel Fellowship)
- Fangcheng (China for Christ Church)
- Five Brothers ("No Name")
- Born Again Movement

Anhui Province House Church Networks (with alternate names)
- Truth (Yingshan, or Zhenli)
- Blessing (Lixin, or Mongfu)
- Little Joe's (name concealed for safety)

Other Networks and Churches
- "YL" Network
- South China Church
- Shandong Province House Church
- Nanyang
- Wenzhou

Sinim was the name of a fellowship of unity and cooperation between many of the networks in the 1990s and 2000s.

8

Tanghe
(China Gospel Fellowship)

To introduce the Chinese House Church networks, we will begin with those that developed in Henan Province. It would be impractical to start with any other Henan network than Tanghe, because it is the best known of the underground networks. It is named after the area where it started—Tanghe County, which is under the administration of Nanyang City. Tanghe Network is often called China Gospel Fellowship. As was explained in chapter 5, the name came from an early leader from Tanghe who commented on the teams that were being sent out to preach the gospel. He felt they were a kind of "gospel fellowship" of believers dedicated to preaching the good news of Jesus Christ.

One of the reasons for Tanghe Network's fame around the world is its huge size. Many people have estimated that the network comprises as many as ten million believers, making it one of the largest churches in history (although Fangcheng Network was considered to be larger at one point). Tanghe has more members than most European countries, yet if someone were to travel to China and ask people at a train station where to find the Tanghe church, he or she would more than likely get odd looks and no answers. Even an Internet search would yield very little information about this network. For example, how can a church with so many members not even be described with adequate information on Wikipedia? At the time of this writing, that popular online source of knowledge contained only one paragraph on Tanghe, while the rest of the information posted had almost nothing to do with the network.

BEGINNINGS OF **TANGHE**

Tanghe House Church Network is widely acknowledged to have been founded by Uncle Feng Jianguo before his imprisonment in 1975. It really began as a loose fellowship of believers who stayed underground and tried to survive. By the time Uncle Feng was released from prison in 1980, a solidified movement existed, having been developed under leaders like Pastor Shen Yiping and Pastor Shen Xiaoming. In earlier chapters, we read Pastor Xiaoming's detailed account of the development of this underground House Church during those years. In this chapter, we will take a more comprehensive look at Tanghe.

Tanghe and Fangcheng networks alike have been greatly influenced by Pastor Dennis Balcombe, who is a legend in his own right. Dennis Balcombe was born and raised in California. In 1969, he moved to Hong Kong to serve as a missionary. By 1970, he had started his Revival Christian Church in the northern area of Kowloon, not far from the Chinese border. When Chinese leader Deng Xiaoping began to open the doors to China, Dennis was one of the first to go, eventually making his way to Henan Province in the latter part of the 1980s. When he arrived, the revival was already very much under way.

The Henan churches were significantly affected by the theologically charismatic teachings of Pastor Balcombe, and—according to the leaders who remember those times well—these Pentecostal practices also brought challenges and division.

However, charismatic influences on Tanghe cannot be credited entirely to Balcombe. Marie Monsen is widely considered to be the matriarch of the charismatic house churches in Henan Province. She arrived in China in 1901, just when the revival meetings in Topeka, Kansas, were taking place (meetings that were the forerunner of the Azusa Street Revival). She served diligently in Henan Province and left her mark forever on the House Church in even the most remote places like Tanghe and Fangcheng.

Before Marie Monsen, there was Jonathan Goforth, who was at the center of revival fires that swept through Korea and much of China in the early twentieth century. He spent some time in Henan and endured great hardships there but was often accused of emotionalism. There was also a well-known Christian general who ruled over Henan Province and brought peace and security to the people there by implementing the righteousness and justice inherent in biblical teachings. In addition, there were many other missionaries who laid the spiritual foundation for Tanghe and, in turn, had an impact on the entire House Church movement in China.

Of all the underground House Church networks, Tanghe has been one of the most active in working with foreigners. Its connection to foreign missionaries and its support from foreign organizations have been among the most prominent of the networks. Its fellowship has been quite inclusive in China, as well. As indicated, Tanghe is mostly charismatic, but the church has embraced even those believers who are more conservative.

In the early days of the House Church, there was no intention among believers in Tanghe to start a church movement. Christians were just trying to survive by whatever means possible. Serving Jesus Christ and staying alive were, at times, mutually exclusive ideas. The original leadership of Tanghe didn't go to Bible school and return home with grand dreams of starting megachurches that would transform their communities. They were just steadfast believers who happened to all live in Tanghe. The place where they were from became associated with the churches that were forming, growing, and then spreading to other areas.

When people would ask, "Where are those Christians from?" others would respond, "They are from Tanghe." Thus, they came to be called Tanghe Church. Even though the church continued to grow to hundreds, thousands, and eventually even hundreds of thousands of converts, they still maintained the simple name of the county where the church had been birthed.

According to Pastor Chen, who is one of the top representatives of Tanghe today, the beginning days of the church were full of trial and persecution. "Christians were always on the run. They would run away from the authorities and hide in the homes of their relatives. Soon, their relatives would become Christians and often have to go on the run, as well, and live in the homes of their friends and relatives. The believers, both old and new, were always looking for new places to hide. That was how the gospel spread in the beginning."[18]

THE INFLUENCE OF **FOREIGN MISSIONS ORGANIZATIONS**

When China began to open in the 1980s, rumors started to emerge that the church inside had experienced growth in the face of persecution. These rumors caused many former missionaries and missionary organizations that had been praying for China to rejoice. When Westerners began to peek inside China and look for any sign of believers, they soon heard about Tanghe and how the Christians there were zealously preaching the gospel everywhere they went.

Foreign organizations from around the world that were hungry to gain status in China were quick to seek them out. As mentioned earlier, Tanghe has probably had the most exposure to Western missions organizations of any underground House Church network in China. Western missionaries and related organizations quickly came with cash in hand to help the church. They offered training, pastoral support, facility funding, distance-learning degrees in theology, foreign mission field training and support, transportation funding, and more.

What Tanghe did not realize was that much of the funding from Western organizations came with its own price tag. While the foreign organizations offered support, they also wanted control. Many foreign missionaries with good intentions of serving the Chinese traveled to China to train them in theology and missiology. Many of them lived with the students, ate with the students, and grew close to them.

However, when the students completed their training, the teachers or missionaries and the organizations that had sent them continued to communicate with them, support them financially, and even direct where they would travel, what they would do, and how they would do it. This completely bypassed the leadership of the local church. The local leadership would arrange for their students to be trained and gain more biblical understanding from these foreign organizations but ended up losing them altogether.

The foreign missions organizations were able to provide more financial support than the local leadership and appeared to have more understanding of how to conduct long-term missions. They also seemed to be quite confident in decision making, so the students eventually became missionaries for the foreigners. (A similar travesty had led to the expulsion of foreign missionaries from China in the 1950s and 60s.)

Here is one illustration of this predicament. In 2008, while Zhang Rongliang (a leader of Fangcheng Church) was still in prison, his son was in charge of the network duties. He came to meet with this author and his coworkers from Back to Jerusalem International in a hotel in Zhengzhou and asked for our help.

"We would like to partner with you to start a training school," he began. We were a little perplexed because we knew that Fangcheng had many training schools in China. Many of these schools were supported and staffed by very talented and dedicated foreign missionaries. "We like the way your organization has always worked with us. Many foreign organizations take our missionaries and provide training for them, but then, when the students graduate, they are taken away and controlled by the foreigners. We have very little contact with them and very little input about the future of those missionaries. In many ways, one more missionary to those schools is one less Chinese missionary from our church."

Once those foreign missionaries and missions organizations had their own "spiritual militia" built up in China, they began to report heavily on their activities to raise more support back in the West. Missions organizations published names, detailed pictures, locations, training goals, and progress in weekly newsletters and magazines. These newsletters and magazines were consumed by Western audiences as fast as they could be printed—but back in China, there were casualties.

Chinese intelligence personnel often scanned those kinds of magazines and articles for information. Their emissaries living abroad were able to obtain many of these church and missions organization publications and glean information from them to use in locating churches, leaders, and workers, and to refer to during their interrogation sessions.

The problems connected to working in association with Western missions organizations were not isolated to Tanghe; they have been experienced by almost every underground House Church network in China. Many of networks have narrowed down the missionaries and missions organizations they are comfortable working with. Newcomers are often sent through channels of middlemen who pose as decision makers. Getting to the leadership of some House Church networks is more difficult today than it was even ten or fifteen years ago.

However, Tanghe Network has still tried to remain as open as possible and continues to work with many foreign organizations at its own risk. In June 2011, we held a meeting with Pastor Chen. We had to be careful about the meeting because Tanghe is one of the most monitored House Church networks in China. These days, the police may not conduct a raid, but they watch who the network is associating with and maintain a list for future use.

THE "**IMMERSION TECHNIQUE**"

Pastor Chen became a believer in the winter of 1989 during a time when miracles were frequent in Tanghe. He was almost immediately enrolled in the underground Tanghe Bible school. After completing the training, he was sent to minister in Hebei Province for a year, Anhui Province for two or three years, and then to Hubei for six months. He clearly remembers that this is how new believers were "baptized by fire" in those days. They didn't have time to get comfortable with the idea of being Christians. Once you became a believer, you were put to work right away.

During a meeting in Baton Rouge, Louisiana, in May 2011, Brother Yun gave a sermon in which he spoke about the nature of this "immersion technique" used by the house churches in China. He stated that the longer Christians wait to be used, the less likely they are to ever be used. He explained that in China, unlike in Western cultures, new Christians are expected to immediately take what they know about Christ and share it with others. He went on to say that many people in the West feel they must first get formal training and a diploma that supposedly gives them legitimacy to preach, and only then *might* they go out and tell others.

The immersion technique is one of the most important practices contributing to the growth of Christianity in China today. Brother Yun often points to the example of Mary Magdalene in this regard. He shows that on the morning of Christ's resurrection, Mary didn't know much about where Jesus had gone or what He had been doing since His crucifixion, but she immediately went and told others that Jesus had risen and that His tomb was empty.

Thus, the longer a believer waits to share his or her faith, the less likely that individual will be to share at all, even after much study. But Pastor Chen of Tanghe did not have to wait long before he was thrown into the heat of battle. Because workers were in such short supply, he was often called back to help carry and deliver Bibles from Guangzhou.

In 2002, he was sent to Beijing to plant churches, and he was able to plant more than thirty churches that are now regularly attended by more than 2,800 believers. Those churches in Beijing are now sending evangelists to Gangsu, Xinjiang, and Qinghai provinces to share the gospel with the Muslim minorities living there.

Pastor Chen does not represent Tanghe by himself. He stands shoulder to shoulder with seven other brothers who help make decisions regarding the network. In March 2011, all the top leadership from Tanghe came together for a strategy meeting regarding the network's future. At that time, they decided to dramatically change the way things worked in their network. Because Tanghe has a massive number of members, it is difficult to adequately oversee the different aspects of future ministry. The Tanghe leadership ended up deciding to assign each representative to one of eight different departments: (1) missions, (2) pastors, (3) finance, (4) children's ministry, (5) youth ministry, (6) worship, (7) education, and (8) administration.

The division of Tanghe into eight different groups is new, and time will tell where it leads them. However, it definitely shows that some of the more chaotic past is beginning to give way to order and planning. Such a development is often part of the cycle of revival. The beginning is usually chaotic, unplanned, explosive, and wonderful; then, as the movement matures, it starts to have more of an outward focus and to take more deliberate steps toward future goals.

Today, Tanghe has Bible schools that are connected with foreign universities to teach practical theology. They have a training center in Beijing currently connected with a Baptist university in Malaysia that allows Tanghe students to receive legitimate university diplomas for completing studies at an underground Bible school. Tanghe was one of the first pioneers in this technique.

Tanghe Network cannot register with the government—not yet, anyway. Many groups around the world have joined in the chant of the Chinese government to convince underground networks like Tanghe to register, but the restrictions that would be imposed on the leadership would basically bring their entire evangelical concept to a screeching halt. Understandably, they have been reluctant to do so.

This means that Tanghe cannot set up any kind of officially recognized training facility for its students. However, partnering with foreign universities and training schools that are formally recognized and sensitive to the situation in China has allowed groups like Tanghe to provide their members with legitimate, formally recognized training.

Today, Tanghe is focused on training missionaries and sending them to countries in the 10/40 Window as part of what is collectively referred to in China as the "Back to Jerusalem vision." In October 2011, I visited one of the Tanghe Bible schools in Beijing. The school has a business in front to act as a cover. While at the Bible school, I arranged a meeting with one of the instructors, with whom I had been acquainted for several years. Christmas was approaching, and we were planning to participate in the "Christmas in China" project with Tanghe. The project involved hand-delivering backpacks to children throughout China; these backpacks would be filled with school supplies by House Church believers. Each backpack would have a picture of the nativity scene and a gospel message, allowing the bags to continue to minister long after they had been distributed.

While discussing the future work, the leader asked, "Do you have connections in Egypt?" Amazingly, we had just returned from Egypt, where work was being carried out with Back to Jerusalem missionaries from China. The leader went on to share that they had a missionary couple working in Cairo that needed assistance. The couple didn't have any income, and their visas had expired. The leader then provided the missionary couple's business card, complete with name, contact information, and designation as pastor. Such openness about the ministry shows that Tanghe is definitely taking steps toward being recognized and is no longer hiding in the shadows. Each year, the network is becoming bolder and bolder.

During another meeting with Tanghe leaders in 2011, the leaders were asked what their biggest needs were. Before even batting an eyelash, they unanimously responded, "Bibles."

"Bibles are one of the greatest needs that we continue to have," Pastor Chen added in response. "Even though your organization at Back to Jerusalem has helped us with Bibles for so many years, it is still a big need. Even to get one or two Bibles is sometimes difficult when you really need to find one. We have begun to focus more on urban ministry, and we know some people at the Three-Self church who are able to help smuggle some Bibles to us, but then they often have problems afterward with accountability. When we minister to the factory workers in the bigger cities, we see large numbers of people coming to the Lord, but we don't have enough Bibles to meet this need. And that does not include Bibles that we need in other languages. We have seen several Uighur Muslims [a minority group in China] come to the Lord, but they have to read the Bible in Chinese. Many of them cannot read Chinese, so we don't have any Bibles to give them. We have an immediate need for one thousand Uighur Bibles."

Tanghe is focusing strongly on the Back to Jerusalem vision. They have set their sights westward to reach out to Muslim countries. They have already trained evangelists and missionaries to take the gospel to the Muslims directly to the west of China.

In 2007, there was a female pastor from Tanghe who was living in Xinjiang Province. Xinjiang is located on the far western border of China and is mostly populated by Uighur Muslims. The people's language, customs, religion, and physical traits all indicate that they are not related to the Han Chinese—the largest ethnic group in China—but are actually Turkic. They are an aggressive minority, and the Uighur regions are always volatile. There are many other minorities in China, such as the Miao, Dong, Mongols, and others, but the Uighurs especially despise being under Han Chinese rule. The ethnic tension there often manifests itself in violence.

The female pastor from Tanghe obtained a teaching position, and she preached the gospel to her students. Seven of the students in her class accepted Jesus as their Lord and Savior. When the school heard about this, they fired the teacher and expelled those students. All seven students were Uighurs and came from Muslim families. They were invited to study at the Tanghe Bible school in Beijing, and every one of them accepted. The Tanghe Bible teachers divided the training into three sections over a period of eighteen months. The Uighur Christians studied the Chinese language, the Bible, and a vocation. After completing the period of training, they were sent back to Xinjiang.

For a long time, the Tanghe leaders did not hear from them. After almost two years, the leaders traveled to Xinjiang to seek out the students and see how they were doing. What they found surprised them: The students had led more than 300 Muslims to the Lord in four different cities. For those familiar with the Uighurs, this is an unprecedented breakthrough.

In 2012, Tanghe started another Bible school in Xinjiang Province. They anticipated having twenty students in the first class. All the students are Uighurs who converted from Islam. Tanghe plans to use this school as a launching base to send graduates as missionaries into Kazakhstan, Uzbekistan, Pakistan, Kyrgyzstan, Afghanistan, and the Middle East.

Having learned some of the inner workings of the Tanghe House Church Network, you can really begin to uncover the mystery of why the underground house churches are growing at such a fast rate.

9

Fangcheng
(China for Christ Church)

Fangcheng Network, also called Christ for China Church, is another good network to examine for gaining a better understanding of the Chinese House Church. This network numbers in the millions. Some estimates are close to ten million, but its leader, Pastor Zhang, stopped giving out numbers years ago. Many people consider Fangcheng to be the largest House Church network in China. Yet, ever since a split among the leadership in the mid-1990s, Fangcheng has been decreasing in size and is no longer the largest.

LI TIANEN

Like Tanghe Network, Fangcheng is named after a county in Henan Province. It is often thought of as the cradle of the underground House Church. Fangcheng was founded by Li Tianen, one of the most well-known patriarchs of the house churches. Li Tianen's father was brought to the Lord by the preaching of British missionary pioneer J. Hudson Taylor, founder of the China Inland Mission.

As a devout Christian who would not deny his faith, Li Tianen was one of the primary targets of the Communist Party, and his family was considered to be the product of "foreign devils." He was continually persecuted by the government and was eventually arrested and sentenced to hard labor in a prison camp because he refused to deny the name of Jesus. While in prison, he took advantage of every opportunity to share the gospel with others.

After his release from prison in the 1970s, Pastor Li made his way back to Fangcheng, his hometown, to preach the gospel and to raise up new leaders. There he met a young charismatic leader and Communist Party member named Zhang Rongliang. Zhang became one of Pastor Li's disciples, and Li began teaching him, having no idea that Zhang would grow to become one of the most well-known and respected House Church pastors in all of China. Though Zhang Rongliang is not the founder of Fangcheng House Church network, he is best known for leading it. The reverse is also true: Fangcheng is well-known around the world because Zhang Rongliang is its leader.

ZHANG **RONGLIANG**

Fangcheng is much stricter than Tanghe with regard to maintaining theological purity within its network. There is more control over the teachings and beliefs of those who belong to it. This could be due largely to the personality of Zhang Rongliang. Although this may not necessarily have been the case in most recent years, generally speaking, this control over doctrine has been one of the characteristics that has set Fangcheng apart.

Fangcheng is one example of a patriarchal House Church network where the leader—in this case, Pastor Zhang (sometimes referred to as Uncle Zhang)—is the "father." After his arrest in December 2004, Zhang spent seven years in prison. His son was seen as the obvious successor in a network where the leadership style is patriarchal. However, Sister Han, a well-respected minister and preacher in her own right, was effectively the hands at the wheel. In many ways, she was the unsung matriarch who held things together while Zhang was in prison.

Zhang's son is generally a quiet leader who gives a first impression of being timid and soft-spoken. The guiding hands of Sister

Han led him down the path of leadership during the seven years of his father's incarceration and helped to protect him from the unforeseen dangers that foreigners can bring.

Sister Han's face is weathered from the years of trials she has endured. She is present at almost any meeting that involves the leadership, but she often sits quietly off to the side and listens intently. At times, if the meeting is full of older men, she will check to make sure everyone has tea. She does not often speak in meetings, but when she does, she is clear, strong, and to the point.

Many of the younger leaders throughout China today have received training from Sister Han. Her life has been dedicated to serving the Lord, and if there is any leader not officially recognized in Fangcheng, it is Sister Han.

When Zhang Rongliang was released from prison in the fall of 2011, we were very hesitant to go and see him. In fact, I initially declined an invitation to meet with him because it was our assumption that missions leaders from around the world would be banging on his door to interview him, thereby causing a security fiasco. When it became known that a trusted friend had arranged the meeting in a secure location, I accompanied Brother Ren to catch up with his old friend Zhang.

During his time in prison, Pastor Zhang had suffered a stroke and endured a terrible fight with diabetes. We were well aware of these facts because we had often provided financial support to help his family and to enable him to purchase his medication. We had also arranged for continued support of the Fangcheng church and would annually meet with his son in China to discuss needs and future goals.

Consequently, we came to the interview expecting to see a fragile man with gray hair and gaunt cheeks who had been half-paralyzed by a stroke. When a healthy, younger-looking man came up to us with his face beaming, and firmly embraced Brother Ren, we were surprised, to say the least. By God's grace, prison had apparently been good to Zhang, and he seemed almost spry enough to jump right out of the room.

When we expressed our shock at his youthful appearance, he moved his hand over one side of his body and said, "You see here? All of this area was paralyzed by the stroke when I was in prison. I couldn't use this part of my body at all, but the day I walked out of those prison doors, it instantly healed!"

He had full use of his body, and had no complications from the diabetes that had given him so much trouble when he was in prison. It was phenomenal—even unbelievable, had we not seen it with our own eyes.

Zhang seemed like a changed man. Before us was a humble, joyful, and introspective man who was very different from the fire-brand we had known in the past. He sat down on the far side of the couch in the small tea room and began, "You are the first foreigners to come and see me since my release from prison." This information was quite shocking, considering that, in the past, ambitious foreign missions workers and reporters would have been beating down his door to meet him. He leaned over to Brother Ren, looked intently into his eyes, and said, "I would like to finally put a book together." Since then, we have compiled a comprehensive memoir of Pastor Zhang and the Fangcheng underground House Church, based on extensive interviews with Zhang and his coworkers. We anticipate the publication of this book in English in the next year or two.

THE FORMATIVE YEARS: "**BLAZING FORTH**" WITH THE GOSPEL

Fangcheng believers have seen many of their leaders taken away in handcuffs, many congregation members beaten, and even some of their dear friends executed. Much of what the world has learned about the situation of the Chinese House Church has come through news of Fangcheng's struggles, which were publicly played out.

In November 2011, we had the rare opportunity to interview several of the founding members of Fangcheng Network. Unlike leaders in many other networks, those of Fangcheng are known for being bold and unafraid of repercussions. No coaxing was required to get them to tell us about the founding of the network; the leaders actually came ready to tell us everything they could remember, and they all insisted that the others sit in on their individual interviews in order to correct them if they confused a date or two.

Between pauses to wipe away tears, one sister recalled the heartbreak she'd felt when she announced to her family that God had called her to join Zhang Rongliang's fledgling network:

> Unexpectedly, when I returned home and told my mother about the whole thing [the decision to go into the ministry], she was extremely upset. Realizing that my mom would not approve of the action I took based on my faith, I decided to leave home. I didn't have much of a choice. I wrote one letter to my parents in which I expressed my strong love and devotion to Jesus; the other was to my young sister, asking her to take care of our parents.
>
> The day I left home, I felt very sad; but, as Psalm 27:10 came to my mind, "My father and mother may abandon me, but the Lord will take care of me," I felt quite comforted. From that day on, I have been walking on the path of serving God.

This sister would go on to be used mightily by the Lord in training hundreds of Chinese missionaries for the field. Those under her care are now serving among minority tribes throughout China and even in other nations, like India. The school she helped to start recently celebrated its tenth anniversary. "Ten years in storms and ten years in thanksgiving," she lovingly calls that time.

Zhang Rongliang also attended that session of interviews and was more than happy to reminisce about the formative days of Fangcheng network. The following is his first testimony to be published after his release from prison in 2011.

I spent seven years in jail, and in 1980, I was released. After going out, I saw many thirsty souls desiring the gospel, so we started to blaze forth preaching the gospel. As we were doing so, the police heard the news and sent people to catch us and arrest us. During that time, many believers had to flee their homes, because if we continued staying where we lived, we would be arrested. One after another escaped.

Later on, as we were asked how we built our team, I replied, "Oh, we have you policemen to thank for it. Because of you, our gospel team was able to form." When they asked when, I said, "It was when you were searching for us to arrest us." That's how we gathered together. Six hundred people were involved in our team; most of them were in debt, terribly poor, and stuck in bad circumstances. These people gathered together and became "David's Army," the army full of might to overcome nations. This is what our team was like.

Most of my companions were home-lovers, but they had to flee their homes. So, when they looked back and recounted their experiences, they described themselves as "unwilling soldiers"—they were caught by God to become soldiers. Just as a Canaan hymn puts it, "God found us from here and there." Since then, we have walked together and become a mighty gospel force in China. We wanted to go everywhere and preach.

The first one who came out in the open was Sister Ding, who was persecuted mainly by her family. The second was Brother Zheng. (If you go to Henan, you will see him.) He is more than seventy years old. I am the third. Then Brother Tian and Sister Han joined us, too. Our team grew very quickly.

At first, there were only five old bicycles for five people; we couldn't afford anything more. Though we lacked money, our churches were extremely consumed with Christ. I can still recall that, after every meeting, we had to run away, because many who heard the gospel wanted to sacrifice their time and life for the cause of the gospel, but the problem was that we were unable to offer them another bicycle. Although many of them were excellent and had voiced their longing to us with tears, we couldn't help any of them, and so we left with tears. We did refuse many. The number grew to one hundred as we continued to preach. This group was just like the tribe of Naphtali, who would dedicate their lives to the spreading of the gospel.

So, as we see, the present China is filled with awakening souls; meanwhile, it grieves us when we think about what God did in our midst in the past. It was God who brought me through it all. At that time, we sent out our companions two by two. Then we started to connect with our town, which included tens of villages, and bound them together to become one church. After the work in Nanyang had finished, we began to target our neighboring areas and helped them to build their own churches or teams.

In 1983, the government gave orders to arrest all Christians. When they got the information that Fangcheng in Henan was the center of a nationwide gospel movement, they immediately sent the police to arrest us. In that year, thirteen people were sentenced to death. As we heard about the bad news, we gathered together to cry to God for help. Deep in our hearts, we felt guilty for doing too little for the Lord.

Days later, a group of life-riskers formed. The main goal of the group was to go to extremes to save souls, even if we had to die for it. However, God kept our lives safe; none of us died. We can live so well because He is our shield.

Until 1987, we hadn't sent any workers to neighboring provinces, but afterward, we went to several provinces, such as Hubei, Sichuan, Yunnan, and Shanxi, Hebei, Liaoning, Heilongjiang, Shandong, Jiangsu, and so forth.

The year 1988 was a special year for our team. There were a lot of amazing things God did in our midst. Sounds of singing, shouting, and praises filled every village. It was clear that God loved the Chinese people so much. We saw many brothers and sisters anointed by the Spirit; they used the gifts they received to sow even more seeds.

Our team grew so fast that it was divided into twenty-four branches; it is a mighty army anointed by the Holy Spirit. Wherever they are—whether at the train station or the bus station, whether on the train or on the bus, or even while they are shopping in grocery stores or eating in a restaurant—they always share their faith. They are just like a blazing fire.

During 1998 and 1999, we started to preach to ethnic groups in parts of China where there were still no existing churches. Our goal was to transfer Han Chinese missionaries to those ethnic groups and help them live as local residents, just as Jesus—in order to preach the kingdom of God to earthly people—came to the world and lived for thirty-three years. Many who had moved to those areas settled down and bore much fruit.

Today, our church has expanded to six countries, mainly neighboring Muslim areas. We feel deeply it is the destiny to which God has called the Chinese church—to spread the gospel to all nations. In the past, many missionaries were sent to China from England; then, this commitment fell upon the shoulders of the United States, and it became the leader of the whole world.

In Deuteronomy, Moses said to the people of Israel that if they obeyed the Lord and faithfully kept all His commands, the Lord God would make them the leader among the nations. In other words, the only way to lead nations is to do what Jesus commanded, making all peoples His disciples.

10

Five Brothers Network ("No Name")

The Five Brothers House Church Network is one of the more modest groups. It does not work with many foreigners and is not talked about in other forums. This underground network has possibly never been examined or written about before, but it is one of the largest networks in Henan Province. Back to Jerusalem International has spent a great deal of time serving the believers in this network, both in China and among the missionaries it has sent abroad.

The Five Brothers is structured just as its name suggests—there are five leaders who share responsibility for the direction of the network. We cannot give the real names of the leaders, because, at the moment, there are no other publications identifying them in the Western world. We do not want to expose names and specific operations, or hinder the progress of any of their work in any way. Their English names are Ezekiel, Barnabas, Paul, Caleb, and Joseph. Of these five, Paul is widely known as one of the most gifted preachers.

This group is also referred to as the "No Name" Network, because whenever people have asked the five brothers what the name of their House Church network is, they always respond by saying, "We don't have a name." These brothers prefer not to attract any special attention, and none of them really wanted to be a leader of a network in the first place. In many ways, they were thrown into the role during a turbulent time for the underground House Church in China.

The Five Brothers Network came out of the Fangcheng Network run by Zhang Rongliang. All five brothers were among Pastor Zhang's closest coworkers. They had been in prison together, had been chased by the PSB together, and had endured great hardships alongside Pastor Zhang for the sake of the gospel. All five trusted Pastor Zhang with their lives, and he trusted them with his. They all saw Pastor Zhang as their leader, teacher, and pastor. He relied on them to carry out some of the most top-secret missionary operations and to oversee large numbers of groups. Some of them even sat on the active board of elders for Fangcheng House Church.

Again, none of these brothers had initially anticipated being a leader of a network. From the beginning, they had all expected to continue serving under Pastor Zhang and to see the people in China reached with the gospel of Jesus Christ through the Fangcheng Network. But things changed in the mid-1990s. In those days, Pastor Zhang was notorious for his quick temper. Although, in meetings with him, I have never seen any evidence of Zhang behaving in any way other than that of a loving, dedicated pastor, other Chinese believers who knew him well said that Pastor Zhang could quickly change moods. Perhaps those traits were characteristics of his younger years, and his recent time in prison and his health problems have calmed his temper.

ROOTS OF A **NEW MOVEMENT**

In the 1990s, Pastor Zhang's power and control were increasing every month as the church grew. The believers of Fangcheng were going out into the highways and byways to preach the gospel, and new converts continued to be added to their ranks.

As mentioned earlier, Fangcheng strictly maintained unified beliefs and compelled others to follow. Pastor Zhang desired to eventually establish a nationwide movement, all of which would fall under the leadership of Fangcheng. From the central headquarters, smaller districts would be established all over China, each of which would answer directly to Fangcheng and even be expected to tithe to it.

It is important to note that this was how all House Church networks functioned in the early years. The main pastor or leader of the original House Church oversaw all the growth and long-term strategic planning for the entire network. No matter how far away the sister churches were planted, it was still customary for them to answer to the mother church. Pastor Zhang was not suggesting the building of a new empire but was merely moving to formalize ties and streamline the system, very much like large church denominations in the United States.

The younger leaders in Fangcheng served in the field and saw the church growing astronomically. These younger leaders listened to the challenges that churches were facing on the lower levels, but they didn't feel that Pastor Zhang was listening to them. As this happened over and over, the issue became increasingly difficult for the other leaders to ignore.

Not only were there leadership problems, but a few moral failures also seemed to be taking place. Even today, most Chinese are reluctant to discuss these accusations, especially with foreigners. The Chinese prefer to handle things in-house and not air their dirty laundry. As the church grew, Pastor Zhang had access to more financial resources than ever before, and this newly found access brought on additional perceived problems. Whether or not there was any corruption in the way Pastor Zhang handled the money is another matter. It was the mere fact that he had sole control over these resources that led to increased suspicion being cast on him.

There were also thought to be some moral failures between Pastor Zhang and some female coworkers, particularly with Sister "D," or Ding Hei. Sister Ding was born in Fangcheng County and became one of the first full-time workers for the Fangcheng Church. After being rejected by her family for her belief in Jesus Christ, she was adopted by Pastor Zhang's family.

My first meeting with Sister Ding took place in Kunming, where she is currently based. At the time, she had just returned from a trip to Jordan and Israel. David Aikman's book *Jesus in Beijing* had just come out, and it included her picture, as well as information about her. When she was shown her picture in the acclaimed book, she just looked at it, quickly nodded in approval, and moved on to discuss the topic at hand. She has been running a training school in Kunming for several years where several Westerners have been routinely rotated through as English teachers and Bible instructors. She also runs a Bible school and a vocational training center. The training center manages a small guesthouse that allows Bible students the opportunity to practice managerial skills in the service industry before being sent to the mission field.

Pastor Zhang and Sister Ding traveled together a lot and served in many different roles together. After a while, several believers began to wonder if there was more to their relationship. Some thought it was inappropriate for Pastor Zhang to be spending so much time with a young single woman. Sister Ding eventually married a man handpicked by Pastor Zhang (quite a common practice in the House Church), but the suspicion persisted even after she had a child with her husband.

Sister Ding insists that nothing inappropriate ever happened. However, to end speculation, she stopped working so closely with Pastor Zhang and set up shop in Kunming, where, as mentioned above, she continues to serve to this day. She is incredibly loyal to Pastor Zhang and is truly a faithful leader. She is admired by leaders throughout China and respected by everyone who has ever worked with her. The fact that she shows so much respect and admiration for Pastor Zhang says a lot about his character, as well.

Today, this matter is not brought up among the leaders of the networks. If you openly ask the five brothers why they left Fangcheng network, they will not mention anything regarding these accusations. To them, the allegations had very little to do with their split from the Fangcheng mother church. They would point to a much more pragmatic reason.

Zhang focused hard on establishing his nationwide movement in which every local church established by Fangcheng would answer to the mother church in Henan and also pay a tithe. The other Fangcheng leaders knew that there was no practical way for them to know in Henan the detailed challenges that would arise on a daily basis in churches several thousand miles away. They also knew that there was no practical way for the Fangcheng leadership to visit these areas on a regular basis. This meant that the only real connection the mother church would have with them would be in collecting the tithe from each church, without any true association with the local problems, growth, or leadership.

The younger leaders felt it would be better if the leadership were localized. A local church established in the city would have its own leaders, and that church would be responsible for the churches that were planted in the nearby countryside. But when the issue of centralized versus localized leadership came up, Pastor Zhang took the firm stance that if you don't agree with him, then you don't support him. In a small farmhouse in Fangcheng in 1995 or 1996, a meeting took place with the leadership of Fangcheng that solidified everything. Brother Ren and his longtime coworker Teacher Zhao were there. Brother Ren related,

> It was around this time that we saw the split take place. We were together for about two or three days discussing the challenges of the future of Fangcheng Church. There were key leaders and pastors who had traveled from far away to be at that meeting. All the key churches had their leadership represented. Altogether, I think that there were about 150 leaders and pastors there.
>
> During that time, the leaders came to the unified decision that localized leadership was the best way forward. It was agreed that there was just no practical way for the mother church in Fangcheng to control churches all over

China in a meaningful way and to expect to receive tithes. With that subject decided, the leaders began to make decisions for how the future would go. They discussed how to dismantle the large-scale operation in a way that would yield more power to the local churches.

Pastor Zhang was not present at any of those meetings. I don't know why. He just didn't come, but he arrived on the last day. Everyone was happy to see him. He listened to the ideas, problems, and proposals, and in one evening was able to turn everything back around.

Pastor Zhang's leadership abilities were in full swing that night. All the top leaders had been able to discuss, decide, and plan how to move forward for the future of Fangcheng. They were all in agreement. But one man, Pastor Zhang, was able to come on the last day and persuade everyone back to his way of thinking, and those who disagreed were compelled to remain silent.

AN UNLIKELY **LEADERSHIP TEAM**

Pastor Zhang was closest to Paul, Joseph, and Barnabas. These three brothers comprised half of the elders of Fangcheng Church. They were three of the top six or seven leaders, so the choice they made was one of the hardest decisions of their lives. They decided to split from the mother church. For many years, their identity had been wrapped up in Fangcheng. They were the principal leaders of the largest House Church network in China, as well as what could possibly be—with over ten million believers—the largest church in the world. These three brothers daringly made a pact with one another to leave their spiritual father and continue ministry on their own—together. Ezekiel, a provincial pastor in Hubei, came along as the fourth partner. There was also a well-known local pastor in Fangcheng County who joined them. His name is Caleb, and he is the oldest of the five brothers.

A sixth brother by the name of Joshua joined them, as well. He is a charismatic leader and preacher who has a gift for strategy and missions work. He came alongside the five brothers and, out of true humble character, serves under Joseph. Joseph has had a lifelong struggle with his health and at times is not able to carry out his duties. When this happens, Joshua rushes to his side to help him until he is well again, then returns to his own area of operation.

The five brothers set up a system of leadership similar to King Arthur's Round Table. They divided China into five different areas (six, including Joshua's area), with each brother being responsible for church growth in a particular sector. It was agreed that no one would make any decisions alone but that they would all come together and decide things as a group. They work together as one team and one leadership body, although each of them is a type of network leader in his own right.

Barnabas is in charge of the work in Xinjiang and western China and rarely leaves the field. He is not always at the meetings but has an equal say in every decision.

When Fangcheng Church split, more than one-third of its members went with the new leadership. Pastor Zhang combed through his ranks to make sure he was not supporting anyone who was loyal to those who had left. A definite line was drawn, and, as a member of the church, you were either on one side or the other.

From the day the five brothers left the Fangcheng mother church, they have avoided any contact with Pastor Zhang. In many ways, Pastor Zhang blamed Brother Ren for the way things transpired. Brother Ren financially supported Fangcheng Church, but he also supported the five brothers in their new ministry. Pastor Zhang felt that the five brothers were encouraged to split because they knew they had the financial support of Brother Ren to lessen the impact of the fallout, a sort of financial safety net.

Brother Ren disagrees, saying, "I provided support to them because I agreed with their outlook on things. They were from a younger generation, and they saw things a bit differently than the older generation. I listened to their hearts and their concerns, and I believed that they were doing the right thing."

Brother Ren continued to provide financial support for Pastor Zhang, but that support was considered suspect. It was thought to be playing both sides of the fence. However, on the day that Brother Ren and Pastor Zhang reunited after his release from prison in 2011, it was evident to everyone that Brother Ren had deep feelings of love, loyalty, and respect for Pastor Zhang. Brother Ren's support of Zhang never wavered, even during Zhang's time in prison. His continued support and concern for Zhang's family, and the personal support that he provided once Zhang was released from prison, were acts compelled by love.

The five brothers are aware of the feelings that Brother Ren has for Pastor Zhang, and they know that Brother Ren still serves the Fangcheng mother church. Pastor Zhang has asked Brother Ren to mediate between the five brothers and himself on several occasions, because he is the one person who maintains deep relationships with everyone involved.

Recently, there have been visual acts of reconciliation between the members of Fangcheng and the leaders of the Five Brothers Network. The five brothers are often invited to different functions at Fangcheng Church and are even asked to speak. Yet between the five brothers and Pastor Zhang there hasn't been any real lasting connection. That could change. As previously mentioned, ever since Zhang was released from prison, there has been a significant change in his personality. He seems to be calmer, full of joy, and thoughtful.

"FULL THROTTLE" **FOR THE GOSPEL**

The five brothers have gone "full throttle" for the gospel since they split with Fangcheng. In early 2000, they held a meeting in Burma where they set goals for the future that continue to have an impact. At the meeting in Burma, the five brothers talked about the need for training evangelists and pastors. That led to the first-ever radio broadcast by the House Church, from the House Church, and to the House Church in China.

To create the daily radio program, they used a lot of the experience they had gained from running their Cassette Bible School. In the 1990s, the five brothers had faced a dilemma. Each one of them had helped to plant churches all over his area of responsibility. In fact, so many churches had been planted that if they had visited one church every day, it would have taken them more than three years to visit them all. These leaders would travel around and meet with each church as much as they could, but eventually they began to record their teachings on cassette tapes. They would leave these cassettes with the teachers, evangelists, and pastors so they could listen to them and use what they learned to teach their congregations.

This practice eventually became known as the Cassette Bible School. The recordings were actually done on DAT (digital audiotape) and were then transferred to cassette tape. Back to Jerusalem workers purchased the cassette copying machines in Hong Kong and carried them across the border to Shenzhen. Since fewer high-quality electronic items were being made in China in those days, the machines had to be smuggled in from the outside.

Eventually, we put everything on CD, and the International Mission Board provided us with CD-burning towers. This made everything much easier. Even today, now that we have put everything into digital format and use simple MP3 players, we still refer to the project as the Cassette Bible School.

From the meeting in Burma also came the most vibrant children's ministry movement in the history of China. The story of the development of this ministry will be covered later in this book. To this day, more than a quarter of a million Sunday school teachers/trainers have been taught using the curriculum that was birthed as a result of that meeting.

The Five Brothers Network has some of the most competent English-speaking missionaries in all of China. This is mainly because of their training center, which was set up by Brother Ren and Teacher Zhao. Teacher Zhao is one of Back to Jerusalem International's top teachers and administrators who has been serving in China for decades. Ren and Zhao put many resources into a training facility that would directly benefit the aspiring missionaries and prepare them for the field. The administrator chosen to run that program put together one of the most challenging and dynamic schools available for the underground House Church today.

One of the difficulties for House Church missionaries is that many of them come from rural backgrounds; many of them grew up poor in the farming communities, without money to go to school. The majority of the workers in the Chinese House Church have not had any kind of secondary education. Some have not even had the chance to finish primary school. Therefore, it is almost impossible to get them formal language training or official vocational training. This is where the primary training center for the Five Brothers comes in. And it has produced some of the most capable missionaries to come out of China. Today, those missionaries are serving in Syria, North Korea, Tanzania, Burma, and Vietnam and are continuing to branch out to preach the gospel in other countries, as well.

FUTURE **CHALLENGES**

As the Five Brothers Network continues to grow, its leaders face certain challenges for the future. One of these challenges brings them back full circle to where they split from Pastor Zhang. As China grows, so does the church, and as the people flock to the big cities, so do members of the underground House Church. Today, the urban centers in China are booming. Cities like Chengdu used to be sleepy little "towns" with barely five hundred thousand people; today, they may boast populations in the tens of millions. There is also a megacity in the works in Guandong Province that will combine forty-two million people into one large municipality.

The urban churches are growing and changing the dynamic of the traditional underground house churches. Although the leaders of the Five Brothers broke from a network they felt exerted too much control, they are now in fact facing a situation in which they are the ones being asked to give up control.

When evaluating the activities and practices of the Chinese House Church today, the importance of the role of Chinese culture cannot be stressed enough. The Five Brothers may have a more democratic approach when it comes to making general decisions for the future of the network, but there is nothing democratic about what goes on within their districts. They are the patriarchs and thus the decision makers. The leaders decide who can or cannot serve as leaders in their districts. They decide who will become evangelists and where those evangelists will go. They decide who will become missionaries and where those missionaries will serve.

If you are a member of their network, they also decide where you sleep, how long you sleep, what you eat, and when you eat. The Chinese pastor is like the father of a family; all respect is given to him, and his words are obeyed as if they were the law of the land. Unquestioned obedience is expected.

It is well-known that arranged marriages are common in China, but what many people don't know is that arranged marriages are also the norm in the Chinese church. The network leader dictates whom you will marry. Not only does he select your future mate, but he also chooses where you will live together, how you will serve the church, what you will do, and how much you will earn as a missionary, pastor, or evangelist.

For example, one time, we were working with Pastor Joshua at one of the network's schools on the North Korean border, teaching the Bible to five young ladies who were studying the Korean language because they were called to preach the gospel in North Korea. These young women had studied at the school for two years and had endured hardships in the process. The school was on a small farm where there was no heat in the classrooms and very little comfort in the sleeping area. The temperatures were almost arctic in that region, which is not far from the infamously frigid Siberia.

One afternoon, we were about to share from the Bible with the young ladies. Joshua and his wife had spent more than two days with them giving them counsel and encouragement. We foreigners walked into the meeting ready to teach the Bible but found ourselves at the tail end of a counseling session.

Joshua pointed to one of the young ladies and said, "You are too fat. How am I supposed to find someone for you if you have gained this much weight?" I looked at the faces of the young women. None of them was shocked or upset. They even laughed a bit, acknowledging that it was true. The young lady whom Joshua was addressing did not look overweight to us. If anything, we thought the other young ladies were a bit underweight and were concerned that they were not eating enough meat to combat the cold weather.

Joshua pointed to the next girl and said, "I want you to take her jogging every morning for about forty-five minutes to lose this weight." The two girls looked at each other, acknowledged the order, and nodded in agreement. The next time I saw the "overweight" young lady, she was fit and trim.

After those five girls graduated from language school and were ready for their assignment in North Korea, we visited the area again with Joshua. At the time, we had a special business platform for a missionary worker—we had an invitation from the North Korean government for someone who could cook. We needed a professional cook. Even though we had five students who had just graduated from language school, none of them was an experienced cook, and we did not have enough time to train them.

There was a member of Joshua's church who was a cook and had managed his own restaurant. He was exactly what we were looking for. We thought it would be a great opportunity to send into North Korea not only a cook but also a translator, yet Joshua disagreed. "We cannot send a young single man onto the mission field with a young single woman," he said. He was absolutely right, but, as Westerners, we thought the answer would be to place a third person on the team. This, however, was not Joshua's solution.

"No problem. I will just have them get married. Problem solved."

In response to the confused look on the foreign faces, he said, "No, no, I know what you're thinking. You think that they don't know each other. I tell you what. I will give them forty-five minutes to meet together before I make my final decision. How about that?"

This was so far from the Western cultural understanding of courtship, romance, and love that it was hard to accept. However, the couple got married and was sent into ministry, and the husband and wife are very happy together.

It is easy for Westerners to look at this kind of situation and be judgmental, but we quickly forget that, in the Bible, most marriages were arranged, and it is made very clear that God's will was being carried out in all those marriages. For example, remember the account of how a bride was found for Isaac. (See Genesis 24.) In fact, it can be argued that the Chinese methodology in this manner is more Bible-based than the Western model. The Western concept of love and marriage is more like a Disney cartoon; and, statistically, Western marriages have a vastly higher failure rate.

Though Joshua exercised a lot of control over that situation, his responsibility is much greater than that of a pastor in the Western world. He travels to meet with missionaries who are about to depart for the field. He and his wife live with them, pray with them, and even cook for them. He sees that everything is provided for them—that they lack nothing. They only have to share a problem with him, and Joshua has to carry the burden to see that all their needs, and even some of their desires, are met.

Again, this kind of control is typical in the House Church. Every House Church leader plays the part of a patriarch. Some are more involved than others, but they all follow this practice. At our training sessions with Chinese House Church missionaries, it is standard procedure for us to tell them why they are at the training and what they will be doing. We don't do this as an introductory formality but because this information was often never communicated to them.

Has your pastor ever called you and said he has a plane ticket for you to fly to Hong Kong, then told you to be at the airport the next morning for the flight before immediately hanging up without conveying any other information to you? Such a conversation is a common occurrence in the house churches in China. It is an everyday experience for a worker in the underground church to get a call with directions to be somewhere at a certain time with no explanation. Although this practice is great for security, it does very little for an information-driven individual.

In the winter of 2011, we had a team of ten students from China who were going to study for six months in the Philippines. When the team arrived at the airport in Hong Kong, none of the members knew what they were there for. They all had been told merely to board a flight to Hong Kong, and that someone would be there to meet them with further instructions. The ten Chinese, most of whom had never met each other, boarded their flight to Hong Kong without question.

When asked how much they knew about what lay ahead of them, none of them knew they would be going to the Philippines, nor did they know they would be gone from China for six months. They also had no idea they would be doing missionary training with foreigners. One of them had suspected she would be going to Vietnam to live. Even so, she had packed only a single suitcase. The students hadn't even known what climate to be prepared for.

Whether or not we agree with this method is not important. Such seemingly blind obedience is one of the contributing factors as to why the church in China is growing at such a rapid rate. China's churches have a patriarchal system that fits their culture, works for them, and is having an impact on the entire world in ways that are difficult for the Western-trained mind to grasp.

However, as indicated earlier, the urban areas are more independent, so the leaders of the Five Brothers are facing this reality when working with and overseeing the churches in those regions. The educated, independent minds of today's urban Chinese are generations away from the traditional rural areas of China. How the Five Brothers Network adapts to these new challenges will undoubtedly determine its future.

11

Born Again Movement (Peter Xu)

The Born Again Movement is the name we have chosen to use in discussing the next underground House Church, although the network has also used several other names in the past. It has been known as the Peter Xu Network, the Weepers, the Criers, the Full Scope Church, Word of Life, and New Birth Church.

The Born Again Movement was founded by Xu Yongze, known in the West as Peter Xu. I have spent a considerable amount of time with Peter Xu and his sister Deborah. Whenever Brother Yun is in California for speaking engagements, Peter Xu and his colleagues always end up staying in his hotel room, often arriving at the hotel at all hours of the night with guests who want to pray with Yun.

Peter Xu has been called the Billy Graham of China, and, in many ways, his testimony is just as compelling as that of Brother Yun. Paul Hattaway, coauthor of *The Heavenly Man*, sat down with Peter Xu and attempted to write a biography about his life. The book has never been published; but if it ever is, it is bound to be one of the most riveting stories ever told, because Xu's life has been packed with adventure and drama.

Peter Xu is a fourth-generation Christian. He was a "rebel" from the beginning. When fanatical students were swarming campuses with Communist propaganda and refused to tolerate any dissent, Xu infiltrated the same campuses with the gospel of Jesus Christ. During that time, the violence of the student movement in

China was intense. A good illustration of this reality may be seen in the early life of Yao Ming's mother. Yao Ming is a retired Chinese basketball star who played in the NBA. His mother was part of the revolutionary guards—a kind of "shock troop" movement that would carry out the most extreme acts of persecution and cruelty on a horrific scale. She was one of the most vocal leaders of that movement and the one whom many feared the most. Yao Ming's mother led the charge against her former basketball coaches. In one of her milder actions to discipline a supposed female dissident, she cut off the woman's hair. She led angry mobs onto campuses like those where Peter Xu was ministering.

Preaching on a vocational campus in China was a huge risk—not just for Peter Xu but for anyone who participated with him. Xu organized reading clubs and used them as a way to introduce students to the Bible. When the Communist regime decided to conduct a sweeping raid on Christians, Xu was one of the top people on its radar. In 1963, he was arrested and questioned for forty days straight. He was later imprisoned four more times.

A FOCUS ON **OUTREACH**

Like Zhang Rongliang, Peter Xu had been a disciple of Li Tianen. Xu, however, immediately saw a need to train and send out disciples to reach the lost in China. He is unique in this way. While the other networks started without an initial intention to go beyond their own homes, Xu was very focused on outreach outside the borders of Henan. He was immediately able to sense the Spirit pushing him toward the outer reaches of China.

The massive House Church networks of Tanghe, Fangcheng, and Blessing were not planned from the beginning, but Peter Xu's House Church network was a deliberate movement. Whenever you spend time with Peter Xu or learn his story, it becomes clear that there is something deep in his spirit that drives him. Today, even in his later years, although he comes across as calm and friendly, there is a spark in his personality that is almost combustible.

A MOVEMENT OF **UNITY**

Peter Xu's strong leadership is one of the many factors that contributed to an autonomous underground House Church. As was stated earlier, when the doors to the West started to open, Christian organizations began to slip through the cracks to see how the church in China had developed. They soon felt compelled to become more than observers, and many had a desire to help their brothers and sisters in Christ. In the 1980s, Christian books other than the Bible began to appear in China. Each church denomination had its own idea of what the church in China needed, as indicated in this excerpt from *The Heavenly Man*:

> These booklets told us we must worship in a certain way, or that we must speak in tongues to be a true believer, or that only if we were baptized in Jesus' name (instead of the name of the Father, Son, and Holy Spirit) could we be saved. Other teachings focused on extreme faith, still others argued for or against the role of women in the church.
>
> We read all these booklets and soon we were confused! The churches started to split into groups that believed one thing against groups that believed another. Instead of only speaking for Jesus, we also started speaking against other believers who didn't conform to our views.[19]

The church in China was being bombarded by the teachings of various foreign denominations. This situation was difficult for them and raised a lot of questions. Many of their colleagues had died in prison for the name of Jesus yet had never been baptized in the name of Jesus. Had they gone through all that suffering for Christ, only to be lost through a technicality? There were many founders of the church who had been persecuted and martyred in the 1960s and 70s but had never spoken in tongues. Were they to perish in hell for never having spoken in tongues? And anyone familiar with the House Church movement today cannot deny the overwhelming number of female pastors, teachers, evangelists, and missionaries. How were they to fit in with some of the foreign doctrines in those booklets?

Peter Xu was one of the first to stand up amid this mass confusion and seek oneness with his fellow believers in China. It was through his leadership that a movement of unity among the Chinese underground house churches was formed. In *The Heavenly Man*, Brother Yun tells the story of how the leaders of two major movements in the Chinese House Church—Peter Xu and Zhang Rongliang—came to meet together. They had arranged for a secret conference, and they had traveled far and taken many security measures to be together. This was a meeting that the Public Security Bureau would have loved to have known about. It would have saved them a lot of trouble to be able to find the leaders of such major underground movements together in one single meeting.

When they met together, Peter Xu received a word from the Lord that he was to go and wash the feet of Zhang Rongliang. "Zhang was praying with his eyes closed when Xu knelt down in front of him and started gently to take his shoes and socks off. Zhang opened his eyes and was amazed. He couldn't believe the great Xu Yongze, leader of the largest House Church movement in China, would ever kneel down and wash his feet! Zhang cried out and wrapped his arms around Brother Xu in a warm embrace."[20]

This one act performed by Peter Xu unified two of the largest underground House Church networks. The two leaders had very strong personalities and leadership characteristics that were so similar they were bound to butt heads. But now the Born Again Movement was joining hands with Fangcheng, and the two House Church networks would act as a beacon of unity for the other networks to witness. This moment of unity cannot be overrated.

The Born Again Movement and Fangcheng came together and called themselves the Sinim Fellowship. Sinim is often thought of as the biblical name given to China in prophecy: *"Behold, these shall come from far: and, lo, these from the north and from the west; and these from the land of Sinim"* (Isaiah 49:12 KJV). According to Brother Yun, this collaboration led to the formation of a fellowship that included most of the underground House Church Christians in China. "In October 1996, five men were elected to be the first elders of the Sinim Fellowship. They were Brother Xu Yongze [Peter Xu], who was voted the chairman; Zhang Rongliang; Wang Xicai [Enoch Wang]; Shen Yiping; and myself [Brother Yun]. Each man represented a different network."[21]

This fellowship embodied the unity of several million believers throughout China, and it caught the attention of the world. Each network was able to maintain its own set of beliefs according to its interpretation of the Bible. Not many churches in the world are strong enough to achieve true unity with other believers in Christ without compromising the integrity of their particular beliefs.

Unity can exist where people have a desire for it, but it cannot exist in an atmosphere of fear. The underground churches desired to be unified in Christ—but not with the official church in China (TSPM). All these brothers were part of the underground House Church but also had the opportunity to unite with the official church. Why didn't they do so? If they'd truly wanted unity among the believers in China, why wouldn't they have chosen to be unified with the TSPM?

The leaders of the TSPM say things like, "Jesus is alive because He lives in my heart." Westerners hear this and are overjoyed and ready to see the Chinese church unified. If the official church in China believes in Jesus, and the underground church believes in Jesus, then that is all that matters, right?

Yet many of the words spoken by the TSPM leadership have a double meaning. For example, the way the TSPM uses the phrase "Jesus lives in the hearts of believers," the idea is much like the belief that when a good person dies, he or she still lives on in the hearts of those who carry on the vision of that deceased person. For instance, if your father died after having established a charitable foundation, you might give a eulogy at his funeral saying something like this: "The world has lost a good man who has done many great things through this foundation. We will carry on the work that he began, and, in this way, he will remain alive in our hearts." Yet, for true Christians, such an idea is not all that it means to have Christ residing in one's heart—but that is what the TSPM means by such statements.

The Christians in the Born Again Movement had a leader who wanted to be unified with fellow believers throughout China, as well as those around the world. But Peter Xu could not trade unity for integrity and allow his flock to be fooled into believing a fake gospel through the TSPM.

As we have discussed, many Western leaders around the world have tried to mediate between the government of China and the House Church in order to get the underground church to register. One of these Western leaders is Luis Palau, an international evangelist. In 2005, he spent some time visiting Christians in China. During his visit, he attended a worship service in Beijing with then U.S. President George W. Bush, and he made some strong statements toward House Church Christians during a press conference. Here is an excerpt from a *Baptist Press* article (quoting the *Washington Times*) about those statements:

> "Mr. Palau told reporters that some reports of religious persecution are unjustified," the *Times* reported, drawing from a transcript it obtained via the Web. The newspaper stated that Palau "suggested that China's unofficial churches should register to 'receive greater freedom and blessings from the government.'"
>
> The *Times* reported that Palau "then compared church registration in China to American tax law. 'Even in the

United States, you can't get away with defying order,' [Palau] said. 'I feel that registering is a positive thing for the followers of Jesus. Believers should live in the open, especially when the Chinese government offers it.'"

Palau continued, "Jesus said that we are the light of the world and that we should not be kept hidden or in the dark. Therefore, believers should share their faith openly. If I were Chinese, I would definitely register. Not registering only lends to misinterpretations and misunderstandings."[22]

Mr. Palau later retracted the statement, but years later, according to his official Web site, he still believed the underground House Church in China should register. After the evangelist made a trip to China in 2010, his Web site reported,

> Palau encouraged Mr. Wang [the director of China's State Administration for Religious Affairs] to make it easier for churches to register in China, suggesting that many do want to register but don't meet the current government registration requirements. Mr. Wang introduced the idea that registration brings churches under financial accountability and oversight, much like those in America. Palau agreed that financial transparency is important for all groups serving the public.[23]

Luis Palau is not alone in encouraging the House Church to cooperate with the Chinese government. In May 2008, one of the top directors of a well-known international ministry asked to meet with me at the airport in Hong Kong. We had been working together to deliver shoe boxes full of gifts for Chinese children for about six years and had a great relationship. "I just wanted to discuss something before you hear about it on the news," he said. His boss had just preached at several churches in China and was present when the earthquake hit Sichuan; while he was in Beijing, he had met with government officials. The director wanted me to know that in response to a question about evangelizing during the forthcoming Beijing Olympics, the ministry leader had said that he would not agree with any foreign missionary or missions group that chose to break the law by sharing the gospel in China (without government consent). He later reiterated his view to a reporter from the *Charlotte Observer* (NC): "I would be against any groups that would be coming in and encouraging people to break Chinese law," he said.[24]

It was quite ironic for him to say that after having worked together with our team of Chinese lawbreakers for so long. Of course, I believe he was just saying what needed to be said in front of the Chinese government officials who had gone out of their way to arrange his tour.

That ended up being our last year of working together. After the Sichuan earthquake, that organization sent an official letter to the Chinese Embassy introducing the idea of delivering the shoe boxes to children in Sichuan Province. Once they solidified their plans to work through official channels, Back to Jerusalem was forced to pull out and support their ministry from a distance. I told the director, "We think what you guys are doing in China is great; we just can't join you in it. You work with the officials and work your way down. We work with the grassroots church and work our way up. One day, we will meet in the middle."

When asked if the government had told the ministry leader to say anything in particular or not to say anything in particular while preaching in China, the director's response was, "No, not really. There was one thing. They said that he should not mention the underground House Church. They acknowledged that it existed but requested that it not be mentioned."

Those words, of course, were greatly criticized by other missions organizations working in China with the underground churches. That director's organization also posted the laws of China pertaining to religion on its Web site, as they had promised the government officials. In its listing of the laws, "State Religious Affairs Bureau Order No. 5" was curiously missing. This order from the State Administration for Religious Affairs states that a Tibetan Buddhist monastery must file reincarnation applications in order for its "living Buddhas" to be legally recognized when they return. Tibetan Buddhist monks or monasteries who violate the government's regulations in this matter can face sanctions or even criminal proceedings.[25]

Westerners who are not very familiar with China are not the only ones putting pressure on Chinese believers. Shortly before the abovementioned events, a funeral was held in Guangdong Province for a well-known "aunty" who had been one of the most respected Bible distributors in the country. I was asked to come and share a few words, but when I observed that Pastor Dennis Balcombe had arrived, I respectfully declined and quietly gave my condolences to the daughter of the deceased. Pastor Balcombe was being watched closely by government security because he is very well-known as a pastor who is focused on China—making him a target. I needed to be "under the radar" on that day.

Joshua, one of the second-tier leaders from the Five Brothers network, who was mentioned previously, asked me why I had declined to speak. But he quickly grasped the situation when he looked out over the crowd and saw Pastor Balcombe's friendly face greeting people as he entered the back room.

Joshua declined to meet with Pastor Balcombe. He had nothing but love and gratefulness for all that the pastor had done for China and Henan Province, but rumors had started to spread that Pastor Balcombe was traveling on an official visa to China and working with the official church. Joshua told me that Pastor Balcombe was encouraging house churches to think about taking the step to register. It was something that his leadership could not fathom at that time. Though I had not been aware of any of Pastor Balcombe's efforts, I could see that Joshua was conflicted.

Today, there are many foreigners who would like to work with the Chinese church in an official manner; therefore, if they cannot work with the underground House Church, they are willing to work with the state church and walk the line dictated by the government. Yet, as we have noted, many believers felt betrayed by the first leaders of the official church in China—especially those in Henan. Consequently, there remains a deep chasm between the House Church and the official church. Memories of past betrayals keep House Church leaders wary of doing anything with their official counterparts.

Peter Xu set a standard of unity with his fellow House Church believers in China, but he refused to bow to pressure from the government to join a movement that underground believers felt to be both immoral and treacherous. Even today, many of the house churches follow Xu's example on this matter.

THE ONGOING INFLUENCE OF THE **SINIM FELLOWSHIP**

The unity that began with the Sinim Fellowship continues to the present time. Yet, today, many people ask, "What has happened to the Sinim Fellowship? It was such a huge thing in the late 1990s and early 2000s, but we haven't heard anything about it lately." As time went by, the Sinim Fellowship continued in name but could not remain active. With five rebel leaders who were always either on the run or in prison, there was no possible way for the fellowship to survive long-term. Brother Yun and his family miraculously escaped China and found asylum in Europe. Peter Xu also left China and found political asylum in the United States. Pastor Wang ended up back in prison. Zhang Rongliang went to prison for making numerous trips abroad on falsified travel documents. Pastor Shen was therefore the only fellowship member left who had not emigrated or been sent to prison.

The Sinim Fellowship served its purpose by uniting the churches in China. What God spoke to Peter Xu set the stage for the unified work that is presently taking place. It is true there are many fellowships and networks in China that do not actively work together. The Sinim Fellowship did not create a utopia of happiness and eternal bliss, nor did it solve all the problems of personal differences between the major House Church networks. Today, there are leaders of different groups who will not hold meetings on the same day in the same city for fear they might brush shoulders with each other. However, what the Sinim Fellowship did do was unite the underground House Church against the foreign denominations that had attempted to control the revival in China with their own sets of ideologies. It also unified the church against a government that attempted to impose its own atheistic-flavored ideology on the House Church. And, even though some of the large networks will not work directly with one another, they will also not actively persecute one another or attempt to print publications ridiculing one another. This fact can be attributed mainly to the impact of the unity established by the Sinim Fellowship.

PETER XU **IN AMERICA**

Peter Xu fled China in 2001. Shortly after arriving in America, he settled in Buffalo, New York. He had been through a lot by that point in his life. His first wife had dissolved their marriage because she could not stand the long periods of separation she had to endure. These periods were not like those experienced by many women who are married to itinerant evangelists or military personnel. While those wives may have to be separated from their husbands for a few months or even a few years, Peter Xu's wife went without seeing her husband for twenty-three years.

Peter Xu had waited to be reunited with his wife, but their marriage was irreparably over when she remarried. In 1996, Xu also remarried, to a bride much younger than he, a move that presented many challenges for his coworkers in China. When he relocated to Buffalo, he and his wife were in dire straits. Brother Ren remembers going to visit them during the first year they were in America.

"Peter and his new wife had just had a baby," he recalled. "They did not have enough money to buy new diapers, so they attempted to hand-wash the disposable diapers in the sink and hang them out to dry—which proved to be an impossible task." Brother Ren gave them some financial support to help with their expenses in the U.S.

Xu's experience of emigrating was in marked contrast to that of Brother Yun, who had benefitted from the consistent support and guidance of Brother Ren after leaving China. Brother Ren had taken on the role of Brother Yun's pastor and advisor and had helped him to cope with living in the West. In addition, Brother Ren had ensured that Brother Yun was able to receive a monthly salary to provide for his family. Yun's speaking engagements were arranged by a responsible mission board. Tax payments and registration of activities were done according to law, and ministry partners understood the mission and vision of the Chinese church.

In contrast, Peter Xu did not have a foreign counterpart to help him adjust to life outside China. It was as if he were swimming in shark-infested waters without a raft to cling to. The only credential he had prior to coming to the U.S. was that of an illegal, unregistered, underground, covert church in China. The idea of establishing a registered nonprofit organization for supporting Chinese missions was a concept that was totally foreign to him.

Consequently, Xu had no way of discerning between the churches and organizations that wanted to truly partner with the Chinese church and those that merely wanted to raise funds for their own projects. During the time when Xu was financially vulnerable, many groups in America saw him as someone they could take advantage of in order to raise funds for their own domestic visions and projects. Once he had served his purpose in their eyes, he was thanked, patted on the back, and sent out the door.

Eventually, Peter Xu moved to Los Angeles, where he continued to raise awareness about the vision of the Chinese House

Church. He still had problems with the idea of registration, and he maintained many of the habits he had developed in China. According to Joy In, who worked with Xu for several years in Southern California, "Peter never really understood the idea of registering with the government in America. At the end of the year, I was getting all of these requests from donors who needed donation receipts from us for their tax returns, and we had nothing to really give them in return. Peter Xu thought that it was just a matter of sending a thank-you letter to those who had donated."

Today, Peter Xu lives in Colorado, where he has started a new mission, with a new staff, called Back to Jerusalem Gospel Mission. It has been a hard road for him, full of ups and downs. He has taken a few falls along the way but continues to believe in the Lord for his strength and provision. Now in his seventies, he has no intention of slowing down. There will be no retirement for this man of God. His new organization in the U.S. is endeavoring to build partnerships and participation between the churches in the West and the East. Xu is focused on working with other churches around the world to connect them with his partners in China.

Most of the information about the Born Again Movement's current situation is contradictory and incomplete. One reason for this is Peter Xu's extended physical absence from China. Xu was a very strong and involved leader, and, without him, a lot has changed. The church has fragmented into smaller groups. These groups are made up of new faces and ambitious young leaders. Many of these leaders from the new generation have never met with Peter Xu and are not familiar with the way things used to be.

Xu can therefore give certain information regarding the Born Again Movement, but because he hasn't been in China for many years, his own idea of the current situation is vague. The nation of China has changed greatly since he left, and it is not easy to imagine the new guidelines that are being used by the present House Church.

A NEW PHASE OF **INDEPENDENCE**

When Peter Xu left China, his role changed from leader to ambassador. It has not been easy for him to leave his position as leader of one of China's largest House Church networks. It wasn't his preference to live in exile, and, if given the chance to return to his coworkers in China, it is almost certain that he would be on the next plane.

Yet, with the new wave of underground churches in China, a phase of independence is sweeping throughout the country. Such churches are more modern, more mobile, and much more self-governing. As China grows, these churches are growing with it. But massive underground House Church networks that are controlled by a single leader, as was the Born Again Movement under Peter Xu, are becoming a thing of the past.

The underground House Church networks that are in place in China today are adapting and continuing to operate, but the chances of a new network developing and growing into several million believers are not as high under the current conditions. In many ways, that is a good thing, because it indicates some exciting developments:

1. The Chinese people have more gospel resources than ever before. In the past, God worked through just a handful of people to share the gospel with many, but today, God is using lots of people to reach many more.

2. Church growth is taking place in more urban settings. Urban areas in China tend to be more transient, with new workers and residents coming and going all the time. By contrast, rural areas, where the underground house churches initially exploded, were made up of

closely knit communities where families had been living for generations. People in these rural communities were loyal to one another when they were animists, and they remained loyal to one another as believers in Christ. Today, the rural communities are made up mainly of children and the elderly, while most of the young adults have left for the urban areas to make money.

It is yet to be seen how these two factors will change the methods and practices of the Chinese House Church networks, but the churches will inevitably adapt as the Spirit leads.

12

The Cave

In part 3 of this book, we will move on to explore the major Anhui House Church networks. Before we do, let us turn to a story that has never been told before about one of the most effective training centers in all of China during the early 1990s, which was located in Henan Province. As the House Church in China grew, so, too, did the need for competent leaders. However, as has been mentioned, many of the Chinese didn't even have Bibles, let alone Bible training, and such training is important for the development of effective leaders.

One major reason for the lack of Bible training was simply that there weren't enough qualified Bible teachers. Many Chinese served God according to what they heard older people in the villages who claimed to be believers say. In addition, they had different perceptions of God, which they had deduced from dreams.

Even if there had been enough competent teachers, there was still a shortage of places where instructors could safely teach. Finding a location to train missionaries in those days was much more difficult than it is today. If Christians met together in secret, they not only had to watch out for the police, but they also had to ensure that even the neighbors didn't see or hear anything. A zealous Communist neighbor could report any activity that seemed suspicious. Congregating in unauthorized meetings was strictly forbidden in China in the early days, probably because it was under similar conditions that Mao Zedong had planned his overthrow of the government. He wasn't going to risk the same thing happening to him that he had pulled on others.

A SECRET **HIDING PLACE**

As we have worked with many leaders all over China, a great number of them have shared their memories of a secret training center called "the cave." Even groups from the Anhui networks had traveled to Henan Province to train there. These leaders were referring to an underground cave, which had been dug out by hand, where thousands of Chinese Christians had been prepared for the mission field. Far from looking like some glorious missionary training center, it was crude, cold, and utterly uncomfortable, but many Chinese chose to be taught there.

Sister H. was the one who had the initial vision for the cave. As of February 2012, she was a mother of five and a grandmother of eight. Her key role in transforming the underground House Church movement has never really been mentioned before. Although she was totally unaware of it at the time, God was going to use her in ways she never could have imagined.[26] The cave eventually made a huge impact on the history of the entire Chinese House Church.

In the late 1980s, Brother Yun had very few people he could rely on to hide him and his family from the authorities. Sister H. prayed for Brother Yun on a regular basis while he was in prison, and was deeply concerned for him and his family. Many nights, she was unable to sleep because she was up praying for him and asking God to keep him safe.

Brother Yun's preaching was full of joy and without compromise, but his whole family had been paying a huge price for the work. The persecution from the government was intense, and it was taxing on them. His wife and children were constantly being harassed and publicly humiliated for his "crime" of proselytizing in China. Even when he was not in prison, Brother Yun was rarely home. His wife, Deling, had to keep the household together all by herself.

In 1989, the revival began to spread uncontrollably. The gospel was moving from the rural farming communities to the more affluent cities, where university students and even government officials were getting saved. In Brother Yun's village alone, several Communist Party members had come to the Lord and begun to preach. As the multitude grew, so did the demand for shepherds to lead them. Pastors and preachers like Brother Yun were so busy that they did not have time to eat or sleep, let alone see to the physical and spiritual needs of their own families.

The people were so hungry for the gospel that they would pack into small spaces to hear the preachers, and they wouldn't leave. The pastors would have to be passed over the crowd in order to get to the next meeting. The leaders realized they could not carry out this task alone, and Deling appealed to her husband to take time to rest, to pray, and to be with his family.

Brother Yun and the other leaders began to pray for guidance and vision. Little did they know that God had already heard their prayers and was preparing a place for them. The answer would not come from a Westerner or a successful businessman but from a humble prayer warrior.

Sister H. owned several homes that were built in a traditional Chinese style. Anyone who has ever visited a traditional Chinese home would recognize the unique layout. Today, most Chinese live in high-rise apartments, but prior to the urbanization of the nation, there was a longstanding tradition in the way houses were built and used.

Every Chinese home had a courtyard surrounded by walls. The Forbidden City in Beijing gives an idea of this concept—though, of course, on a much larger scale. Traditional Chinese homes always have a wall that provides the courtyard with privacy. The homes also usually have three different living quarters in the shape of a horseshoe, with the most senior family members living in the center home, and the younger families living in the homes on each side.

Sister H., who was born and raised in Nanyang County, had one of these traditional Chinese homes in a place called Jingwa Town in Nanyang. Her house was at the base of a mountainside. She was the first person in her family to become a Christian. Her conversion took place in 1979 when she was about thirty years old. Her mother knew that she had been an angry young lady who was always getting into fights. "My mother knew that it must have been a miracle. Anything that made me turn from a hateful, angry person into a loving person had to be the work of God, and my mother immediately became a believer," Sister H. said.

"I remember a need during those early years to create a secret hiding place for books and things like that," she related. "So, my husband and I dug out a small place in the side of the mountain and covered it with rocks so that it would look like the rest of the wall."

God began to tell Sister H. to use her home as a place of refuge for Brother Yun. Beside her stove in the kitchen was a stack of firewood that she would use for cooking and for heating the home. She had the idea of removing the firewood and creating a small, secret space big enough for one person to enter. The entrance could then be concealed with firewood.

Behind the place where the firewood was kept was a soft limestone area of the mountain; this permitted Sister H. to dig out, by hand, an area that was big enough for two people to squeeze into. God moved on the hearts of Brother Yun and Deling to take a time of rest and just pray before the Lord. Sister H.'s small cave seemed to be the safest place for that purpose. Brother Yun traveled back to Henan, met with Sister H., and began to use the "prayer closet" she had prepared.

A CLANDESTINE **CONSTRUCTION PROCESS**

The prayer closet did not remain a prayer closet for long. Brother Yun loved the idea of having a place to go and pray, but anyone who is familiar with him knows that he also loves to be around other people. He always shares everything he has with others. Soon, he started to envision this prayer place being used for much more.

Brother Yun began to express the need for training others, and he also emphasized the fact that the leaders needed to be more attentive to their own families. He argued from Scripture that one who does not properly care for his own family cannot possibly take care of the church of God. (See 1 Timothy 3:5.) In the life of a Christian, God must always come first, family second, and ministry third. Unfortunately, several House Church leaders opposed Yun in this teaching, and the problem of ministers choosing ministry over family continues to be one of the major weaknesses of the Chinese house churches.

Soon, the work to build the prayer place into a larger area for people to pray and train together was begun. Brother Ren remembers well when the cave was being constructed: "I sat down with the Chinese brothers and sisters, and we designed the training facility in the cave. My background was in construction engineering. I focused on the need for electricity, air circulation, and structural integrity. We designed the cave with the idea that we could fit more than one hundred people inside. I remember that we would sleep in the house and crawl through the secret door by the oven during the time that we were building it. We began to call the mountain *Tian Shan* (Heavenly Mountain). We would send as many people as possible with rocks and dust from the cave. Everybody would put dirt in their pockets or rocks in a bag or backpack and take a walk toward the other village and empty their bags and pockets along the road away from the construction site."

There was a nearby rock quarry that masked a lot of the activities, but no one wanted to take any chances. Even though the debris from the cave construction would have been largely unnoticed because of the excavation taking place at the quarry, there was no room for error. This place would need to remain a deeply guarded secret. To prevent infiltration, only the top leadership and those closest to them could be a part of this training facility.

Small tractors were also used to move rocks, but this could be done only at night. All the digging was done with crude hand tools. There were only four people who were responsible for building the entire cave—Sister H., her husband, her husband's friend, and her son. Sister H. and these three men hammered away until their hands were cracked and bleeding. Their joints would still have the vibrating sensation of pounding a hammer into rocks even hours after they had stopped hammering. They were unable to enjoy a good night's sleep during those days, but the hunger to have a place where people could come and pray, sing to the Lord, and learn more about Him drove them to work around the clock.

They would use a metal chisel and bang away until they had chunks of rock large enough to shovel out. If they hit an area of soft rock, they would stop hammering and change direction. They used the areas that felt safe and stable.

Many believers encouraged them to enlarge the area even more after they had finished. "It would not have been safe to make it any larger," Sister H. said. "The cave felt pretty safe and secure, but if we would have gotten greedy and tried to make it even bigger, then we could have had the entire thing come down on us."

Even today, Sister H.'s hands are rough and callused from hard work. "If the police would have known what we were doing," she said in a recent interview, "they would have—" (She put her fingers up to her head to imitate a gun being pointed at her temple.)

"They would have killed you?" asked the interviewer.

"Absolutely. During those days, if the police would have known that I had a secret cave where I hosted meetings like this, they would have executed me."

Joshua of the Five Brothers Network visited the cave many times. "In the beginning of the 90s, we would have our training there in the cave. It was in this cave that many people fell in love with the Lord. We had many precious times of prayer. Many of the missionaries who were trained in this cave went out and served the Lord full-time. We were so excited to finally have a safe place that would allow us to learn, sing, and worship without fear. We would even abstain from eating food and drinking water so that we did not have to leave the cave to use the bathroom. There wasn't any place inside the cave to go to the bathroom. When you went in, there was no way to leave until everyone left, so it was important that you planned around those times."[27]

TWELVE THOUSAND **MISSIONARIES TRAINED**

As intended, when the cave was completed, there was room for more than one hundred people. The door was about one square meter and was located at the bottom of the wall next to the floor behind the woodpile. To get to the secret cave, one had to go into the kitchen and move the woodpile out of the way. A blanket was often hung over the hole, giving the appearance that it protected the wall from the woodpile.

To get into the cave, one would have to crouch down and fit through the one-square-meter hole. Then, one would crawl or scoot about ten meters down a small corridor that led into the main room. The ceiling was about two meters high in the highest spot. The measurements were not exact, because there was not one single right angle in the entire cave. There was increasingly less head space the closer one came to the outside edge.

There was always the challenge of preventing noise from coming out of the cave. A thick blanket was thrown over the hole to keep the sound from getting out, but that also restricted the airflow.

"Most of the time, we would train for only three to four hours at a time inside the cave because of lack of fresh air," Joshua remembered from his time there.

In the beginning, they used candles to provide light, but this was not a long-term solution. Brother Ren used his engineering skills to solve the problem. He arranged for a generator that would provide for lights and a fan.

"We could not use the local grid for electricity," Brother Ren said. "The local officials would notice right away that an unusual amount of electricity was being used by a small family. This suspicious activity would have led to the discovery of the cave, so we needed a way to provide the electricity. I arranged for a gas-powered generator to be used, instead."

Although the fan circulated the air, it did very little to combat the suspension of dust and dirt. So, Brother Ren also arranged for a dehumidifier. When the cave was new, the students and teachers would come out of the cave after a day of intense training looking like zebras, their faces black-and-white, as if they had been working in a coal mine all day. A large pipe was later installed that allowed for more air circulation.

Soon after the cave was built and began to be used as a training facility, foreign preachers and missionaries started to come and teach there. This development presented an additional challenge for security, but the leadership was hungry for the Word of God. Around the mid-1990s, more people in Western nations began to use cell phones. Not many Chinese had access to cell phones in the early days, and any foreigner with a mobile phone was closely monitored by the Chinese government. A rule was quickly made that no mobile phones were allowed in the cave. Foreigners were told to remove the batteries from their phones so they would not give off any signals to the PSB.

Not long after a visit from Pastor Dennis Balcombe, the PSB was able to obtain video footage of the underground cave from the inside. The police did everything they could to locate this cave. Several leaders were arrested and interrogated to obtain information about its whereabouts, but the location was never disclosed.

"There were some close calls," Brother Ren remembers. "Several years after we completed the cave, a Finnish organization donated a solar panel that we could use for electricity. This, of course, was much quieter than the gas-powered generator. One day, a patrol officer was walking through the neighborhood when he noticed the solar panel on Sister H.'s roof. During those days, not many people in Nanyang had solar panels on their roofs. He came around to Sister H.'s main entrance and confiscated it. He never followed the wires from the solar panel to see where they led. If he would have followed those wires, it would have led him right to the cave!"

A TEN-YEAR **MIRACLE**

The cave was used for about ten years. "I would estimate that there could have been as many as twelve thousand missionaries trained in there," Brother Ren said. "It was one of the safest places that we had for training during those days. You could sing, you could dance, and you could preach without much fear of being heard or caught."

"We had a lot of amazing times in that cave," Joshua said as he reflected over his cup of tea at an interview. "You know, I saw my first black person in that cave. I don't remember who arranged for him to speak and teach. I don't know if he was a black American or an African. All I remember was that I had never seen a black man before. I found it amazing that so many people from all walks of life came and shared the Bible with us in that little cave. Brother Ren and Teacher Zhao came to speak there many times, and I have fond memories of those days. That is where I learned so much about the Bible, and much of what I learned in those days I teach here in my school today."

Sister H. recalled, "The police were looking and looking for the cave, but they never did find it. Zhang Rongliang had visited the cave with some of his partners. Soon after he left, word began to circulate that the police were intent on tracking him down and arresting him. My husband and I felt that the cave had served its purpose. We felt that ten years without being discovered for a place so big was a real miracle. We also felt that there could be a chance that Zhang Rongliang would be caught, tortured, and forced to tell about our cave. With so much on the line, we decided that it was time to destroy it. Around the entrance to the cave there were wooden supports. We pulled out the wooden supports and let the entire entrance collapse, closing off the entire cave."

In those days, there were about three hundred people living in Sister H.'s area. In 2000, the rock quarry workers came in and excavated the mountain. Today, there is nothing there. The land is flat and barren. There are no new houses or any building projects where the mountain once stood, but the memories of the cave that was there during the 90s still echo throughout China.

Part 3:

Inside the Anhui
House Church Networks

A worship service in Wenzhou

Children at a Dove training session

Introducing Dove to the Anhui House Church leaders

13
Truth (Yingshan, or Zhenli)

Many of the Henan networks have tried to move past the county names they were branded with, but old habits die hard. Therefore, we usually refer to the county name when speaking with members of Tanghe or Fangcheng. However, we almost always call the Anhui networks by the names they have since adopted. We call the church in Yingshan County Zhenli, or Truth. And we call the Lixin County church, which we will explore in the next chapter, Mongfu, or Blessing.

The churches in Anhui Province are not as well-known as those in Henan. Very few people have learned anything about them, let alone their historical background. Despite our organization's having served the churches in Anhui for over a decade, we still know little about their history. We support their evangelists, missionaries, and Bible distribution efforts, and we have also been helping their Bible schools for years, but somehow we have hardly ever seemed to find the time to share a meal with their top leaders. Even on the rare occasions when we have met with the leaders, we have almost never talked about things like church history. We know these leaders and are familiar with their current projects, overall vision, and how they operate on a day-to-day basis, but our meetings with them are generally focused on working out the nuts and bolts of projects, rather than racking their brains for stories.

In fact, no one in China really talks about the history of the underground House Church. This is a tragedy, because a new generation of Chinese Christians is growing up with no knowledge of its own spiritual roots. In the West, we can walk into any Christian bookstore and buy plenty of books about Martin

Luther, John Wycliffe, Jonathan Edwards, or church history in general. Westerners can purchase vast volumes about European and American church history that could take several lifetimes to read; but in China, there are virtually no books about the formation of their churches. As a result, countless stories of martyrs and others who made immense sacrifices will never be told.

Westerners actually have more material about the history of the Chinese House Church available to them than Chinese believers do. Informative books about the church in China, such as *Jesus in Beijing*, *Back to Jerusalem*, and *The Heavenly Man*, are simply not available for purchase in China. Undoubtedly, this book will not be available there, either.

A CHURCH **SHROUDED IN MYSTERY**

Truth Network, in particular, is shrouded in more mystery than any other underground network. Very little information is available about its founder, history, leadership, or activities. Accordingly, very few people around the world—including those familiar with China—know anything about it. This chapter will give a brief introduction to the Truth Network. Although it is not as famous as the Henan networks or even as well-known as its Anhui counterpart, Blessing Network, the Truth Network is one of the most important underground house churches in China and will play a major role in determining the future of the House Church.

More than likely, some nonprofit organizations around the world that consider themselves experts on the House Church in China will disagree with some of the information presented in this chapter. Many so-called China experts came to the conclusion years ago that the Henan networks are the largest in China, and their assumptions are advanced by major Internet Web sites such as Wikipedia. However, this author would once again like to caution that virtually everything related to China is constantly changing. What was true in the year 2000 is not necessarily true at present. Many experts today still rely on studies that were conducted more than fifteen years ago. These studies are outdated and need to be replaced by new ones so that the facts can be reported as they are currently—not as they used to be.

Actually, all statistical reports coming out of China are incomplete because of the political situation, and all facts that are presented are based on the degree of exposure of those reporting them. The organizations that are working in China have various limitations to their exposure to the House Church, and those who have maximum exposure provide very few (if any) reports. Therefore, any report coming out of China, including the information given in this book, needs to be evaluated in relation to the amount, duration, and dates of exposure the researchers have had. Keeping those factors in mind will help you to evaluate the actual situation of the Chinese House Church today.

"THE STRONG, **SILENT TYPE**"

Truth will be the last large network covered in this book, although we will also look at several smaller ones. As we have noted, while Tanghe is likely the largest church in China today and is often thought of as such, there is information about the amazing church in Anhui called the Truth Network that few people are aware of.

If the Truth Network were an individual, it would be labeled "the strong, silent type." Truth does not make much noise or garner much public attention, but, without a doubt, this network is making the largest impact for world missions today, if measured by the amount of money spent or the number of missionaries sent out from China. Truth Network has continued to grow exponentially, and for the last few years has been producing more missionaries and evangelists than any other Chinese network. In 2011, Truth operated more than sixty Bible schools throughout the nation, and, every year, it graduates more than 1,500 evangelists and missionaries. This does not include its pastoral programs, its grassroots worker training programs, and its Sunday school teacher program.

The 1,500 evangelists and missionaries are supported and organized through the network and strategically sent out to various areas that have needs. The network sends out missionaries in groups of ten to twenty-five at a time, and it has appointed two missions directors to oversee the implementation of the work. These two missions directors are supplied with nearly U.S.$200,000 per year entirely from the house churches—not from foreigners.

Two hundred thousand dollars may not sound like a lot of money compared with the budgets of large missions organizations in the Western world, but Truth Network is based in rural Anhui Province, and most of the church is made up of poor farmers. This means that it does not have a large headquarters facility or other buildings to rent or keep up every month. In addition, the $200,000 does not include the outside resources and financial support the network receives from foreign organizations, which is much more than the sums it is able to raise in-house. The amount of its resources raised domestically shows how important world missions is to the Truth Network.

The church's dogged and determined focus is just one of the factors that has contributed to its growth in China and abroad. Truth Network currently has more missionaries in the field than any other network. It is even possible to say that, in 2011, Truth had more missionaries in the field than all the other networks in China combined.

THE **EARLY DAYS**

In our fifteen years of working with Truth Network, we have met with the leadership on a regular basis, but we had never asked about their history or background until one night in February 2012, while we were gathering research for this book. We spend most of our time working with the lower leadership, so it was exciting to meet with their senior leader, Pastor Chen, in Shanghai. He is a stout man with a comb-over hairstyle and strong, round facial features. We began talking about the projects we had completed together in 2011 and the vision for 2012.

After we had discussed all our projects, I asked him to provide a brief history of his church for this book. He was caught off guard and obviously had not been asked that question often. However, once he got started, he told stories for over two hours about the Chinese church of previous decades and the founding of the Truth Network.

As we munched on mandarin oranges, China's main winter fruit, Pastor Chen talked about the political situation in the early days, which was basically the same for all the networks. He began,

> After the 1960s, it was not easy for any of the Christians left in China. They had relied a lot on the foreign missionaries. The foreigners had read the Bible for them. They had preached for them, led the churches, and led the prayers. When they left, the old Christians were not sure of anything. They didn't know how to pray. They didn't have a strong understanding of the Bible. They knew only that Jesus was God.

MIRACLES OF **HEALING AND DELIVERANCE**

Unlike the church in Henan Province, which had leaders with strong personalities who can be identified in relation to its founding and history, the history of the church in Anhui is not as straightforward. The Truth Network cannot be traced back to the work and efforts of one man or missionary. For example, in Henan Province, there were giants of the faith like Jonathan Goforth, Marie Monsen, Li Tianen, and others, but the same cannot be said of Anhui. Undoubtedly, there were key players who "cultivated the land" there, but, again, their imprint is not as strong or as traceable.

Pastor Chen was born in 1956, and his family lived close to the banks of the Huai River in Yinshang County. He was raised during the darkest years of Chinese history. "I cannot really point to one person who really came and shared the gospel with us," he recalled. Even though he was clearly well-versed in Chinese history and church history in China, he was not able to identify a central figure who had ignited the fire of church growth in Anhui. "During the days of Mao Zedong, the area where my village was located was one of the poorest in China. The villagers went insane. They were demon possessed. We didn't know it then, but there were entire villages that were possessed by demons."

The reason the villages in and around Yinshang County had so many people who were out of their minds is that the people had lost all hope. There were no hospitals to go to for diagnoses, and there was no money to pay for any treatment, even if the diagnoses were clear.

Pastor Chen's family had experienced its share of hardships. His family had a history of cancer and deafness. His grandfather had gone deaf at an early age and died of cancer. His father had gone completely deaf and died of cancer at the age of thirty-one. Pastor Chen remembered,

> When I was younger, I realized that I, too, was going deaf. In 1979, I was almost completely deaf in both ears and was showing the early signs of cancer. I was sick and too weak to move. I knew that my time on earth was not going to last much longer. One of my in-laws came and shared the gospel with me, and it was at that time that I accepted Jesus as my Lord. On that day, I was completely healed. No one could explain it. We didn't know how it worked. We knew only that it was the name of Jesus that had healed me.

That is how the church grew in Yinshang in the early days. Those ten years between 1980 and 1990 were full of revival throughout that area. The biggest attraction was the casting out of demons. People were bringing to the Christians their demon-possessed family members who were out of control, and the demons would immediately leave.

In Yinshang, ancestral worship and appeasing demons were deeply rooted cultural practices. Demon possession may not be a common visible occurrence in the Western world, but in China, it was very real and visible, and the appeasement of demons dictated every aspect of life. People's lives were focused on pacifying the demons so they would not torment the family. Houses, rooms, and all other structures were built in ways deemed inoffensive to demons.

The Chinese practice of feng shui is based on the idea of creating good *qi* so that all forces will flow naturally without stopping the flow of dragons or demons. The positioning of wind chimes and mirrors is very important in the feng shui practiced in Anhui. Even today, in Hong Kong, no one would dare to offend the demons and risk getting bad luck. Feng shui has been adopted and implemented in places like Hong Kong Disneyland, and dragon dancers are hired to scare away evil spirits at upscale shopping malls throughout the city. Large Western companies spend millions of dollars to hire experts to create an auspicious environment that will not offend the demons.

Pastor Chen continued to recall those earlier days:

> So many people were being set free from demons that there was no doubt about the power of the name of Jesus. We didn't know how to pray. We didn't have a Bible. We didn't know anything except what the old Christians told us regarding crying out in the name of Jesus.
>
> During the 1980s to 1990s, there wasn't a farmer left in the field on Sunday. Everyone flocked to the name of Jesus. Our village went from a village with no believers to a village where everyone was a believer. Even today, if you travel to Yingshan County, you will find that almost everyone you meet is a believer in Jesus Christ.

TRANSFORMED **LIVES**

As with the other networks discussed in earlier chapters, the revivals in Yingshang County did not start off with the purpose of becoming a large movement. They were just the natural flow of the power of the Holy Spirit.

> I can't really say that there was a defining moment where we began to adopt the name "Truth" as the name of our network. Maybe I wasn't even there, but the best that I can remember was that there was a pastor from Taiwan who was arranging a large meeting in the mid-90s. He asked us what the name of our group was. We didn't know. We just referred to people who came from our county as Yingshan. The pastor told us that we needed a name that we could use to register, so we used "Truth." I mean, we believe in the truth of Jesus Christ, so it sounded natural to me.

The churches grew rapidly during the 1980s, especially where people like Pastor Chen had seen miracles of God performed. The villagers were too poor to buy medicine or to see a doctor when they were sick, so their only hope was the prayers of the Christians. They were not disappointed. Many people were healed and had their lives transformed, never to be the same again.

Our church continued to grow. Every time I was arrested, I saw the Lord blessing the church of Yingshan more and more. In 2003, I was arrested, and the arresting officer told me that I was one of the most wanted men in all of China. Out of all the criminals in China, I was among the top six in all of eastern China.

> Even though the government sought to destroy us and to stomp out our church, they were not able to. Even if you go to the Three-Self government church in our area, you will quickly understand that they are the minority. The unbelievers and the official church in Yingshan are the minority group. Our House Church makes up most of the population.

Truth has started an officially recognized school that provides education for children from kindergarten all the way through high school. Upon learning about the school, some locals were concerned and immediately began attempts to sabotage the efforts. Pastor Chen said,

> They didn't want us to have a school that taught children. The government immediately had problems with the facility and said that it didn't meet their standards, but I knew that it was more than that, so I called up the officials. I asked them if we were being stopped just because we were Christians. The officials emphatically denied that they were trying to stop anything. Eventually, we got our school up and running, and, today, we have more than one thousand students, not including kindergarteners.

Truth Network has stepped onto a new frontier in China. The network is not registered, but it is recognized and respected by the local police and officials. Pastor Chen has come a long way since being the "sixth most wanted criminal" in all of eastern China. Today, he has missionaries in many different countries, such as Ethiopia, Pakistan, Cambodia, Myanmar, Nepal, Uzbekistan, and Laos. At the time of this writing, he had ten students at the Back to Jerusalem training facility in the Philippines.

Truth also has students attending universities around the world to be equipped with the tools they need to train others for the future. They are in prestigious universities like Oxford and Cambridge and are dedicated to returning to China and using their skills to aid the Back to Jerusalem movement.

When asked what Truth Network's greatest need was, Pastor Chen replied, without hesitation, "Bibles! We still have a huge Bible deficit everywhere we go."

Pastor Chen has a passion to get the Bible and other teaching resources into the hands of believers. In 2011, we received the following testimony from a young believer named Brother En who had been handed a Bible directly by Pastor Chen:

I had my back to the wall, and there was no hope in my life. It was at that time that I received a Bible from Uncle Chen. He said to me, "If you want hope in your life, read this." That night, I started to read the Bible that he gave me. I read it all night long. When I read in Matthew 8:17, "He took our illnesses and bore our diseases," I began to weep. I cried so loudly that it woke up my family. They came to me asking why I was crying. I could not say anything. I could not stop crying. Instead of asking more questions, they just joined me and began to cry, as well.

Before I was a Christian, I had a disease in my throat that prevented me from eating normally, but after that day, I was completely healed. The next morning, I woke up and brushed my teeth and sat down to eat real food. I had been completely healed. Hallelujah! My family could not believe their eyes. As soon as they saw that I was healed, they immediately began to believe in Jesus, and they, too, became Christians.

Thank you for sending the Bible to me. May God bless you in every situation. I ask God to bless your [Back to Jerusalem] team.

Here is another letter given to us by the Truth Network after we had delivered Bibles to Brother Hua:

Dear Brothers in the Lord:
Peace to you!
The reason I am writing this letter is that we have seen so many people blessed by your support. Today there are 236 believers in our church, and they all now have their own Bible! We have Bible studies together every evening and morning. How precious His Word is to us! In Psalm 119:11, it says, "I have stored up your word in my heart, that I might not sin against you." I have seen most of the people at our

Bible study have their lives completely changed. Today, there are many believers who are praying with us who used to be thieves, liars, and gamblers. Some of them would fight with anyone and everyone at every opportunity. All of us are new in Christ and have been changed forever.

We have had several women in our group who could not have children, but after coming to the cross and following Jesus, they were able to get pregnant and have a baby. There are so many testimonies in our small group that I could write all day. I just want to say thank you for your gift. Because of your support, we have seen an incredible increase in believers. We have many testimonies and new believers here. God bless you!

The results of the collaboration between Truth Network and Back to Jerusalem International to deliver Bibles in China have been amazing. We sometimes receive letters from the network that actually confirm that people became Christians when they received a Bible, such as this letter from Sister Han:

First, I give thanks to our God! Thank you for supporting our church for all these years. I remember when I received my first Bible. It was provided by you. When I first received it, I didn't know what it was and what the book was about. I thought that it must be a history book or a biography. After I read it and studied it, I gave my heart to Christ. Because of your contribution, I was able to obtain life, as well as strength and courage to minister to others.

Truth Network continues to break barriers in China. As with the other underground House Church networks, its leaders are delivering Bibles as quickly as they can. There has been a direct relationship between the delivery of Bibles and the growth of the church in China. The Back to Jerusalem Web site and Facebook page are regularly updated with stories and testimonies related to Bibles being delivered in China.

14

Blessing (Lixin, or Mongfu)

Apart from keeping portions of their church history secret for security reasons, Chinese Christians just do not have the time to sit around and talk about the amazing works of God they have witnessed. The leaders of Blessing Network, for example, have never approached anyone with a glossy, full-color brochure that describes their church of five million believers. They wouldn't even think of mentioning that they are one of the five largest House Church networks in China, or that they are one of the largest movements in all of Anhui Province, with more congregants than the entire nation of Norway.

Accordingly, it actually took much prodding to get the information for this chapter out of the leaders of Blessing Network. It was largely extracted from a report they gave us on Bible distribution in June 2011. Back to Jerusalem usually connects with them twice a year to talk about Bible delivery with their network.

PERSECUTION OF CHRISTIANS IN **CHINA TODAY**

A story leading up to our meeting with the leaders of Blessing is quite typical of ministry life in China. One of the leaders was coming from a training session for workers from ten different provinces—and he almost didn't make it out of the session. On the second day of instruction, a teacher was present whom no one had ever seen before. He ended up being an undercover policeman who had infiltrated the meeting. No one is sure how it happened. The training session was raided by the local police the following day, but the leader who attended our meeting had left the gathering just before the raid.

After the police burst into the training session, the other leaders were detained and questioned. Before they were released, their names were recorded in the local logbook to document their unregistered meeting and illegal activities.

It is important to realize that this raid did not take place during the Cultural Revolution of the 1970s but in June 2011. There is still very real persecution taking place on a regular basis in China, and most of it goes unnoticed because many foreign organizations and nations are turning a blind eye to it in order to maintain a good relationship with China.

Several years before that police raid, in another meeting that included representatives from Blessing Network, a group of foreign supporters of the Chinese House Church got to have a small taste of the real situation of persecution in China. While the historic meeting was under way, a large group of uniformed police officers came down the hotel's spiral staircase toward the room where we were meeting. A local Chinese brother who had worked with the police department in the past noticed them and alerted the Chinese leaders at the meeting. Those leaders immediately exited out a side door opposite of where the police were and quickly blended into the crowd on the street, while most of the Westerners waited to see what would happen. One woman in the back of the room panicked and started to become hysterical.

The police officers walked down the staircase toward our meeting, but then they quickly turned aside and went into the massage parlor. The conference room just happened to be directly adjacent to a Chinese spa. Even though it was a false alarm, for a brief moment, several foreign Christians felt what it is like to be a Chinese believer in a normal prayer meeting. For just a few seconds, those Westerners were able to relate, in a very small way, to what most Chinese go through every time they meet for worship.

ORIGINS OF **BLESSING NETWORK**

At about nine in the evening after that training session had been raided by the police, the leader from Blessing Church arrived at our hotel. Almost immediately, we began to discuss the need for Bibles in China. We had provided tens of thousands of Bibles for Blessing House Church in the past, so they wanted to discuss the future need. After talking about the projects, as usual, we intentionally steered the conversation toward the history of the network. The situation was awkward at first, and all the leaders in the room knew that it was a strange request, but they graciously gave us a brief history of their church. The founder of Blessing Network, named Enguan, sat back against the couch. He had been so taken off guard by our inquiry that he had to pause a moment to organize his thoughts.

In 1976, when Enguan was fourteen, his father became ill and soon died. Two years later, his mother came down with a serious illness. She had been demon possessed for a long time, as well. In addition, his older brother had serious issues with his ears, but the family was too poor to pay for treatment. Enguan's family hadn't had the money to help his father when he had become sick two years earlier, and they still didn't have enough money to help his mother or his brother.

"I believe that God used poverty to teach me to trust in Him," Enguan stated matter-of-factly.

Six Christians lived in his village at that time. None of them was educated, and they could not read. Enguan's uncle was one of those Christians. He would often sing old hymns to his God, but he did not have a Bible or any significant formal education. Even though Enguan was not a Christian, he was comforted during those most trying times by hearing his uncle's songs. He asked his uncle to teach him the hymns that he was always singing. Once he learned them, he found comfort in their words and peace in their melodies. Even before he was a Christian, he would share the hymns with others. He could see how God was using him, even though he was not yet a believer.

He wanted to ask the Christians to come to his home and pray for his mother because of her demon possession, but in China it is customary to feed houseguests. He didn't have any food to offer them. Since the family couldn't afford rice flour, Enguan eventually made flour out of sweet potatoes and offered it to the Christians in his village when they came over to pray.

During their visits, he would listen carefully to every word they prayed. Since he couldn't afford to keep asking them to come and pray for his mother, he memorized the words of their prayers and prayed them over her himself. One day, he knelt down and began praying for his mother, and she was suddenly healed and set free from demon possession. All the local Christians who heard about it rejoiced.

Enguan was saved in 1978 and immediately began to preach the gospel in his area. At that time, the Christians there didn't have any worship services, so Enguan began to hold meetings at his home, and this became the very first house church of Lixin County. The formation of Blessing House Church Network had begun.

Other families in the area also had members who were completely out of their minds with unexplainable insanity. Word began to get around that this kind of uncontrollable behavior could be demon possession. Enguan started to get requests to travel around and pray for those who were afflicted in this way. Again, all he knew were the hymns taught him by the old believers in the village. Whenever there were people who needed prayer, he would pray the few words that he had heard prayed before in the name of Jesus and sing the hymns. People were set free from the demons, and entire families came to the Lord. He began to see miracles take place. It was unexplainable.

Enguan did not have a Bible; thus, he had no way to reference any of the prayers he was praying, nor any way to formally introduce people to the God who was setting them free from demon possession. To him, Jesus was only a name that demonstrated power of deliverance, and he placed his faith in the name of Jesus.

It is not easy for believers from that generation to explain how things happened in those early days, but people saw the miracles and believed. They believed in Jesus as their Lord and began to call themselves Christians. It was one of the few signs of hope in the dark days of Mao Zedong, when evil seemed to consume all of China.

That first house church in Lixin that met in Enguan's home was more of a hospital for the sick than a gathering place for believers, because sick people who had no other hope for treatment would travel there from distant places to be miraculously healed. They came because they had heard rumors of other sick people being cured. Enguan prayed for them, and they were indeed healed. This led to even more people believing and even more people telling their friends, family members, and acquaintances about the miracles.

Although these things were taking place, and the church was growing, the believers still didn't have anything more than mere songs to rely on for their faith. They cherished those songs and held close to the prayers in the name of Jesus that demonstrated power to heal the sick and perform miracles. Yet no Bible was to be found anywhere. No one had even seen a Bible or known anyone else who had seen one.

In the 1980s, a man who was a Christian was seriously ill and about to die. One day, his wife, who was also a believer, decided to get baptized. She thought that if she was baptized, Jesus would see her and bless the water surrounding her. After her baptism, she immediately collected the water around her in a bottle. She brought it to her sick husband and asked him to drink it. Amazingly, after he drank the water, he was healed. Without a Bible, there was no possible way for the people in Lixin County to understand the meaning of the miracles they were experiencing and witnessing, but God responded to their misguided acts of faith anyway.

After some time, the believers were finally able to get their hands on a Bible. The problem at that point was that they weren't able to understand it. They were so excited to have a Bible, but they were not exactly sure what to do with it. However, they connected the Bible with healing from God, and the believers practiced two general methods of healing in conjunction with their Bible. First, when sick people came to the House Church meeting, they would place the Bible on the bed in one of the rooms. Then, they would tell those who were sick to go into the room and place their forehead on the Bible and then lie on it. Sometimes, the people would use the Bible as a pillow, and sometimes they would pull it to their chest and lie on top of it.

Second, the Blessing Church people would get those who were sick to stand still, and then they would take the Bible and actually hit them on the head with it. Amazingly, both ways worked. Those who did these things were healed of their sicknesses. God continued to be gracious to the believers in their ignorance.

In 1984, Dennis Balcombe gave Enguan his first Bible. Enguan recalled,

> Bao Dani [Dennis] would often bring in groups, sometimes up to fifty people, who would bring in the Bible. It was not easy to get a Bible during those days. We didn't have mobile phones to contact people, and a delivery of Bibles often involved a lot of waiting and misunderstandings. During one delivery of Bibles, Mr. Z.—one of the delivery-truck drivers—was arrested. The police took the entire truckload of Bibles into custody. On another occasion, Mr. Z. drove the Bibles to the location that he was given. He dropped off the Bibles and returned home. The next day, he called the leaders, only to discover that he had dropped off the Bibles at the wrong location.

In the 1980s and even into the 1990s, the believers went from home to home and county to county spreading the good news of Jesus Christ. Enguan was given a bicycle and would ride it from six in the evening until noon the next day just to minister in various areas.

Like most of the other House Church leaders we have discussed, Enguan never assumed that the small underground House Church gatherings that took place in the middle of the night would ever grow to anything other than just a few saints coming together to sing praises to their King. The believers never dreamed that their small meetings would spread beyond their backward, poor, rural region of Lixin County.

"Since the founding of the church in 1985 in Lixin, we have seen the number of people coming to the Lord every year grow and grow. There is no way we can possibly keep count," Enguan said. In 1994, he had tried to calculate the number of people in his church; at that time, he estimated it to be about three million believers. The network has continued to grow drastically, so it has not been easy to determine how many people currently belong to it. In 2012, those familiar with the areas Blessing was working in and how many leaders they had in those areas estimated the numbers to be between five million and seven million believers.

INTENSE **TRIALS**

The Blessing Network became notorious among the local police in Anhui during the 1980s and 90s, because most of the Christians who were arrested during that time were from that network. Enguan recalls,

> We were one of the most heavily persecuted churches in all of China. The police regularly swept through our area and conducted sting operations. Every year, more than one hundred leaders would be arrested. Christians in our area

were not Christians for long before they were rounded up by the police. You would have one believer who had been a believer for six years and had served five and a half of those years in prison. It was not uncommon to have believers who were baby Christians only be saved for a month or more before being martyred for their faith. This was life in the Lixin [Blessing] Network. Those were hard days.

In 1998, I remember that we had a large meeting with so many leaders who came from all over China. They were all referring to themselves as Lixin House Church workers, but many of them were not from Lixin County, so, in 1998, when we were in that meeting, we came together and made the decision to change our name from Lixin to Mongfu [Blessing]. It seemed to be more appropriate than Lixin.

In 1998, we actually came together to focus on training up other leaders. All of us in the top leadership positions were positive that we would all soon end up in jail. We were concerned for the future of the church in Anhui if we all ended up in jail at the same time. The Public Security Bureau was searching for us, and we knew that it was only a matter of time before we were caught. We could not run forever.

All of us leaders came together and began to talk about the bare essentials that a replacement should know in case anything ever happened to us. A young man at the meeting wrote down everything that we dictated to him. He wrote up a list of everything that would be needed in our absence. The young brother also wrote down all the names of everyone at the meeting. Unfortunately, that brother posted it on the Internet and caused us all a lot of problems.

Because of intense persecution, Enguan still keeps a low profile. When the filmmakers who made the documentary *The Cross in China* came to China, he did not want to be interviewed by them. *The Cross in China* is a set of stories and interviews about the Chinese House Church; it was put on DVD and sold around the world.

PROGRESS AND **CHALLENGES**

In the 1990s, the Blessing Network began to arrange more formal training for its leaders. They would study the Bible, as well as methods of evangelism. Upon completing the training, the students were sent out to areas all over China. People from Anhui tend to be good stage performers; therefore, many students went to minority areas like Yunnan Province and arranged stage productions that presented the gospel in small villages. These young men and women used a traveling theatrical show to go from village to village sharing the gospel.

A great many people came to the Lord through that ministry, but it did face challenges. Due to China's one-child policy, there are not enough females for the men to marry, and, on a couple of occasions, female evangelists from Blessing Network were invited to villages to perform their play, only to be kidnapped and forced into marriages.

In 1999, Enguan was arrested, and he went to jail for two years. During that time, he was constrained to make boxes for Haier Electronics. Today, Haier is a famous brand in China and is even becoming popular worldwide. During his time in prison, Enguan shared a cell with about forty other prisoners. He stated, "I was never really bothered by my time in prison, to be honest. I really felt that since all my coworkers had already gone to prison or were still in prison, it was my turn now."

Enguan clearly remembered one particular brother who was in prison with him. He had been put on death row and was there for only about eight months. This brother knew that he was about to be executed; however, instead of living every day in fear, he put his trust in the Lord and preached the gospel to everyone else on death row. Even though those prisoners were in the most hopeless situation, with no light at the end of the tunnel, they found love and mercy in Christ. Everyone on death row in that prison became a Christian.

Enguan knows Pastor Zhang Rongliang from Fangcheng Church because Pastor Dennis Balcombe introduced them. There were some major problems between the Fangcheng and Blessing networks, but the two leaders met, talked through their problems, and prayed about the challenges together. Those challenges usually arose when evangelists from the two networks would arrive in the same place to preach the gospel and end up in competition, but a solution was eventually worked out. Today, the two brothers are highly respectful of one another.

In the past ten years or so, there have been some major shifts in the way the Blessing Network conducts its operations in China and abroad. Its members are better prepared and are given many more tools to use in the field than they were in the past.

Today, one of the visions closest to their hearts is the Back to Jerusalem vision. The young people in Blessing Church are truly passionate about taking the gospel to the darkest regions of the earth and seeing those who have never before heard the gospel of Jesus Christ saved. The network's evangelists have been heading out in large numbers to share the gospel in areas like Tibet, Guangxi, Guizhou, and Yunnan. Some of them are working at the universities and preaching the gospel to the students. In the beginning, many of these workers were able to get financial support from Teacher Zhao and Brother Ren. However, in 2008 and 2009, the support decreased because of the drop in donations from the West.

This decrease affected the number of workers Blessing was able to send to the western regions of China, but the workers who did go survived on faith. Today, the network is encouraging the local churches to support the workers with what they have. Some of the areas in southwestern China have been doing well for ten years, and they really thank Teacher Zhao for his hard work and dedication in ensuring that they had extra support to cultivate those areas at the beginning.

Many of the churches that were planted ten years ago have grown and flourished remarkably. Guangxi has been one of the areas of heaviest focus for Blessing Church. It has not been an easy road, because the evangelists from Anhui are Han Chinese and don't speak the minority languages of the mountain villages in Guangxi. Evangelists from Blessing have had to overcome numerous cultural and linguistic barriers to do ministry there.

Blessing Network now has Bible-training centers all over China. The network is also starting to get involved in humanitarian projects in poor areas; these projects can be used as avenues for preaching the gospel. In 2011, they began to work on helping people in a small rural village obtain clean water. Previously, the villagers had to walk about ten kilometers to get drinkable water.

Enguan compared China's past with its present, saying, "Things are changing in China. Before, there were so many police after me who wanted to arrest me and throw me into prison. Today, I am a bit older, and so are they. Instead of chasing me, we might even go out and have a cup of tea together. Of course, if we have a meeting, they will not be happy about it and will come and break it up. They are obligated to write down the names of everyone present, but, for the most part, we have come to terms with each other."

Enguan had just received his first passport. He was able to travel to Hong Kong, and, in March 2011, he was able to travel to America for the first time. "I didn't have anything to do there," he chuckled. "I just wanted to go and see what it was like."

Before we parted after the interview that night, Enguan asked me to share one message with the West on behalf of the Blessing House Church Network: There is still a desperate need for Bibles in China. "Please share with your partners in America and Europe that believers in China still need Bibles. This is one of our daily challenges, and we cannot do it alone."

15
Little Joe's Network

Little Joe's network is named after its founder. Although "Joe" is obviously not his real name, nor the name of his network, to use the real names would jeopardize the safety of his church. Little Joe's name comes from the Chinese way of saying "Junior." In Western terms, his father would be "Joe Senior." The Chinese say *xiao*, meaning "little," to denote sons who share names with their fathers.

Little Joe's network has never been written about before. Its leader works with very few foreigners. In fact, we don't believe Little Joe works with any foreigners outside of those partnered with Back to Jerusalem. His church is considered to be a fragment of the Blessing Network that has gone "rogue," meaning that it split from the main network without official authorization from the leadership. Little Joe's father had always been quite an independent pastor within that network, with a different way of doing things. He was the original patriarch of this splinter group, yet, when he was imprisoned in the 1990s, Little Joe began to be recognized as the one taking the reins. Under Little Joe's leadership and organization, the group developed into a network.

Little Joe's church is one of the smaller networks in China; it is estimated to comprise eight hundred thousand to one million believers. The network is mainly established in a rural part of China, with most members residing in Anhui Province.

Little Joe is relatively young for a network pastor, having been born in Fengyang County, Anhui Province, in May 1973. Among all the House Church leaders in China, he is one of the most dependable when it comes to financial reporting and project clarity. I have traveled extensively with Little Joe for several years and often share a hotel room with him. Thus, I have spent much time sharing stories and discussing future plans and visions with this pastor.

Little Joe first visited the United States in 2011, soon after receiving his first passport. It is not easy for House Church pastors to obtain a passport, since most of them have a criminal record, but somehow Little Joe was approved to receive this valuable travel document. When he made his trip to the U.S., it was only the second time he had been outside of China. Because we knew that his chances of getting a U.S. visa would improve if he had already visited another foreign country, our organization had arranged his first trip abroad, as well.

MIRACLES OF HEALING, PROVISION, AND THE FIRE OF GOD'S PRESENCE

Little Joe had always wanted to be a pastor, like his father, and he first started preaching in the 1990s. He remembers the early days when he felt the Lord calling him to preach the gospel in different areas far from home. At the outset of his ministry, the only support he received came from his parents, who were extremely poor. Naturally, a father who is habitually being arrested is not the most ideal source of ministry funding.

The beginning of Little Joe's network was similar to that of other Chinese networks—marked by miracles, including many sick people being healed.[28] In those days, they set out to start a church in a rural part of Anhui that was known to have many sick people. The farmers outside that village had to walk a long way to attend the meetings, and it was a very hot summer. There was one woman in particular who had heart problems and who actually suffered a heart attack brought on by the strain of walking so far in the hot sun. Little Joe and his coworkers prayed for her, and she was immediately healed. She said that she had suffered heart attacks in the past and had needed to be taken to the hospital to get an injection in order to be revived, but this time she was immediately and completely healed.

Quite a different story came from another village in Jiangsu Province. A sister there had stomach cancer. She had believed God would heal her when she got saved, but her condition actually grew worse after her salvation. When the doctor said she had only a few days to live, she was greatly discouraged and wanted to give up the faith. Little Joe and some elders went to the hospital to pray for her. She had formerly been an idol worshipper, and it was clear that the demons didn't want to let go of her. While Little Joe and the elders were praying, the nurses came in and started yelling at them, saying, "What are you doing? Why are you starting a fire in here? You could burn the whole building down!" Evidently, the presence of God was so strong in that room during their prayer that the nurses saw flames coming through the closed door. The darkness lifted, and the woman repented, saying, "Lord, even though You didn't heal me, I will believe in You whether I die or not." She went to be with her Lord that same week.

In those days, along with miracles such as these, there was also supernatural provision. Little Joe felt called by God to go preach the gospel in other villages, but he didn't have any money to do so. He needed bus fare to travel to other churches that were in desperate need of preaching. There were occasions when he was able to visit churches in other villages but didn't have the funds for a bus ticket home. One time, he had to stay in a village and preach there for almost a month—not by choice, but because he didn't have any money to enable him to leave. Other churches needed him to come and preach, but he had no means of making his way to their villages.

He loves to recall the story of how, one Sunday, he preached at a service in one village and had only half the required bus fare to get to his next preaching engagement. He decided to ride the bus as far as his money would take him and walk the rest of the way to the meeting. Unbeknownst to him, there was a fellow believer on the same bus. When he attempted to purchase a ticket before boarding, he was informed that his ticket had already been paid for in full by a sister who just happened to be on that bus.

After preaching in the next church, he prayed, "God, You fed Elijah. Please provide a way for me to go home." Soon after he prayed, another Christian sister arrived on a long-distance bus. She walked alone in the dark to where Little Joe was staying, because she was determined to meet him. She told him, "God led me to see you now." After talking for a while, this sister said, "God told me you don't have any transportation money," and she insisted on giving him twice what he needed for the trip home.

This testimony may seem insignificant in comparison with others that have been related in this book, but it was through this small provision that Little Joe learned at an early age to trust in the Lord. Through this experience, he got a deep impression that God really does provide.

LITTLE JOE **IMPRISONED AND INTERROGATED**

Little Joe's lowest point came in 2000 when he was arrested in Anhui Province. The police confiscated his phone, and he was deeply distraught that they would go through his address book and find all the phone numbers of his coworkers. This bothered him so much that he wasn't concerned in the least with his own safety or what would happen to him. He felt personally responsible for bringing disaster on his beloved coworkers. Later, however, he found out that the police never looked up the numbers, and no one else was arrested.

The judge sentenced Little Joe to three years in prison for preaching. It was arranged for him to be sent to an infamous coal mine labor camp to serve out his sentence. This was the same dread labor camp that his father had served in years earlier. Little Joe recalled,

The prison that my father went to was especially hard on Christians. I know that many Christians like to tell the stories that end in wonderful testimonies about God's amazing grace and power bringing them through the most trying times, but that was not always the case.

The coal mine was torture for Christians serving time there. Coal mining is one of the most dangerous and physically demanding jobs in China. [The Chinese government] likes to use Christians and political dissidents for labor in the coal mines. Many go in, but few come out. There was a brother who was in love with the Lord and was arrested in Anhui, then sent to the labor camp. He was told to deny the name of the Lord. He refused. He was sent to the coal mine. He was again told to deny the name of the Lord. He again refused.

The guards beat him for refusing to deny the Lord. Every day, every prisoner has a quota to complete. If they do not complete their quota, they will be punished. After the brother was beaten, he was not able to complete his quota the next day. He was beaten again and kicked in the head. He was kicked so hard that it caused him serious damage.

He was not able to handle it any longer. He used a light in the shower room, took the lightbulb out of the socket, and then turned on the water and killed himself. He just couldn't take it anymore.

Torture for a few days or even weeks might be bearable, but when there is no end in sight, there can be times when the human body and mind just quit.

Little Joe had a friend in politics who was able to get his sentence reduced to one year, and he was never sent to the coal mine. While he was in prison, the guards would interrogate him night and day. "They would suddenly take me from my cell and interrogate me at the most unexpected times. They especially liked the middle of the night!" They chose the odd hours of the night and early morning to catch him off guard, hoping to get him to incriminate himself. But with God's help, he was able to endure the questioning. "I truly learned the truth of Luke 12:12, *'For the Holy Spirit will teach you in that very hour what you ought to say.'*"

"BUSINESS AS **MISSION**"

Little Joe's underground House Church network has one unique asset that deserves special recognition. The leaders have a clear understanding of "Business as Mission" (BAM). In fact, in 2011, Little Joe was one of the main speakers at a Back to Jerusalem Business as Mission Conference held in America's Bible Belt.

Many missions organizations and leaders often define the concept of BAM in narrower terms than Back to Jerusalem does. Yet our intention is to keep the parameters open when defining, teaching, and using BAM on the mission field. The vision of sharing the gospel drives everything we do—including business. Definitions based on rigid Western models often limit the method's effectiveness in practice, because flexibility is key in both international business and missionary service.

For example, at the 2010 Lausanne Conference in Cape Town, South Africa, a sixty-page report about Business as Mission was issued, entitled "The Business as Mission Manifesto (revisited from 2004)." To us, the troubling part of the document stated,

> Unfortunately, there is sometimes a confusing misuse of the term BAM. Let's be clear: BAM is not "Business for Mission," a fundraising activity facilitated by the profits generated by business. Neither is BAM "Business as Platform" (i.e., an attempt to obtain visas to do "real ministry"). Rather, genuine BAM is the practice of business as a calling and ministry in its own right—a manifestation of the Kingdom of God."[29]

We must respectfully disagree with this description of BAM because of the limitations inherent in it. The definition has to be changed to be more inclusive.

What is the definition of Business as Mission as practiced in China by Back to Jerusalem workers and underground House Church networks like Little Joe's? Well, defining anything Chinese isn't easy, because definitions involve absolutes and a commitment to terms with defined parameters—concepts quite foreign to Chinese business.

However, from observing House Church networks like Little Joe's, it can be concluded that—at least for the Chinese—BAM is: (1) business leaders using their influence and position to share the gospel; (2) church missions directors using business to fund their ministries; (3) missionaries using business as a platform for ministry. In light of these three facets, the following may be the best "working definition" that can be given at this point: "BAM is any opportunity to use business to further the gospel of Jesus Christ."

Little Joe's network has been using business to support many of its ministers and ministries in China. For the most part, with groups like Little Joe's, BAM is a means to an end. Little Joe and his team of "undereducated missionary misfits" maintain a concept of BAM that is in the minority in mainstream Western thought, but they are taking advantage of the mainstream trends in countries in the 10/40 Window where mixing business, religion, and family is a common practice. The underground church in China is recognizing and responding to God's call to take the good news of Jesus Christ to the whole world, *especially* to those areas that don't want it, and business can often facilitate an opening to do so.

It should be noted that the organization Youth With A Mission (YWAM) has rightly admitted that BAM as it is taught and defined by the Western world doesn't do very well in the 10/40 Window:

> One of the biggest hurdles for BAM businesses around the world, especially in and around the so-called "10/40

Window," is securing investment capital. BAM is not built upon traditional models of charitable fundraising and donations, but upon a foundation of the disciplined allocation and return of capital.[30]

Basically, since the Western concept of BAM doesn't allow for businesses to be funded by ministries, or vice versa, BAM projects in the 10/40 Window have a very hard time getting off the ground. Along these lines, one of the difficulties for BAM projects there is a lack of investment from Christian businesses. This isn't surprising, because legitimate businesses that focus on financial returns alone have to evaluate the capital and risk involved. Yet most of the countries in the 10/40 Window are volatile and have no real stability for a thriving business, making long-term predictions impossible. In that region of the world, most business plans last less than a week after registration, because things are always changing.

The distinct threefold model in the Chinese view of BAM is essentially the following: (1) business *as* mission; (2) business *for* mission support; (3) business as "platform." Even these three terms need to be used flexibly, because they are often in harmony with each other in different stages of an outreach. For instance, in Egypt, a Chinese businessman saw an opportunity to start a grocery store. He was a Christian, but his investment was mainly financial, not necessarily spiritual. He began to have problems with the business and found himself in jail. Soon afterward, he met Brother Yun, who helped bring focus and purpose to his life by reintroducing him to the heavenly Father who ordains our steps. The businessman then decided to use his business as a platform to give visas (and jobs) to Chinese missionaries. The believers who left China to work for him did not care if they were going to work in a grocery store or to clean toilets at the local zoo—they were just looking for any opportunity to go to Egypt, because they felt a strong calling to share the gospel with Muslims there.

The Back to Jerusalem missionaries employed by the grocer work hard to earn their pay, and they are not dependent on other sources to sustain them; thus, the grocery store has become a business for mission. This kind of "business metamorphosis" occurs often with the Chinese. It isn't uncommon to see all facets of the threefold model in operation at the same time.

The Chinese understanding of BAM is not a definition cooked up by those who have done years of research, study, and analysis of mission trends. Rather, it is part of a new trend that is becoming more and more common as the number of Christians in China increases. Little Joe's network is part of this new trend, in which truly legitimate businesses are willing to donate to missionary projects that are, in turn, using business on the mission field. Such businesses aren't necessarily expecting a return on their investment; they are most interested in taking advantage of viable missions opportunities.

It is this concept of BAM that Little Joe brings to the Western world as he travels with Back to Jerusalem representatives. He often shares about the BAM structure in China and uses examples of businesses in Shanghai that are intricate parts of his ministry vision.

16

Other Networks and Personalities

There are several underground House Church networks that are often overlooked because they are not as large as the better known ones in Henan or Anhui provinces. However, these networks are playing an important role not only domestically but also internationally. Some of them deserve special recognition for their huge impact on the growth of the Chinese church.

"YL" NETWORK

In China today, there are many younger leaders who operate in a fashion similar to pastor "YL," who has rolled up his sleeves and is tackling the huge challenge of evangelizing in Shenzhen. YL is one of the leaders who was under the tutelage of Peter Xu. Although he still considers himself to be a disciple of Xu, he has an independent vision and focus for Shenzhen.

For many years, Back to Jerusalem International has supplied Bibles to this network throughout China. YL has planted churches among minority groups in places like Guizhou, Guangxi, Yunnan, and Sichuan. Although he planted those churches more than ten years ago, he still visits them on a regular basis to continue their cultivation. He sends many of his workers out of Shenzhen to witness and to plant churches in the minority villages. He also had the vision to start the very first House-Church-run Christian magazine in China.

When the earthquake hit Sichuan in 2008, YL's network was one of the first groups to respond. Ministry workers from the church traveled into the areas that had been hit the hardest and worked together with the locals to help them rebuild. They provided counseling and assistance. They printed many of the testimonies and stories from the earthquake's aftermath in their new magazine and then distributed copies throughout the country. The publication helped to build understanding between Christians and the unbelieving Chinese public at large. It also helped many of the earthquake victims in the midst of their grieving process as they read the amazing stories of some of the survivors and how they had found Christ in the darkest hour of their lives.

YL is currently living in Shenzhen, and his network is heavily focused on the many workers who have flooded southern China to work in offices there. He has several hundred thousand people in his network throughout China, but in Shenzhen specifically, he is seeing more than fifty people per month come to the Lord.

SOUTH CHINA **CHURCH**

Like YL, South China Church comes from Peter Xu's network. Some have estimated the number of South China Church members to be over fifty thousand, although it's impossible to know for sure. This network continues to grow, even though many of its leaders are in prison. Gong Shengliang was considered to be one of its top leaders and was sentenced to death, but his sentence was later commuted to life imprisonment.

At the same time, alleged and even confirmed wrongdoings by Gong Shengliang have limited the impact of this church. These would include allegations that he had inappropriate relationships with some female followers and had authorized imposing unorthodox methods on those who were not deemed loyal to his church.

Pastor Gong is often beaten in prison, and his face is scarred as a result. During family visits, other inmates have had to carry him from one place to another because he was too weak to walk. It has been reported that he was beaten so badly in 2003 that he nearly died.

Leaders like Xu Fuming and Sun Minghua are in prison, as well. Sun Minghua's mother was a believer and played a major role in bringing her daughter to salvation when she was nearly twenty years old. After she became a Christian, Sun Minghua almost immediately began to serve the Lord and share the gospel with others. She was arrested in September 2001 for "organizing a spiritual cult" and influencing direct disobedience to the laws of China. She was sentenced to life in prison, but the sentence was later reduced to twelve years. Other members of her network also suffered. During that same year, more than five hundred full-time evangelists from South China were detained and beaten, had their homes raided, and had property confiscated.

During this particular crackdown in September 2001, the government had pulled out all the stops in persecuting the South China Church. They had planned to secretly execute seventeen of its leaders without a real trial. At that time, members of the church contacted Back to Jerusalem, asking if we could help save the lives of their leaders. We started to send out prayer requests by e-mail, but, clearly, more was required. We began looking for a lawyer to help with the case.

We engaged a lawyer to help fight for the lives of these leaders, but it was to no avail. Chinese lawyers were not able to make any headway without the aid of international pressure. By God's grace, that pressure came from an unlikely source: United States President George W. Bush.

Unfortunately for those who wanted to swiftly and quietly snuff out the leadership of the South China Church, President Bush was scheduled to visit China the next month. We asked the family members of the imprisoned leaders to write letters about the situation, and then we asked one of our influential Southern Baptist friends for the American ambassador's personal phone number. We made the call, and the following conversation ensued:

"Hello?"

"Hello, I have some very important letters that I need to send to you via fax. We have friends who are in prison and will be executed in China for their Christian faith. We need to get a message to the president. Do you have a secure fax line?"

There was silence on the other end of the line. Everything had been laid out on the table from the start.

"I am sorry, who is this?"

"I am a friend of a friend."

It was beginning to sound like something from an old spy film, but, amazingly, the ambassador replied, "Okay, here is the fax number...."

Once we had the number, we faxed the family members' letters to the American embassy in Beijing. We later learned that the messages did get through to President Bush and that diplomatic channels were employed on behalf of the leadership. There were immediate results. We were able to hire a team of lawyers to fight for the lives of the seventeen members of the South China Church leadership, and—after much pressure and a new court case—none of them was executed. Unfortunately, we later found out that some of the Chinese government's accusations against Pastor Gong were indeed true, so he wasn't released.

Ten years later, on Christmas Day 2011, Li Ying—a Christian newspaper editor and the niece of Pastor Gong—was released from prison as one of those seventeen members whom God had rescued from execution. The South China Church leaders may never know how many brothers and sisters in Christ were praying for them and acting on their behalf during that crucial time.

BENJAMIN

Just a few miles north of YL's headquarters is a small group in Guangzhou that was started by a young man named Zhao Ming, or Benjamin (his English name), who never knew his father. This young man's wife was born and raised in Taiwan. Both of them are rather famous singers today. Benjamin is not a network leader, but he leads several groups in China and has greatly influenced the house churches with his music. He also started a small Bible study group in his home in Guangzhou in the late 1990s.

In the early 2000s, Guangzhou was a booming city experiencing exponential growth every year, and many young educated Chinese were coming to the Lord in the wealthier suburban areas. Suburban areas were a new concept in China at the time. A television sitcom called *Jia You Er Nu* [Home with Kids] was released beginning in 2004 and captured the attention of this new culture. It is about a Chinese suburban family that has one son and one daughter and lives in a moderately wealthy area.

Benjamin pushed the limits of what China was ready to accept as a society when, in 2003, he went on national television to participate in a singing competition much like *American Idol*. He and his wife sang a Christian song with their two children,[31] a boy and a girl, in front of several million people. The audience was blown away when they heard the family sing about loving one another.

Benjamin won the competition and moved to Beijing, where he began working on a recording contract. There he met with the well-known actor and movie producer Shaun Bao.

SHAUN **BAO**

Shaun Bao is not a traditional House Church leader, but he is having a huge impact on the church in China. He is an iconic leader who has made headlines around the world.

"They call me the last actor of China," he said in a 2006 interview at his home in Beijing. It was a tongue-in-cheek reference to the movie *The Last Emperor*. Shaun is very energetic, and his enthusiasm is contagious. He is continuously pushing the boundaries in China. He oversees several house churches throughout Beijing and has built a massive facility for training tomorrow's Chinese Christian leaders. In 2007, he legally published a biography of Jesus, which was overtly evangelistic in nature. Today, he teaches business concepts for Christians in China.

Shaun was born into the Chinese royal family—a three-hundred-year-old dynasty that quickly found itself being persecuted in Mao's new China after 1949. His family, like any educated or wealthy family in China during the rise of Communism, was considered to be a part of the "black class." This class was made up of professionals, such as doctors, professors, and business owners. All their wealth was stripped from them, and they were forced into reeducation camps and farm labor.

Shaun's mother and father had to go to different areas to serve in the field for the "betterment" of China's masses. However, in his youth, Shaun caught the eye of Mao's wife, who thought that he should be a film star. As a result, Shaun starred in the very first movie to be shown in China after the Communist revolution. Shaun later starred in twelve additional films over a period of just eight years.

As one of the few Chinese privileged enough to go abroad at the time, he left China at the age of twenty-five and moved to New Zealand. With no money or resources of any kind, he took jobs cleaning floors, doing laundry, and babysitting to support himself.

He had no future in New Zealand. He was living off minimum-wage jobs in a country that was not his home, and he lacked family and friends to support him financially and emotionally. However, returning to China would have been even more of an embarrassment and would have marked him as a complete failure. Shaun seemed to have hit rock bottom, with no hope in sight, but then he was attacked by a rabid German shepherd, making his situation even more desperate.

After the attack, he was approached by a believer who spoke Mandarin and introduced him to Christ. Shaun had never heard of Jesus Christ before. The only godlike personality he had ever heard about was Mao Zedong. After meeting with Christians, he was amazed at the love and care they had for him. He felt accepted and loved. He gave his life to Christ and immediately became focused on his homeland. Shame was no longer an overwhelming factor in his life. Instead, returning to China to share with others about the Jesus he had never heard about until he moved to New Zealand became a primary focus.

Shaun saw the need for Bibles in China and began to help get them into the country while leading several missions groups to Beijing. He eventually moved back to China and started preaching the gospel. He initiated a home group that began to grow beyond the house's capacity. He then sent representatives out to start other churches throughout the city.

Today, there are more than fifty churches throughout China that are directly connected with Shaun, and there are even more in his vast network of connections. These churches are in more wealthy areas, and the Christians have been active in sending and supporting missionaries abroad.

Shaun Bao and Benjamin are now making movies and music that reach out to China's new generation and appeal to a wide audience among the urbanites. They are creating high-quality entertainment with a strong gospel message, and the response has been amazing. These creative endeavors are surely helping to change China one person at a time.

Shaun Bao and Benjamin are among the more youthful urban leaders in China who are leading the charge to see China officially embrace Christianity. Unlike most House Church believers, they see themselves as Christian ambassadors, and they try to make everything open and legitimate. They are fighting the good fight and are slowly gaining ground.

XIAO **MIN**

Benjamin and his Bible group in Guangzhou worked together to make one of the first Christian music videos ever produced in China for the underground House Church. Benjamin took the music of Xiao Min—one of the most famous underground Christian songwriters in all of China—and performed her songs in different settings to distribute to the underground churches. The VCD (Video Compact Disc) was called *Canaan Songs*.

We worked with him in those early years to print and distribute tens of thousands of those music VCDs throughout China. In the Western world, a believer can go to a Christian bookstore or shop online for Christian materials, but things are much more complicated in China. This was really the first time such a project had ever been done.

Though Xiao Min is not a network leader, her songs have strengthened millions of believers in China's House Church. The Canaan Hymns are the most popular songs among underground house churches in China today.

Those who want to get a taste of the suffering and pain that the Chinese church has gone through need only to listen to the messages in these songs. They were written by a young girl who was born to poor peasant farmers in Fangcheng. It is only by God's grace that Xiao Min has been so influential. She is not outgoing or educated; rather, she is very shy and doesn't seem to know the first thing about music. She doesn't play an instrument or have a flashy stage presence; nor does she sit around with other great recording artists and discuss the ins and outs of the music business. Here is someone so meek that her singing voice cannot be heard by others unless the entire room is silent. She is just a simple farm girl whom God used to write more than one thousand hymns that have been sung by persecuted believers all over China.

When Xiao Min was born, she was unwanted by her parents. They desired to give her away, but a big flood hit their village and prevented them from following through with their plan. Xiao Min dropped out of school when she was young and started to work in the cotton fields to help support her family. It was there that she heard the gospel for the first time. While working in the field with a friend, she was invited to her first church meeting, and, at that meeting, she gave her heart to Christ. Xiao Min became a Christian completely against the wishes of her family. She attended the church meetings without telling her parents.

In 1990, she felt the power of the Holy Spirit during one of those secret underground meetings, and it was after that meeting that she wrote her first hymn. She later sang the hymn to a little girl in her village, and the girl went around singing the song. When others asked the little girl where she had heard the song, she replied that she had learned it from Xiao Min.

Xiao Min's songs began to spread like wildfire. Unlike the hymns that had been taught by foreign missionaries many years earlier, they were unique to Chinese life. Xiao Min wrote hymns that expressed exactly what the Chinese church was going through, and they ministered to the leaders who were being persecuted at that time.

Xiao Min is a prime example of the unique qualities of the Chinese House Church. She has neither education nor wealth. Despite all her worldly shortcomings—or rather because of them—God has used her to move His people in China.

After seeing how her songs were reaching people in China and helping them through hard times, Xiao Min began to pray to go to prison. She actually prayed that God would send her to jail for the sake of the gospel so that she could better identify with those who were suffering for Christ's name. Her prayers were answered. On December 7, 1992, two years after she became a Christian, the police burst through the doors at the prayer meeting she was attending and apprehended everyone. The shy, quiet farm girl became the object of intense interrogation. She was slapped around and beaten, but she insists that she was not treated as badly as the others were. A Christian magazine in the West reported,

> After being arrested, she wasn't scared at all.
>
> Furthermore, she said that on one summer day when it was extremely hot she requested the guard to let everyone wash their head, but she received a rude response telling her to ask the Lord Jesus to wash for them.

Despite the rude response, the Canaan Hymn author was not discouraged, but she used this as an inspiration to write the number 56 hymn "Lord, We Know Deeply" in the Canaan Hymns series.

In this hymn, Xiao Min wrote, "Lord, we know deeply that in every moment your love never, never diminishes, Lord we know deeply that in every moment, our only friend is you, our hearts long for you, our hearts long for you, because you're the first in millions, no one can be compared with you, no one can be compared with you."[32]

During Xiao Min's time in prison, her parents began to blame her for their problems. A message was sent to her from her father, stating that he was losing weight worrying about her and that the family really needed her help on the farm to survive. She was told by her family to give up her silly beliefs, deny Christ, and get out of jail. Xiao Min lovingly declined. She clung to the name of Jesus and refused to let go of her faith in the Lord.

Her family abandoned her, and her country was punishing her. Her release would have been as easy as saying, "I don't believe in Jesus anymore." All her problems would seemingly have gone away if she had just denied Christ. But, instead of fleeing from her problems, she provided comfort to her fellow inmates and began to sing in the midst of it all. When the other prisoners heard her, they, too, began to rejoice.

Today, Xiao Min continues to write songs that speak directly to the underground House Church, and she is greatly influencing the direction of tomorrow's Chinese church. She has a desire to go and preach the gospel in Africa, as well as the Middle East.

Benjamin, Shaun Bao, and Xiao Min are able to work with any of the House Church networks—or independently. They have the unique position in China of being able to go between networks to build bridges, as well as to pave the way for more religious freedom in China for tomorrow. This dynamic trio is making an especially huge impact in the capital city of Beijing. There are churches today in Beijing that started out as simple, independent home groups and have grown into more formal church gatherings. They are not registered, but they are not hiding their identities, either. They are also not intentionally provoking problems. They purposely don't do things they know will highlight their illegal activities, and the police purposely ignore them. It is a mutual understanding of convenience.

The police do not want a bad name with the people, and the people do not want problems with the police. The people do, however, want to be free to worship Christ, and they would like to introduce others to Him, as well. Groups like these continue to push the boundaries.

There are many bookstores in Beijing that are actually illegal Christian bookstores. But since they are legally registered and are selling Christian books that have been legally printed in China, they are left alone, for the most part. They are recognized as bookstores and allowed to continue their operations with very few, if any, problems.

When the first few Christian bookstores opened, about the years 2003 to 2005, there were raids and arrests by the police. Yet, after the dust settled, other such bookstores began to come in and find a way to work around the system. After some time, the effort to shut down the bookstores became tiring to the police; in addition, the police had more important problems to deal with, so they left the bookstores alone.

A SHANDONG **NETWORK**

Things are much different in Shandong Province, where remnants of the early twentieth-century movements are still strong. We cannot mention the cities where Shandong Network works, because to do so would indict its leadership. There are Christian gatherings in these cities that are open secrets; to mention places or names would jeopardize the operations there. This network in Shandong is pushing forward a strong movement that is also going against the local authorities.

Unlike Beijing, the area of the network's activity is not a large, progressive metropolis. In fact, it more closely resembles Fangcheng in Henan Province or Blessing in Anhui Province. Its head, Mr. C., is an older leader who remembers the revivals in China from years ago and can still sing the songs of those early church meetings.

Mr. C. is well-known among the brothers in Henan Province. When Brother Yun and his wife were on the run from the police and were forced into hiding, Mr. C. and his wife took care of Yun's two children, Isaac and Yiling.

Mr. C.'s activities and network have never formally been written about. He has built up an extensive network, although its numbers are not quite clear. From the rural farm areas of Shandong to the tourist cities, such as Qingdao, a massive movement has been created, with connections to people in many different walks of life.

Mr. C. is a businessman, as well as a House Church pastor. He doesn't look for support from his church because his business takes care of the expenses for all the needs of the ministry. Mr. C. uses the profits from his business to further the work of the kingdom.

Shandong Church reaches out to the rural schools by taking Christmas gifts to the children who live in the small villages. When the gifts are delivered, the House Church representatives openly preach the message of Jesus Christ—in Communist public schools. They are able to do this because they know believers who are teachers and principals at several different schools. This network continues to grow among the business and farming communities. It has just started a training school that holds classes at the meeting place it recently finished building.

This church is also training missionaries to be sent abroad. The daughter of Mr. C. has been studying Korean and is preparing to preach the gospel to people on the Korean Peninsula.

NANYANG **NETWORK**

In addition to the Born Again Movement, Tanghe Network, and Fangcheng Network, there is another independent movement in Nanyang that is one of the oldest networks still surviving in China. Hardly anything is known about it, because its members have very little contact with foreigners. It is one of the most buried underground groups in the nation. According to Paul Hattaway, the Nanyang Church was founded by Elder Fu after he moved to Nanyang in the 1960s.[33] Brother Yun is one of the more well-known leaders to emerge from this group, but he was very connected with other leaders in China during his time as an active leader there.

It isn't easy for a Westerner to meet with people from this group in Nanyang, because the leaders are still very entrenched in the rural areas; consequently, they would show up to meetings wearing work clothes and muddy shoes, making them conspicuous in a hotel. Another reason is that this group's leadership seems to be less centralized.

Although Back to Jerusalem has financially supported this group's evangelists and has provided them with cameras to film their current activities, their past history is not as well documented as those of the other networks. From what we been able to gather from field reports, the leadership is elderly and still strongly focused on rural evangelism. Although it is difficult to know for sure, today, their evangelists appear to be working on farms and maintaining moderate church growth.

It is also hard to get an idea of this church's number, scope, and influence. Brother Yun is one of their main representatives, and he still maintains a very close connection with the elders. However, now that he lives outside of China, it is difficult for him to acquire hard data from them. They are still affectionate toward him and care about him deeply. Their bond with Yun must not have been easy to maintain after his long absence from China.

Nanyang seems to be lost in time. All over China—even in remote places like Tibet—the country is changing. Yet somehow Nanyang has been passed by and is still one of the most tightly controlled hotspots in China. This atmosphere no doubt contributes to the current security situation of the Nanyang Church.

What is certain is that this church continues to aggressively share the gospel, with almost no foreign support or connections. Its members also have a deeply passionate affinity for the Back to Jerusalem vision.

ENOCH **WANG**

Enoch Wang has been a controversial figure in China, and he remains so to this day. The information that Back to Jerusalem has about Wang is mainly thanks to our relationship with his eldest daughter and her family. Susanne and her husband were missionaries in Egypt for more than five years, and their son was born in Cairo. We helped them to get visas and a funding base in Egypt. The couple is currently living and studying at a Bible school in California.

Though Enoch Wang is a controversial figure, the amount of suffering he has endured for the gospel is more than most people can imagine. One night, while sitting by the Nile River on a warm evening in Cairo, Susanne shared about the hard times her family went through in China for the sake of Christ. She began to cry as she recounted what she experienced in her early years.

Her father was a follower of the teachings of Watchman Nee, a famous author and Christian leader in China who died in prison at the hands of the Communists. Enoch Wang was viewed by the authorities as a traitor. He had been a leader in public service to the People's Liberation Army and the Communist Party, but when it came out that he was a Christian leader, he was sent to prison for thirteen years.

"My mother and I felt abandoned," Susanne said. "I was rejected from every school. We were yelled at and forced out on the street. We had nothing to eat or any way to get food. My mother and I were forced to beg. They were hard times for all of us."

After Wang was released from prison in 1994, he tried to make things better for his family, but the immediate demands of the ministry drowned out his family's needs. He was arrested again in 1997 and spent another three years in prison, but not before tragedy struck their family.

In 1997, when Susanne was eighteen, she was at home caring for her little sister. She was holding her sister when she got too close to the balcony of their fourth-floor apartment and lost her grip on the squirming child. The little girl fell and landed on a pile of bricks and stone rubble below. Her skull was cracked open, and her brain was exposed. Blood was everywhere.

Susanne's guilt was indescribable. She had killed her sister! Because the family was on the run from the police, they couldn't even think about taking the child to the hospital. All hope was lost. The dead girl was carried back into the apartment.

However, after a day of prayer while Enoch was away at a unity meeting with Sinim Fellowship members, Susanne and her mother saw the girl begin to show signs of life. Air filled her lungs, and her heart began to beat again, putting color back into her face. On the third day, the girl began to walk again, and eventually she was totally healed. Today, she shows no signs of having any brain damage. In response to her family's desperate prayers and hopeless situation, God had raised her back to life and completely healed her.

Enoch Wang struggled with family problems, and, today, he is estranged from Susanne and her mother, but he has kept on serving the Lord in China and focusing on the Back to Jerusalem vision.

Like all the leaders of the church in China, Enoch Wang is not perfect, but he is in love with Jesus Christ and has the track record to prove it. Much of his adult life has been spent in prison for preaching, but he continues to lead people to Christ. He also helps Chinese missionaries go to other countries. He now has a passport and is able to travel around the world giving counsel to help Chinese missionaries become established in the nations between China and Jerusalem.

17
Wenzhou

This chapter focuses on the Chinese church in a particular city, Wenzhou, which is a powerhouse port south of Shanghai. Because of its good harbors and favorable location, it is a natural center for trade. In the year 192 B.C., Wenzhou was the capital of the Kingdom of the Eastern Ou. During those days, it was called the City of the White Deer. As folklore has it, when the city was being built, a white deer passed by with a flower in its mouth.

Shortly after China's embarrassing defeat in the Second Opium War, several foreign-occupied cities were established on the mainland. Wenzhou was one of those foreign treaty ports, but, unlike places such as Shanghai, it was never really occupied by foreigners. The Chinese themselves ended up developing this port for trade.

In the past, Wenzhou was well-known for producing paper, silk, shoes, belts, and tea, as well as for shipbuilding, but today it is the largest producer of cigarette lighters, eyeglasses, and leather products.

A SPECIAL **SITUATION IN CHINA**

Wenzhou is also well-known for the huge number of Christians who live there. The city was one of the first places in China where the Communist government openly admitted defeat in its confrontation with Christianity. The number of Christians in Wenzhou was just too high, and, after thirty years of persecution, the authorities came to the conclusion that the persistent faith couldn't be stamped out. According to the *New York Times*, at one point, the Chinese government reported that 10 percent of all Christians in China were in Wenzhou alone.[34]

Unregistered churches in Wenzhou built meeting places throughout the city with large red crosses prominently displayed on the steeples. The government attempted to destroy all these buildings in the 1990s and bulldozed many to the ground, but they have been rebuilt and are packed with believers today.

The Chinese government's main excuse for giving up in the area is that there were already large numbers of Christians in Wenzhou prior to the rise of Communism. Similar to the minority areas in Yunnan and Guangxi provinces, where cultural traditions and religions are allowed to continue, Wenzhou Christianity has been accepted as part of the culture. There are more than 1,200 registered churches in Wenzhou that enjoy a special situation in China. Despite a government crackdown in the spring of 2014, most of these churches are allowed to operate in quasi-registered mode yet maintain a high level of autonomy.

PASTOR **PHILLIP**

Pastor Phillip leads a registered church with about five thousand people in the heart of the city. His church is a perfect case study for understanding the situation in Wenzhou. As a registered pastor, he is supposed to be controllable. He is not allowed to travel to lead churches in other areas or to run Sunday schools for children. However, Pastor Phillip is not being held back by the government in either of those areas.

His situation demonstrates the degree of autonomy given to the church in Wenzhou. It is not something that is discussed in the government-sponsored *China Daily* or paraded at annual meetings in Beijing, but this freedom is allowing churches in Wenzhou to have a huge impact on China and the world.

Even though some of the churches in Wenzhou are legal, many of them send out missionaries and evangelists—activities

216 The Underground Church

that are highly illegal. In 2002, Pastor Phillip was in need of assistance in regard to one of the poorer provinces in China, and he contacted Back to Jerusalem International for help. He had sent out a missionary who was working in rural areas and required help establishing some orphanages. We met with Pastor Phillip and his wife in a distant part of western China. Most of the underground House Church leaders in China do not have good relationships with their spouses, because, as we have noted, they are often absent from home for months or even years at a time. It was nice to see that Pastor Phillip had a great relationship with his wife and that their ministry together was powerful as a result of their unity. They are also an amazing example to others.

After meeting at the train station, we traveled together to see the local politicians to discuss the possibility of building orphanages. Having worked in China on similar projects for many years, we had assumed it was clear to everyone that ministry would have to remain clandestine.

We met with the local government officials, and they drove us to a rural mountain area with very bad road conditions. Our first stop was a small roadside building in a rural town.

"We are here at the first church," the driver announced. We thought that maybe there was a misunderstanding, but Pastor Phillip confirmed that we were indeed at the first church that a missionary from his church had planted in the area. The van left us there, and everything seemed suspicious—to the point that we were considering exit strategies for when the police returned. It was then that Pastor Phillip told the whole story.

You see, one day at our church, we had a young man who had come to Wenzhou to make money. After some time, he felt empty inside and felt a strong desire to come to our church and give his life to the Lord. After learning about the love and mercy of Jesus Christ, he knew that he couldn't remain in Wenzhou and make money while his family back home was on their way to hell. He came to me and told me that he felt a calling to return home and preach the gospel to his family and the other surrounding villages. I told him that our church would support his efforts if he would go and share the gospel in this unreached area.

A few months later, he was arrested by the police for evangelizing, but then something strange happened. Instead of being sent to court to face a prison sentence, he was asked about his Christian beliefs. You see, the local police live in this poor area, as well. They are not some foreign group sent here by the regime in Beijing. They are minorities with families at home who have to endure the same poverty as everyone else. They are looking for truth, just like everyone else. The police had never met a Christian before, but they had heard that Christians help people who are poor, so they approached the evangelist that our Wenzhou church sent here and asked him if he knew anyone who would be willing to help orphans. The evangelist called me from prison, and I called you, so we are now both here. This is one of the first churches that our Wenzhou church helped start.

Since this was such an unbelievable situation, our workers were very skeptical until an hour later, when the government vehicle picked us up as promised and proceeded to take us to one church after another. None of these churches was registered, and the believers were not meeting in registered facilities. These were clearly unregistered churches engaging in illegal activity, but no one seemed to care.

Over dinner that night, the local governor was clear about his need for help with the orphans. And Pastor Phillip was clear about his need to share the gospel—no matter what he did and no matter what subject we were talking about. If the governor talked about how nice the day was, the pastor would agree and say, "This is the day that the Lord has made. I will rejoice and be glad in it." If the officials complimented the pastor and his wife on how young they looked, he would reply by saying, "The joy of the Lord is my strength."

This banter-like dialogue reached a climax when the foreign Back to Jerusalem representative exclaimed, "Mmmm, this Coke is good," and the pastor replied, "You know what else is good? God! God is good." Then, with a full audience of every local government official in town—including the chief of police—he began to speak.

Do you know what I find amazing? As you look around at China, what do you see? I see poverty. I see lack of originality. I see poor people begging for scraps from Western countries. To build an orphanage, we have to depend on the kindness of strangers from Western countries.

What do you think makes these countries wealthy? What do you think makes these countries blessed? You know, I grew up in a Communist society just like every one of you here did. I listened and believed everything that my teacher told me about God being a crutch for the weak and the opiate of the masses. I believed them when they told me that there is no God and believing in a fantasy will only make my situation worse.

Look at Europe. Their history is rooted deeply in the belief that Jesus Christ is Lord. Does that make them weak? Does that make them poor? How are they doing compared to us?

Look at America. They are a Christian nation. Does that make them weak? Does that make them intellectually inferior to us enlightened ones who think that God does not exist? Why are their academic institutions, which started off as missionary sending schools, now some of the best in the world? Why are the schools and hospitals that missionaries started here still the very best in China?

Everything is better in America. Their educational facilities, their medical facilities, their working conditions, their programs for the poor, and even their leisure activities are some of the most sought-after in the world.

Are Americans smarter than the Chinese? Many Americans come from Chinese descent, so that cannot be the reason. The reason is that they believe in Jesus Christ.

Look at Korea. North Korea and South Korea are on the same peninsula. They have the same history with the same language and the very same culture. One end of the peninsula has freedom for Christians and has the world's largest church, and the other enforces atheism. Which Korea is poor? Which Korea has dilapidated medical and educational facilities?

If we want to see China blessed, if we want to see our nation succeed, then we must accept Jesus Christ as our Lord and Savior. He is the Way and the Truth. There is nothing in this world truer than He and the blessings He provides.

Every person in the restaurant stopped what her or she was doing for a brief moment while Pastor Phillip was talking. It was amazing. They were all nodding their heads in agreement with what he was saying.

We ended up not going through with the orphanage project but instead supported a water sanitation project that brought clean water to a mountain village where the evangelist was working. After we completed that project, our representative traveled back to that area with Pastor Phillip and his evangelist. Almost the entire village had become Christian during the few months that it took to build the water sanitation plant and get running water into every home for the first time. The village leader hosted all the church services in his home. The people had abandoned their animistic beliefs and had begun following Christ.

Soon afterward, the local governor got saved, as well, but he was summarily fired when government higher-ups heard about his conversion. He was replaced by someone else whom they thought would not be as susceptible to the teachings of the team from Wenzhou.

Since that first visit to the area with Pastor Phillip, the church in Wenzhou has sent several missionaries to the same minority area to conduct Christmas programs. They go from village to village performing Christmas plays. In some places, they have even started churches where they perform the plays and lead people to Christ.

A WORLD-CHANGING **SUNDAY SCHOOL PROGRAM**

The church in Wenzhou has also played a pivotal role in changing the way children are taught in Sunday schools. In the year 2000, an aforementioned meeting was held in Burma in which most of the main leaders of the underground House Church came together and talked about the needs of their churches. One of the main needs was a good Sunday school teacher training program.

The leaders were very much aware of the need to reach out to the children in China. They collectively went to Brother Ren during the meeting and commissioned him to help meet this need. The job was passed to Sister Huang and this author. Sister Huang was in charge of the whole project.

Sister Huang is a remarkable missionary from Europe who has devoted herself to the people of China. She has been living and working in China for most of her life. Her full Chinese name can be directly translated "The one who loves Chinese people." She has never been married and doesn't have any children, but, in China, she has more children than she could ever have physically given birth to. No book has ever been written about her, and she isn't known by those outside her ministry, yet she has changed more lives than can be counted. A coworker testified of her,

I began working with Sister Huang when I was helping the poor minority people in Yunnan Province and Tibet. We worked together to build schools and implement teaching programs, and Sister Huang showed me how to serve the Chinese in the best way possible. She would walk up to one of the rural village schools, and children with dirty faces would see us coming and become timid. She was not Chinese, so the children did not know how to react. She would just begin to show love and joy, and in less than five minutes, the children would fall in love with her. Her joy is contagious, and no one is ever able to resist it.

When Sister Huang was asked to take on the job of creating a training program for Sunday school teachers in China, it was not a small task, and she knew it. None of the Chinese House Church leaders had ever attended Sunday school. The Chinese knew only of life on the run. They knew only what it was like to survive as a church, and they'd had only underground, illegal, clandestine church meetings for the past fifty years. Entire generations had come and gone without ever having been exposed to children's ministry. The only thing the Chinese knew is that they didn't want their children's program to look like it did in the Western world, which they considered to be a babysitting program while the parents were in the main service. The Chinese wanted a children's program that represented the real needs in China and on the mission field.

Sister Huang knew that she was not qualified, that she lacked experience, and that her language skills would be challenged. By God's wisdom, all these characteristics ended up being perfect for someone running the program, because "experts" on China never really make it far. They usually seem to know too much to allow them to be used by God, and they end up creating barriers that break the spirit of the people before they even start.

Sister Huang collected Sunday school training curriculum from around the world and presented it to the Chinese for review. Most missions organizations would have used their own judgment, selected materials, and forced it on the church. Instead, Huang painstakingly searched out training materials from across the globe and let the Chinese leadership decide. After several months, they finally found one they liked.

The main husband-and-wife team in charge of teaching the materials was from New Zealand. The church in Wenzhou became the fertile ground for creation. Pastor Phillip and his church took the project on as their main focus, investing everything needed for it.

Sunday school teachers from different networks were carefully selected to travel to Wenzhou to train with the Kiwi instructors. The Sunday school teachers had one main focus: learn the material inside and out and then do what China is notorious for—copy it.

They would learn the material and master it in every way from a Western perspective, then modify and adapt it to make it fit a Chinese cultural setting. When they were finished, it would look nothing like what it was in its original Western format.

The training was intense. It went on for several weeks at a time, over a period of more than a year. The New Zealand teachers poured their hearts and souls into the training and gave their students everything they had. The Sunday school teachers/trainees never wavered but studiously took notes and eagerly drank in every word being taught.

There were many business owners in the Wenzhou Church who were able to provide perfect cover for the training sessions within their own facilities. At one point, we were in a factory that made Oakley sunglasses—whether they were genuine or cheap Chinese knockoffs is uncertain. The factory owner allowed us to use the facility as our training area, and an entire floor was cleared out for us. We would sneak in early in the morning before the sun came up and quickly be ushered through the factory and up the stairs.

We trained and ate in that space. While we met, workers above and below us busily made different types of sunglasses.

One day, we heard a noise downstairs and thought the police had come to arrest us. Pastor Phillip was called into the local police station for questioning. It ended up being all right. The guards had been walking through and inspecting the work area when they had seen someone breaking the security rules. Pastor Phillip knew the police well, and they knew him. He never dealt with them as if they were enemies but showed joy and love every time they were together.

Once the Chinese Sunday school teachers had gleaned from their New Zealand instructors all they had to offer, they began to teach the material back to the trainers, to ensure that they had learned it all correctly. Every session was filmed and immediately burned to a VCD that was, in turn, copied and handed out to the Chinese teachers so they could take it back home and review each course over and over in their own language.

It was decided that the Chinese would use what they had learned to create an entire Sunday school training curriculum of their own to be distributed throughout China. Along with the training curriculum would be sixteen hours of training module videos. All of the training, development, and filming was done in Wenzhou. The goal was to instruct Sunday school teachers who could go out and train other teachers. Each teacher allowed into the program would commit to train at least ten other teachers.

Sister Huang led the entire operation, despite its being one of the most dangerous projects ever attempted in China. To this day, sharing the gospel with anyone under the age of eighteen is illegal in that country. The Chinese are very protective of the minds of children. They begin the Communist indoctrination process in their citizens as early as age three and continue the atheistic brainwashing for the rest of their lives. Any attempt to challenge this indoctrination by proselytizing a child is considered a grave offense and is dealt with swiftly and firmly.

The young leaders in Pastor Phillip's Wenzhou church didn't flinch at the opportunity. They stood up and committed to a training program that would eventually become one of the most widely used Sunday school training programs ever.

Pastor Phillip bravely recorded the introduction to the curriculum. We filmed him sitting at a small desk in a Wenzhou hotel room. He called it the "Dove Training Series." They developed a small black briefcase for each trainer to carry that contained the books for the students, the training manuals for the teachers, and the sixteen training module VCDs. Many foreigners had different ideas for the name of the program, but the church decided that "Dove" was the appropriate title. They created a small dove logo to go on the outside of the briefcase.

Pastor Phillip's church was one of the first churches to begin using Dove, and the children's church saw amazing growth. Children even began to invite other children to attend who would then go home and share the gospel with their parents.

This situation did not escape the notice of the local police department in Wenzhou. The police threatened Pastor Phillip's church and forbade it to teach children about Jesus. Such teaching would not be allowed under any circumstances. Surprisingly, Pastor Phillip seemed willing to obey this rule—under one condition. "Every Sunday, we have several thousand people come and worship at our church. Isn't that legal?" he asked the authorities. Knowing that his church was a legally registered church in China, the police agreed.

"Every Sunday several thousand people come to our church, so what do you want us to do with their children? According to you, they cannot sit in the service with their parents, so we have to create another activity for them. If you will not even allow us to do this, then I propose that, every Sunday, before those several thousand people come to our church service, we will ask them to first drop off their children with *you* here at the police station."

The police chief did not like the idea of several thousand children being dropped off by their parents on the way to the local church, so he reluctantly agreed that the church could have a program for the children.

As of 2012, almost 250,000 Sunday school teachers/trainers had been instructed in China using the Dove program. It was the first curriculum ever developed by and for the underground House Church.

As the number of those participating in the Sunday school training program became astronomical, Sister Huang decided that this was her last big project in China and that it was time for her to retire and return home. She walked into the boardroom during a Back to Jerusalem meeting in Austria and announced her plans. "It has been a great time in China, and now this project is coming to a close for me," she said softly, with a smile on her face that signified she was a bit nervous. "I think that it is time for me to retire now."

The board members were quiet for a moment as they pondered her announcement. The chairman of the board broke the silence by simply saying, "No."

Everyone looked up at the chairman. He continued, "No, we don't accept your retirement. The Lord is not done with you yet, and neither are we. The Lord still has plans for your life, and we are excited to see what is next. What God has done through you has been utterly and truly amazing, but even greater things than this are yet to come."

Dove has left the hands of the church in Wenzhou and has begun to bless other churches around the world. There are multitudes of training programs for Sunday school teachers out there, so perhaps you are wondering what makes Dove so special or different from the other programs on the market. Is it just because it is Chinese?

If you were to listen for only a few minutes to Sister Huang introduce the program, the difference would quickly become apparent. The Dove training series does not merely teach children little Bible stories with cute coloring books. It is not another Sunday school program that teaches the best way to entertain children in a manner that will keep them occupied until they are back

226 The Underground Church

in the custody of their parents. The Dove program emphasizes the responsibility of children to become evangelists and preachers. It is structured in a way that puts the burden of missions and the Back to Jerusalem vision on the hearts of children. It is designed to teach the children how to have a direct relationship with Jesus Christ and to learn to trust in Him.

In the video clip that Sister Huang often shows to introduce the Dove program, you can see children weeping before the Lord and having a genuine burden to be forgiven for their sins and to be used by God. Believers in many countries around the world have seen how this training program has had such an impact on children in China and have pleaded to get it in their own languages.

The Dove training program has been translated into several languages, and a team from China has been sent to train Sunday school teachers in Hong Kong, Macau, the Philippines, Vietnam, Ethiopia, Egypt, India, and Pakistan. The Dove training program has even been used to wake up the churches in Scandinavia. Churches in Finland, Norway, and Sweden have adopted the methods used by the Chinese. The influence of Wenzhou Church on churches throughout China and around the world can best be understood by the impact of the Dove training series.

18
Missionary Training

It was well past sunset when the cargo ship's gangplank dropped on a remote island in the Philippines. Waves gently crashed against the old ship's hull as a former U.S. Marine stepped onto the dock. He waded his way through the sea of industrial vehicles that were exiting the boat and hopped in the back of a small container truck. He was on his way to a Chinese House Church missionary training center where he was going to put the students through the wringer. These missionary students, who had been training for months in the Philippines, were in for a long night, and they had no idea what was coming.

UNUSUAL **TRAINING METHODS**

Another reality to be uncovered about the Chinese House Church is the various methods of training it employs. Several years ago, many Western churchgoers were alarmed to hear from people like Brother Yun that Chinese missionaries were being taught how to release themselves from handcuffs and how to jump out windows to escape from the police. Such statements made it sound as if Chinese missionaries were more like secret agents and fugitives than emissaries of the gospel.

This misunderstanding underscores the striking difference between Western and Chinese House Church missionary training. In fact, training methods became a problem for us while we were setting up the Back to Jerusalem Foundation in the United Kingdom. Our first application was rejected after government officials read the introductory material about our organization. It seemed that the UK government was not interested in registering a charity organization that taught missionaries how to break out of handcuffs, jump from moving vehicles, and escape from prison. Those registration papers were later modified to the liking of the UK government so that we could register.

WHAT CHINESE **BIBLE SCHOOLS ARE LIKE**

There is very little about Chinese House Church training that resembles anything in the West. For example, instruction at Chinese Bible schools does not take place on campuses with beautifully manicured lawns, quaint chapels, and administration buildings. Graduations are not celebrated with smiling parents taking pictures and waving obnoxious banners. Deans in colored gowns are not present to give long, drawn-out speeches, occasionally interjecting them with well-rehearsed jokes.

The first Chinese Bible schools were held in churches located in the countryside, but that changed as China opened up and it became possible for people to travel to major cities. The cities became choice locations for Bible schools, because such gatherings are not as likely to be noticed in a noisy city. Bible schools often take place in small, simple apartments, located in dingy high-rise buildings towering over overpopulated townships covered in coal dust. An apartment as small as six hundred square feet (almost fifty-six square meters) may be used for a Bible school with as many as thirty students. To keep the neighbors from growing suspicious, the students will move in and stay in the apartment for months at a time without leaving. Usually, one person will be assigned the job of going out to purchase food and supplies. Occasionally, a teacher might be seen coming and going, but the students will remain as stationary as possible.

Every window will be covered, and no one will open the door to a visitor before looking out the peephole to make sure the visitor is not the local police or a curious neighbor. Although most House

Church believers are charismatic, they will muffle their prayers and sing at almost whisper volume to keep their voices from being heard outside.

Quite recently, however, the need for vocational training for missionaries has caused many Bible schools and missionary training centers to start moving back to the rural areas. These areas allow for lower overhead expenses, as well as the space needed for the vocational training, especially training that involves agriculture. Other benefits of rural training are that security can be monitored with less difficulty, and activities are not as easily noticed. The downside is that routes to and from the rural training areas can be very easily monitored by the authorities.

The Back to Jerusalem school in the Philippines was selected as a place to give Chinese missionaries exposure to serving in a foreign land. It gives them a chance to work in a country that has a different culture, language, and history. The Philippines is an ideal location for training missionaries because it is a Catholic country that is open for preaching the gospel. In addition, Chinese missionaries have the opportunity to work with militant Muslims, Buddhists, atheists, and animists there. It is unique to find a country where there is freedom to share the good news with people of such a variety of religions.

The other benefit of training in the Philippines is that most educated people there speak English, which is the primary foreign language the missionaries are taught at training centers in China. Although the missionaries may be trained in other languages, as well, English is quite often their first foreign language. The Philippines is one of the few places within easy traveling distance from China where Chinese are able to work with the locals, using English as the common language.

Like most other Back to Jerusalem training centers, the facility in the Philippines is atypical compared with other training programs. The concept is based on the first-century church. Students are given a strong practical missions focus that includes a brief introduction to the local minority mountain tribes, some practical guidelines, and hands-on evangelism experience in those areas. The Chinese live in the villages, preach the gospel, and work with the locals for a week or more before returning to the classroom. Upon their return, they discuss what they did, saw, and experienced. The students discuss which strategies worked and which did not. Then, a week later, they are sent back to the "bush" to minister to the same villagers.

There is an undeniable tendency in our age for those who have more theological training to be less evangelistic. It seems as if the more theological degrees a person has, the more likely that individual is to spend his or her time debating doctrinal nuances with other believers instead of reaching lost sinners. With training that focuses on hands-on evangelism rather than merely sitting in a classroom listening to a lecture, Back to Jerusalem missionaries are able to maintain their emphasis on the people they are ministering to rather than become distracted by theological debates.

SURPRISE **INTERROGATION**

The following account, from the former Marine we left riding in the back of a container truck at the beginning of this chapter, describes another aspect of Chinese missionary training that may be controversial in the West.

As we drove down the narrow island road, the evening breeze was coming through the windows. The mountains were silhouetted in the moonlight. We pulled up to the first guard checkpoint. The guards knew the friends I was traveling with well. They knew we were on our way to meet a couple of their colleagues who had worked with the police department in the past.

Their colleagues were going to help me with the interrogation. The students knew me, but they had never met these former policemen. After meeting with the former policemen and going over the interrogation schedule with them, it was time to start waking up the students to be interrogated.

None of their leaders in China was even told about this training, for fear that it would compromise the element of surprise. None of the curriculum even alluded to the fact that tonight they would be put through a surprise interrogation. They wouldn't even know that it was only training! Having a background in special operations from the U.S. military and making the training curriculum with a friend who had U.S. Army Special Forces experience allowed for a unique program.

Around midnight, we sent for the first person to be interrogated. One of the English teachers went into the dorm room and woke up a brother. "Wake up. The police are here, and for some reason they want to speak with you," he said as the student was waking up.

The first student to be interrogated was taken to a separate location where the police were waiting. They were very friendly and welcomed the student into the interrogation room. We had secret cameras set up that allowed us to film the entire event.

"Sorry to wake you up and disturb you," the first officer said as they shook hands and he directed the student over to a chair.

"We just have a few really quick questions, and then you can go back to bed."

The Chinese student was visibly nervous.

"Can you tell me about the nature of your training here?"

"I am here for language training. I am studying English."

One of the officers spoke in a low, calm, friendly voice, and the other officer strategically remained quiet for the perfect "good cop, bad cop" tactic.

I viewed the entire interrogation from another room and closely monitored the situation for the best way to move forward to extract information from the student. Every five minutes, one of the officers would leave the room, and I would hand him a piece of paper with the next line of questions.

The first questions were mainly to allow the students to incriminate themselves. We let the students talk about how they were learning the English language and the reasons why they chose to study in the Philippines. We encouraged them to talk about things that they didn't need to talk about and fueled small talk.

Every time I gave the police a new batch of questions, they were progressively more intrusive, and, within an hour, we began to have our first contradiction. We noted it for future reference and moved on. We then had our next contradiction, made a note, and moved on.

Soon we had a circle of stories that were exploitable, and it was time for us to pounce. I began to tell the interrogators to ask about Back to Jerusalem.

"What do you know about Back to Jerusalem?" the interrogator asked.

"I hear it's a beautiful city," the student replied. I had to keep myself from laughing. It was such a great stall technique by the student.

"No, it is a Chinese movement to go into other countries and subvert the population through religious and ideological teaching. Isn't that right?"

I signaled for one of the officers to come out so I could coach him to go harder after the student. When he exited the room and shut the door, I put my hand on his shoulder, looked into his eyes, and told him to close the space.

"For the last hour, I have told you to get progressively closer to the student. I wanted him to feel his space being invaded by you as your questions became progressively more intrusive. Now I want you to be up in his face. I want him to feel threatened. I want you to threaten his safety. Take away his feeling of security."

I didn't realize that my idea of threatening and his idea were two different things! He stormed back into the room, got up in the student's face, and maintained strong eye contact.

"You need to start telling me what I want to know, or I am going to stab you and then cut your throat!"

"Yikes!" I frantically began to wave for the interrogator to come back out into the hallway. I started to have misgivings that this entire interrogation could go very wrong. After more time had passed, I began to hand the interrogators pictures of the students' leaders back in China. We also presented them with flight schedules to Muslim areas where they had flown earlier to share the gospel. At the very end, the interrogators presented a picture of me.

"Do you know this man?" they asked.

"I am Chinese. Is he Chinese?" the student asked.

"No, he is American."

"How would I know an American? I am Chinese," the student quickly shot back.

The interrogators questioned the student over and over about information on me until finally I walked into the room. When I entered the room, it was already several hours into the morning, and we had been conducting the interrogation all night. I greeted them with a friendly "Ni hao" and explained everything.

"This has all been a test. Training. These guys are our friends and are not real police."

One of the students was a quiet young lady. She was one of the youngest in the entire group and was as thin as a twig. When the students first arrived in Hong Kong, I asked them to stay for one week so that I could get them prepared for the training in the Philippines.

We would often hike up the mountain behind Hong Kong International Airport, pray together in the mountains,

234 The Underground Church

and have Communion together. This young lady literally had to be carried up the last part of the hike. She was so weak and lacked energy. She was used to being in the city dorms all day and was not accustomed to much physical exercise.

I assumed that she would be the easiest person to crack. Getting her to break down would make the night go much faster. It would also have been great to have her reaction on camera so that we could later show the tapes to the rest of the class and talk about what to do and what not to do.

She was woken up in a separate living area and brought into the interrogation room. I don't know how she saw the cameras so fast, but she did and immediately sat in the interrogator's chair. The two interrogators were being nice and polite and asked her to sit in the other chair.

"Thank you," she said politely. "I am fine."

"No, you need to sit here," they insisted.

"Thank you so much, but I am fine." She stood up and led the interrogators by the hand to sit. They followed her instructions!

I could not believe my eyes. This young lady, who seemed to be as timid as a mouse, had just fooled our guys into sitting exactly where she wanted them to.

The interrogators began with their line of instructed questioning. As the questions got more intense, she began to make signals of having to go to the bathroom.

"Can I go to the restroom?" she asked.

The interrogators came out and told me that the student needed to go to the restroom. "No. We need to use this to our advantage. Tell her that she cannot use the restroom until she answers all of our questions. Maybe that will expedite the process."

As night turned into morning, it was clear that she was smarter than all of us. She took every question and turned it around on the interrogators and did it in the nicest, sweetest

way. Her sweet words and demeanor masked her clever
tenacity.

I ended the interrogation prematurely. It was not going
our way. After I finally ended it and told her that it was only
training, I then offered her a chance to use the toilet.

"I don't have to use the toilet," she said softly. "I just made
that up so that I could make a run for it."

We called it a night, and then the following day, we began
teaching about interrogation. One of the underground
church pastors from China came to assist me. I talked about
methodology and techniques, and he talked about his experiences. This pastor had been arrested several times and had
been interrogated in China on many occasions. He talked
about the different ways he was interrogated, what the police
were looking for, and the different ways that he was able to
deflect their questions for short periods of time.

Many Westerners may find this kind of training a bit
overboard and unnecessary, but the truth is that many
Chinese have never been outside of China. They get nervous
when going through immigration checkpoints. We needed
to prepare them for at least the basic questioning used at
immigration.

Although we would never do these things, we taught the
students that in areas where interrogation is not developed,
beatings and physical abuse usually serve as the primary
means of interrogation. We explained that outside of clever
questioning, the other means of breaking down barriers are
food deprivation, sleep deprivation, beatings, family manip-
ulation, isolation, long-term discomfort, and pain infliction
without markings.

I told them, "When going through interrogation or immigration, you have to adopt a personality different from the
one you have now. Before God, you are used to admitting
your guilt and asking for forgiveness. Your guilt is assumed,

and you come before God asking Him to forgive you, but to be forgiven you have to admit your sins. This attitude needs to be left at the door during interrogation. Remain emotionless at immigration and interrogation. Most hardened criminals do not have guilt and believe in themselves. Practical interrogation manuals are generally based on the extensive experience of interrogators and offer allegedly effective techniques for breaking down a suspect's resistance."

The main point of our interrogation class was, "Don't give up information easily and never lie. Make yourself like an onion. Make the interrogators peel off each layer."

"Forget your guilt. If you want to be successfully interviewed and walk away clean, you have to remain guiltless," I taught. "You have to say to yourself, 'I didn't do anything wrong. I didn't say anything wrong. You are wrong. You are at fault. This has nothing to do with me.' Watch your body language. Move as little as possible and be disciplined. Occupy your thoughts with something else. Don't think about the situation unless you are preparing your story.

"Rule number one that you must never forget is never lie. Just don't tell the whole truth. Your story never has to change. You don't have to lie; you just don't have to tell them the whole truth."

At this course, we teach about the "good cop, bad cop" technique, as well. We also teach maximization technique, which is based on imposing maximum fear for not cooperating. We also instruct on the use of undercover informants, which was one of the tactics used by the Eastern Lightning in China when attempting to convert the Tanghe leadership.

"A plainclothes officer is one of the best ways to get information," I said. "Whether in prison, secondary immigration, or even in your daily activities, this method can give a lot of information to people who interview you so they can give you the illusion that they know everything. The interrogation takes place during conversations without your knowledge. Even if they already know everything, make them work for it. Make them work for every piece of information. Don't give up anything for free. Don't get cocky. You don't do this for a living. Your best policy is to shut up. Keep your mouth shut. Silence is the best policy, above all else. Silence is the best policy. Don't talk with your mouth, and don't talk with your body.

"Deflect! Deflect! Deflect! You have no rights when being interrogated. If you do, they will try to tell you early on, and they will not repeat any rights you might have. When they tell you, you probably will not be aware of it. Always insist on talking to someone else at every turn. Say you want an attorney of your choice, or to talk to your family. The best way to get out of guilt is deflection. Deflect to the guilt of your interrogators and to talking to someone else!"

We teach the students about behavioral observation and different techniques to discipline the body from giving away information that interrogators are looking for.

"Micro-expressions lasting less than one-fifth of a second may leak emotions someone wants to conceal, such as anger or guilt. At the same time, signs of emotion aren't necessarily signs of guilt. An innocent person may be apprehensive and appear guilty, but don't be that person. Take control of your body and voice. Learn techniques that work for you."

Although some might find this type of interrogation training excessive, it is the best way we have found so far to help prepare Back to Jerusalem underground missionaries for countries that aggressively oppose proselytizing. It is just one of the many ways that underground House Church missionaries differ from their Western counterparts.

$Part$ $4:$
The Future of the Chinese House Church

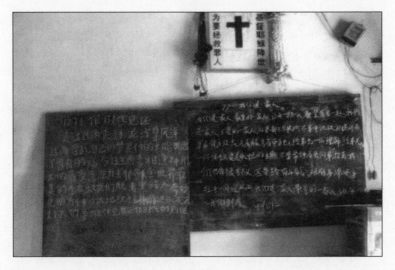

Inside a Blessing Network Bible school

Blessing Network missionary training

Xiao Min, writer of the Canaan Hymns

19

The Back to Jerusalem Vision

This chapter explores the future of the underground house churches in China and reveals more about the current status of the Back to Jerusalem vision than ever before. Since sharing about the present situation and future plans of the House Church could put others in danger, much restraint and caution have been used, but the information given here is as much as can possibly be shared with the public. It is being revealed because those who are supporting the Chinese efforts from abroad need to know how better to pray for them, and they may even learn from their endeavors. A portion of the following material has been covered in previous chapters, but it is necessary to repeat it here in the context of this discussion of current and future trends.

THE RAPID **URBANIZATION OF CHINA**

We have noted that the origin of the underground House Church movement in China was rural in nature but that the Chinese church's future is bound to change due to the rapid urbanization of the nation. During the twentieth century, Christianity took hold in the rural areas and spread like wildfire. The rapid rate of growth has been hard to calculate, and it continues in those rural areas even while it jumps to the urban areas. According to World Bank estimates, 52 percent of China's population was living in urban areas in 2012.[35] That percentage is expected to climb to between 60 and 70 percent by 2030.[36]

Currently, according to our own estimates, China is nearly 10 percent Christian. This number might seem inflated, because it would be obvious to anyone in China that one out of every ten people on the street there is not Christian (unless it is a place like Shandong, Anhui, or Henan). However, the estimate becomes tenable when Henan—formerly the most populated province in the nation with a high percentage of local Christians—is factored into the mix. In addition, there is a growing number of Christians in the minority areas around Guangxi, Yunnan, and Sichuan, where entire people groups consider themselves to be Christian, which also contributes to the national percentile. Ever since the Sichuan earthquake in 2008, the number of Christians in that area has been quickly increasing.

Places like Sichuan and Henan had been the most populated provinces in China for years, but this situation has recently changed. Urbanization has led to the separation of Chongqing from Sichuan Province, and Guangdong has surpassed Henan as the most populated province in China. People from rural areas throughout the nation are racing to production powerhouse provinces like Guangdong. Large numbers of rural Christians have also started moving to the urban areas and are filling up factories, roadside shops, and office buildings throughout the cities, taking the gospel with them.

EVANGELISM IN **URBAN AREAS**

The Lord is definitely using the mass migration to the cities for His purposes. It is almost as if the Chinese evangelists were not moving fast enough to get the gospel to areas outside their own provinces, so the Lord sped up the process by sending the missionaries to single locations—the cities—and then starting to bring the rest of the country to them.

Until now, the general control and leadership of the House Church has been largely centralized. Yet urbanization is leading the churches toward more decentralized leadership. However, one factor must be kept in mind: Most of the traditional networks have been focusing on aggressively evangelizing the urban areas, and this has led to the formation of many groups that seem to be independent but are not really autonomous in practice. This is the case because the Five Brothers, Tanghe, Fangcheng, Truth, Blessing, and Little Joe's networks are all working in the urban areas and have planted several churches in homes, factories, and universities. Even the pastors over some of these urban groups are not always aware that their fellowship was actually a strategic plant from a major network.

Consider the following example: Suppose the Five Brothers sees a need for evangelistic outreach in Chengdu, a major city in Sichuan Province. They send a team of four evangelists and fund their efforts. These evangelists then divide their efforts and focus on migrant workers and minority groups. In the migrant worker community, a few older workers get saved and join a Bible study with one of the evangelists, remaining totally unaware of the fact that the evangelist is part of a much larger network. After a year, the migrant worker fellowship consists of more than fifty believers, and the original migrant workers are the elders of the church, actively sharing with others. After eighteen months, the Five Brothers Network reevaluates the situation and decides that that it would like to send those four evangelists to participate in training in Thailand. Once the four evangelists graduate, they are sent to Kunming, leaving the churches that were set up in Chengdu to stand on their own. However, the evangelists who now live in Kunming travel regularly to the ongoing ministries in Chengdu, preach at the churches, and still guide the vision of the fledgling network, all the while taking orders from their leaders in Henan Province. Again, according to this illustration, which is a common scenario in China, it is possible that the pastor of the church in Chengdu would not even know that he is part of a network based in Henan.

A SHIFT IN **LEADERSHIP**

The current leadership of most of the groups will most likely never agree to register with the official church in China. There are some leaders who may be more open to registration today than they were yesterday, but the majority of them will refuse to register because of the obvious restrictions that doing so brings.

Earlier, we covered the reasons for their refusal to register; many of those reasons are linked to personal experiences of persecution and suffering. We also noted that within the underground House Church, the leaders are extremely reluctant to share their personal stories. It is a strange phenomenon that those who have been through so much and have seen so many things share so little about themselves. To cite another example, Joshua of the Five Brothers Network is one of the leaders that Back to Jerusalem International has been working with closely for several years. He has traveled to different countries with our members, and we've even shared hotel rooms together, giving us many hours to discuss all aspects of life.

However, he has never once mentioned some of the miracles that happened to him when he was in prison. He never speaks of how he was detained and beaten and had his limp, broken body thrown on the floor of the prison cell, only to wake up on a bed, miraculously healed, with a beam of light shining down on his body from an unknown source. This miraculous light and his healing led everyone in Joshua's prison cell to repent and believe in Christ. Joshua never preaches or shares openly about this testimony. Whenever we've asked him to write about it, he's gently said, "Maybe one day."

Again, this reluctance is common among the Chinese House Church leaders. However, their reluctance to express their experiences creates a certain partition between the generations and their perspectives on the issue of registration. Because the current leaders do not speak about these experiences, many of the younger leaders aren't familiar with what their older leaders have gone through, nor have they had to endure the same experiences. Though there is still persecution in China, it is not the same as it was twenty years ago.

A parallel scenario is taking place with the younger leaders in the Chinese government. They were not part of the generation that severely persecuted Christians. In fact, many of them have traveled to Western countries and have attended Western universities where they were exposed to Christianity. They are not familiar with the Communism that actively and aggressively oppressed the church. In recent years, instances of government persecution of the church have been largely covered up rather than publicized as triumphs against "class enemies," as in the past. Even the recent mass arrest of members of Shouwang Church in Beijing for singing Christmas carols in public received more publicity outside China than within the country. Chinese society remains largely unaware of such issues because its news media is not allowed to report on them.

Yet, as time goes on and members of the current generation move into primary leadership roles in the church and society, there is bound to be a policy shift in both the church and the government in regard to ideas about registering and conducting more open activities.

EXPOSURE TO OTHER **COUNTRIES AND IDEAS**

Another factor that will have an increasing impact on the Chinese House Church is that Chinese are traveling out of the country more today than ever before. This exposure to other nations is giving them a different perspective about the meaning of individual freedom. If this trend continues, and there is every indicator that it will, the Chinese will continue to learn from the freedoms that they enjoy abroad and will start bringing those ideas back home.

Even when Chinese are visiting a country that is not free, they themselves are afforded freedoms that the country's citizens are not given, simply because they are foreigners. When Chinese travel to Egypt, for example, they are able to attend a church or a home prayer group without fear of harassment—activities that are totally prohibited for the local Muslim population. The same is true when they travel to Malaysia during Ramadan.

Even exposure to nearby areas like Hong Kong, Macau, and Taiwan has had a lasting impact on Chinese mainlanders who travel there. These three areas have many freedoms that most Chinese do not experience. At first glance, Hong Kong, Macau, and Taiwan may seem to be just more expensive versions of mainland China, but, after some time, it becomes more evident that these areas are very different from the mainland in other ways. They have access to foreign news, books, and magazines that cannot be obtained in China. They are also immune to the "Great Firewall of China," having access to all the Internet Web sites that are blocked on the mainland. Anyone who has encountered the Great Firewall knows from a quick browsing session that several Web sites popular everywhere else in the world cannot be accessed in mainland China. Chinese visitors to Hong Kong, Macau, and Taiwan are therefore exposed to an endless world of blogs, opinions, and social networks where people freely express themselves. This kind of exposure is helping the younger generation to shape their ideas of freedom and individuality, and it is changing the church, as well.

A GREAT-COMMISSION **MOVEMENT**

The zeal of the younger generation in the underground House Church is just as strong and tenacious as that of its predecessors. This gives us reason to believe that the dedication of the church in China to carry out the Great Commission will continue for many years to come. The primary way Chinese believers are pursuing this commission is through the Back to Jerusalem movement.

The unifying vision of Back to Jerusalem is showing signs of increasing in size and scope. To review, "Back to Jerusalem" is most simply defined as the vision of the Chinese House Church to preach the gospel to the unreached peoples in the eastern provinces of

China and in all the countries between the border of China and the city of Jerusalem. It is a rallying call to wake up China to become a missions-focused country.

There is excitement in the air when young people in China share about the Back to Jerusalem vision. Many Chinese see the present time as their turn to be responsible for carrying out the Great Commission, as so many others have in the past.

Many books and reports on what has happened in China are focused on the revivals that took place in the 1980s and 90s, leading some China experts to conclude that the revivals in China are dying down and coming to a close. However, these reports usually fail to take notice of a new wind sweeping throughout the nation. How is most of the world missing it? Foreign Christian delegations and potential missionaries are seeing the bright lights of Shanghai and the tourist attractions in Beijing, and are exploring the huge shopping areas in Shenzhen, without getting a true picture of what God is doing in China. Though the churches are growing at amazing rates in these cities, there are new revivals taking place in less-frequented parts of the nation. Places like the northeast are experiencing an awakening that has not been seen since the days of Jonathan Goforth. Young underground House Church leaders are one of the main factors contributing to those new revivals.

The following is one example of current circumstances that have led to revival. In August 2010, floods struck Jilin Province. The Chinese in Jilin asked for help from foreign aid organizations, but many of them were not able to help; many foreign Christian organizations were fatigued from other emergency aid efforts. The Chinese church therefore began to pool together its resources to provide aid to Jilin Province. The results have been amazing. Aid was handed out by believers while they preached the gospel on street corners. Believers in Jilin began to attract people from all over the province to hear the gospel, rumors of miracles began to spread, and people reported having had visions like the "Macedonian call" (see Acts 16:9–10), in which they instantaneously started speaking the language of the nation calling them. "In the city of Jilin alone, we have been seeing areas with an average of fifty people per day coming to the Lord," reported one pastor involved in the relief effort.

The revivals springing up in Jilin Province are not isolated events. In December 2010, Teacher Zhao traveled to Hong Kong for meetings with Back to Jerusalem International. He had just spoken at several different churches inside China and came to give us a report on those gatherings.

Teacher Zhao is from a Pentecostal background but is rather conservative in his views and observations. He is not someone who has a tendency to dramatize or exaggerate. If anything, the opposite could be said of him. Groups like Keymedia in Finland, IBRA Media in Sweden, AVC in Switzerland, and other large organizations around the world have relied on him for the most accurate reporting about the House Church in China.

At this particular meeting, he was bubbling over with excitement as he began to describe the nature of what he had just witnessed in China. "These young people are so on fire. I haven't seen anything like it. I mean, they were crying and repenting, and you could just feel the power of God. It was unlike anything I have seen before."

Less than a month later, in January 2011, we met with three leaders from the Five Brothers Network and with Little Joe. We were there to arrange for missionaries to be sent to Kazakhstan and had representatives from the local church meeting with us, as well. One of the leaders, Ezekiel, began to tell of what he had just experienced prior to arriving at our meeting.

> In 2010, we have seen a huge revival take hold in all of China! I was there in the 1980s when China began its famous days of massive revivals, but I tell you that this revival is even stronger. This spiritual revival is happening everywhere, and we have received a clear vision from God.
>
> Before, it was our goal to train missionaries in languages and cross-cultural skills, but many of the missionaries who

had been trained couldn't go because they felt too weak and incapable. Missionaries have been training all over China for years, but most of them have never had a clear vision of where to go in the Muslim, Buddhist, and Communist world.

Now we are having prayer meetings where God is talking to us clearly and telling us where to go. God is specifically calling people to the western borders and to the minority groups. In the past, Chinese Back to Jerusalem missionaries would go to other countries and cultures to preach the gospel, but the vision and the calling were never really clear. The leaders often appointed people to go to different areas because of availability, not based on the calling of the Lord.

Now, believers all over China are seeing visions like the ones that the apostle Paul had. These visions are of specific people in specific countries speaking specific languages. Some of the believers who are having these visions are even being told specifically that they will be martyred.

One night, I was in western China, and the Spirit of the Lord filled the room. Everyone fell to their faces and started crying and calling out to the Lord. During these meetings, I couldn't sleep for two days and two nights. I couldn't stop praying. The Holy Spirit was so strong. Young people began to call out, "Yes, Lord, I am willing to die in that country for You. Yes, Lord, I am ready to have my name put into the Lamb's Book of Life."

One night, during one of these meetings, a young man came to me and asked me to pray with him. I told him, "Everyone is praying. Why do you want special prayer? Just join everyone else." The young man was persistent. He told me that God told him to go to Palestine and preach the gospel, but he was afraid. He said that God was telling him clearly that Palestine will be the mission field that he will be sent to, but he was afraid of the violence toward Christians there. I told him not to fear, because, if God had called him, God would be with him and would strengthen him. I placed my hands on him and began to pray. After praying, he replied, "God has told me clearly that I am to go to Palestine. It is there that I will be martyred, but I will not fear. I will preach the gospel of Jesus Christ, because it is the Truth for all mankind. It is the power that saves!"

As this young man stood there, his young wife came and stood beside him. She quoted from Ruth and said, "Where you go, I will go; and where you stay, I will stay. Your people will be my people, and your God, my God. Where you die, I will die, and there I will be buried. May the Lord deal with me, be it ever so severely, if even death separates you and me." That night, forty-four young people came forward and said that they, too, were willing to sacrifice their lives, if need be, in Muslim countries.

Revival has also been taking place in the hard-to-reach areas like Xinjiang. Since 2008, not many foreigners have been living in Xinjiang. Many of those who were living there prior to the Beijing Olympics were forced to leave. At that time, many of them were given only forty-eight hours to sell their car and apartment, find places for their clothes and furniture, and arrange everything to get to their next destination.

Back to Jerusalem partnered with the underground House Church to help start a hotel among the Muslims in Xinjiang Province. It is one of the most difficult places to share the gospel because there is not only aggression against Christians but an overall hatred for Han Chinese, as well.

When many of the foreigners were forced to leave in 2008, there were very few local Christians. It was not easy to find more than one or two. Today, in the small city of Kashgar and the surrounding area, there are an estimated four hundred to five hundred believers. This may not sound like a lot, but to have that many Muslims come to Christ in such a short time is evidence of an amazing revival among the Muslims in western China.

These revivals are getting Christians excited about the new role of China and the Back to Jerusalem vision. The vision has a flavor that is unique to the Chinese. The impact that God is having on China and the spiritual fruit of Chinese serving around the world are already very visible.

CHINESE BACK TO JERUSALEM **MISSIONARIES**

The future and longevity of the House Church can be better understood by looking at firsthand information from Chinese Back to Jerusalem missionaries working in other countries. The following is rarely disclosed information about just a few countries in which they are now ministering.

BHUTAN

Many people have never heard of the country of Bhutan, which is hidden in the Himalayas. It is sandwiched between the two giants of China and India. For generations, this country actually lied about its population, keeping it artificially inflated to discourage its neighbors from invading. Back to Jerusalem has been working closely with the underground church in Bhutan. Representatives from Back to Jerusalem were present at a meeting held somewhere between the cities of Paro and Thimphu that took place in 2006 to establish the Christian Alliance of Bhutan.

The nature of our project with the Chinese underground missionaries cannot be given in detail here, but the Chinese are using their experiences in Tibet to relate to, connect to, and serve the church of Bhutan.

NORTH KOREA

Not many countries have as close a relationship with North Korea as China maintains. Chinese Back to Jerusalem missionaries have been working inside North Korea since 2007. Today, several missionaries are living and working in that nation, preaching the gospel and using small electronic Bibles to help spread the Word.

In April 2011 alone, Back to Jerusalem missionaries were able to produce and deliver one thousand handheld video players that had been preloaded with several hours of Christian movies, gospel teaching, and an entire audio Bible in the native dialect. At the end of October 2011, another thousand were sent in.

During that year, Back to Jerusalem missionaries were also able to deliver food to starving families located throughout North Korea. Food distribution is not an easy task, and large donations are often redirected to the military or government officials. But this is something that the Chinese are better able to monitor, and they are dedicated to doing so to help share the love of Christ.

SOUTH SUDAN

In September 2011, the first Chinese Back to Jerusalem missionary traveled to the world's newest country, South Sudan. South Sudan was officially recognized as a free, independent nation on July 9, 2011. The road to independence has been a long and hard one. Even in 2014, the new country was suffering from civil war, political instability, and famine. Christians have a history of being severely persecuted by the Muslims in Sudan. According to *Touchstone* journal, in the period between late 1983 and the middle of 2004, "Over two million black African Christians and others from central and southern Sudan have died, and about six million have been displaced." Those who died were either killed or succumbed to disease and/or starvation after fleeing their homes.[37]

Sudan was one of the first countries in the world to provide slaves to other nations. Since the early 1980s, more than 200,000 Christian and other non-Muslim women and children in Sudan have been enslaved by Arab Muslim militia groups, and there may be as many as 35,000 still living in slavery.[38] In the early 1990s, people were "often sold as property in a thriving slave trade for as little as $15 per human being."[39]

Today, Africans from Sudan are still being sold as slaves, but most news media outlets around the world still fail to report on it. While Chinese Back to Jerusalem missionaries were visiting South Sudan, they were able to spend much of their time with the Dinka tribe. The enslavement of the Dinkas in Southern Sudan may be one of the most horrific, well-known examples of contemporary slavery in the world. Joshua, the Chinese House Church pastor mentioned several times in this book, was greatly moved by the church in this area.

After spending some time in Sudan, the Chinese evangelists said, "We believe that God is moving mightily in this country. Sudan played an important role in the beginning times, and it will play an important role in the end times. We must return the hate of the Muslims with the love of Christ. We must stand with our persecuted brothers and sisters in Sudan and let them know they are not defeated, and they are not alone. The church in China stands together with them, and we will not say it only with our words—we are willing to display it with our actions."

There is currently a team of five Back to Jerusalem missionaries living and serving in South Sudan. And we have a vision of moving 300 workers to Sudan and Somalia.

NEPAL

Today, there are a couple of teams made up of more than twenty missionaries who are living and working in Nepal. Several of them were trained at our main base in the Philippines. The first team that arrived there to set up for the other teams came through the main vocational training programs run by Back to Jerusalem in Tibet.

Prior to their departure for Nepal, we met with them and listened to their challenges and concerns. It was important that they knew what to expect, because other Back to Jerusalem missionaries had encountered difficulties in that country that discouraged and shocked them. The previous missionary couple, who had moved to Nepal in 2007, did well for the first part of the year, but after a while, the living conditions there became very challenging for them. When the wife became pregnant, they left Nepal and returned to China. They have not been back since.

The missionaries who are there now are actively studying the language and working in the open market to share the gospel.

INDIA

India is the top desired destination for most Back to Jerusalem missionaries in China—at least in theory. At any given Bible school, one can ask the students what country they feel called to, and, most of the time, India will be the response of the majority of the class.

The main reason for this answer is that most Back to Jerusalem missionaries have not been formally educated and have never been to secondary school. India is really the only other country that many of them know of or have heard anything about.

We have traveled with Chinese missionaries and leaders to India on shorter trips. In addition, in 2012, a team of Back to Jerusalem representatives from China went to India to work with a local church and started an Aquaponics training center in Nagpur. Aquaponics is a sustainable farming technique that recycles water and waste to grow vegetables and fish in a contained soilless system. Today, Christian leaders from all around India are being trained at the center.

TANZANIA

Back to Jerusalem missionaries from China were sent to Tanzania and have successfully helped to serve the local church there for more than six years. These Chinese missionaries started off as assistants in an orphanage and then began serving the international church.

PAKISTAN

Pakistan shares a border with China, and its leaders are actively engaging China for a broader partnership. Pakistan sees China as key in its rivalry with India and likes to court the Chinese whenever possible.

Ten Back to Jerusalem missionaries have been working and serving in Pakistan for four years in three different locations. They finished their language training and are actively serving the church. Back to Jerusalem missionaries have also sent in hundreds of audio Bibles in Urdu, the local language, that are being used for teaching the Bible to illiterate Christians and for evangelizing Muslims.

In addition, the Shandong Group currently has a team of ten missionaries in this country. This is the first team the group has sent out. There is also a new Back to Jerusalem team living in a Taliban-controlled area.

EGYPT

There are about twenty Back to Jerusalem missionaries from China living and working in Egypt. They have set up businesses and are serving there even amid the political turmoil, and they have seen a few people come to the Lord.

These missionaries have utilized a wonderful idea for business that allows them to have daily interaction with Muslim women who are not permitted to leave their homes without a male escort. The Chinese missionaries have engaged them and are able to minister to them in a unique way.

During a trip to Egypt, our representatives were able to enjoy a meal on the Nile River with a team of Back to Jerusalem missionaries. We also spent time with a local Muslim whom the Chinese missionaries had befriended. This local resident was more of a cultural Muslim than a practicing one and was very open to the gospel, even joining us in prayer before our meal.

SYRIA

Ever since terrible civil turmoil began in Syria, fewer and fewer missionaries have remained there to share the gospel. However, Chinese Back to Jerusalem workers are still ministering in this country. They were able to set up a small business because of the training they received at one of the Back to Jerusalem training centers. Today, there are five Back to Jerusalem missionaries still living and serving in Syria.

IRAN

Back to Jerusalem missionaries are highly motivated and focused on the country of Iran. In 2011, Back to Jerusalem partners were successful in printing and delivering thirty thousand Bibles to this nation. China's House Church networks are concentrating their efforts on moving into Iran and its neighboring countries in order to bring the gospel to the people of ancient Persia. There are currently five Back to Jerusalem missionaries in Iran.

CAMBODIA

There are twelve Back to Jerusalem missionaries ministering in Cambodia. Five of them are working for an American clothing brand. The boss of the company in Cambodia is a believer and uses this platform to provide visas for the Chinese. The American side of the company has no clue that their factory is being used for this purpose.

Five of the missionaries are from one House Church network in Henan, and the other five are from a network in Anhui. These two groups are working completely independently of one another.

The group from Anhui spent the first year learning the language and the second year living in small villages to learn more about the language and culture. The third year, they were commissioned by their home church to start a church. They ended up establishing three churches in the first six months.

In addition to the above, Brother Yun's daughter and son-in-law are missionaries in Cambodia.

LAOS

There are currently five Back to Jerusalem missionaries living and working in Laos. They have opened a service business to serve the local community and are using that business as their platform.

Places like Laos are easier for the Chinese to transition to because there are buses from China to Laos, and many of the country's imported products come directly from mainland China. Most of the locals have been working with Chinese businessmen for generations, so there is already a natural connection there.

This is not an exhaustive list of Back to Jerusalem projects. There are more missionaries living, working, training, and preaching abroad than we can be aware of. It is impossible to know exactly what every network is doing in every country. Back to Jerusalem missionaries are also in countries like Yemen, Vietnam, and Ethiopia. There are actually more Chinese missionaries living in Myanmar than in any other country.

This list also doesn't take into account the large number of Chinese Christians living abroad who aren't officially missionaries. Thousands of Chinese who had never been exposed to Christianity in China are getting saved in 10/40 Window nations on a regular basis. A sister in Guangdong Province who now oversees the production of many of the Back to Jerusalem electronics became a Christian while working for a company in Saudi Arabia. At a Christian home group in Egypt, we met some Chinese who were all working for foreign companies there. The fellowship of about fifteen people had all come to Christ while living in Cairo.

AN EXPANDING **MOVEMENT**

By looking at the past and present situation of the underground House Church and identifying obvious patterns and trends, it is possible to make some projections regarding its future. The main prediction is this: Considering the urbanization, transformation, and globalization of China and the House Church movement, it is clear that the movement will continue to expand and bring the message of Christ to every tribe, tongue, and nation between China and Jerusalem.

20
Nine Significant Features
of the Chinese House Church

In this book, we have explored the history of the underground House Church, surveyed the main networks within the movement, and identified various elements that have helped to propel its growth. We have read personal testimonies of Chinese believers and looked at some of their experiences and trials, all of which have helped to bring their history to life. Through these examples, we can better understand concepts and situations pertaining to the Chinese church that are otherwise completely foreign to outsiders.

As discussed in previous chapters, the last few decades of Chinese church history were directed largely by the great work of God flowing out of the Nanyang region in Henan—through the networks of Peter Xu, Tanghe, Fangcheng, and others. A foreign visitor to that area would most likely look around and immediately wonder why God would choose such a place to pour out His grace. In many ways, Nanyang is about ten years behind the rest of China. It does not contain any notable foreign communities, and any foreigner visiting there is stared at and sometimes pointed out by local children who shout, "*Laowai!*" ("old foreigner"). One House Church worker from the Five Brothers Network described Nanyang in this way: "There are four areas of unrest for the Chinese government: Taiwan, Xinjiang, Tibet, and Nanyang." It is hard to imagine that this county has had such an impact on the entire world.

When Christians in other nations and cultures learn the mysteries of the Chinese House Church, it can help them to reflect on their own relationships with Jesus Christ. The history and testimonies of the underground Chinese believers are encouraging, because they show us what God can do in a country that declares war on His people, as the Chinese government has done. Even though China tried to eradicate the Christians, Jesus never left them. He never abandoned the Chinese people and is actually using them today in amazing ways to fulfill the Great Commission.

Looking into the secrets of the Chinese House Church can also shock us into seeing the truths of the Bible without using the cultural spectacles that sometimes dilute and pervert the Word of God. At first glance, several elements of the Chinese church might look like the results of bad judgment, but, upon closer evaluation, many of these elements are actually closer to the Jewish culture Jesus grew up in than the Western culture that dominates most foreign churches.

Upon evaluating the Chinese House Church's hidden treasures, we can recognize at least these nine characteristics that are unique to it and have contributed to its growth in one way or another.

1. THE EXPERIENCE OF **PERSECUTION**

Persecution is not unique to the Chinese underground House Church. If persecution was indeed the only requirement for a revival, then China would not be alone in seeing massive numbers of people come to the Lord. However, the Chinese persecutions have been somewhat distinct in that the government actually implemented a plan for the systematic destruction of the church among its people.

Chinese persecution was a direct assault on the Christian leadership in that country and aimed to erase the name of Jesus Christ from Chinese soil forever. Christians were not merely included in a massive, widespread effort to stamp out all political opponents of Communism but were specifically singled out for annihilation.

Many church leaders and other Christians in China initially agreed with and supported the tenets of Communism. The Communist Party had the backing of many Christians who were happy to see the tyrannical Nationalists replaced by those who claimed to support equal distribution of wealth and resources. In theory, equal distribution was already being practiced in the 1940s by indigenous Christian groups like the Jesus Family and the Back to Jerusalem Evangelistic Band. The Communist Party of China had an early ally in this regard.

It was the Party that first viewed the church as a natural enemy. Again, the persecution in China did not only inflict pain on Christians but was also an attempt to dilute, pollute, pervert, and completely destroy the church. The government persecuted the church with a rarely seen vile hatred that can be explained only as demonic in nature.

The movement of Sino-Christianity was determined by the Lord's changeless will; the enemy saw the future and potential of the Chinese church and moved to prevent it. Yet, could the enemy have predicted that the very acts that were intended to eradicate Christianity would be instrumental in bringing about church growth that would not have been possible otherwise?

2. THE INFLUENCE OF **MAO ZEDONG**

Despite all his anti-Christian propaganda, hideous orders of destruction upon the church, and systematic attacks on Christian beliefs, Mao Zedong undeniably put into place the very factors needed to assist, nurture, and facilitate the growth of the world's largest revival.

First, he insisted that everyone in the country become responsible for the sins of his or her neighbors. Everyone was accountable to know if the neighbors were involved in foul play—creating a very transparent society. Confession sessions were arranged for the Chinese to come forward with valuable, incriminating information about themselves or their neighbors.

According to Mao Zedong, you are your brother's keeper. The confession sessions were implemented to create an atmosphere where no one would ever attempt to go against the Communist Party for fear of being caught by family, friends, or neighbors who, in turn, were afraid not to report an illegal activity for fear that they, too, would get into trouble. Yet this atmosphere actually created the perfect environment for healings and other miracles of God to be witnessed and shared. In such a confessional society, news spread very quickly—even the good news of Jesus.

Mao also standardized the Mandarin language for everyone in China, enabling believers to spread the gospel to many people without the need to learn other languages. This policy removed a huge barrier that hadn't previously been possible to overcome.

Mao also connected the country with a road and railway system that allowed missionaries and evangelists to travel around quickly, preaching the Word of God to everyone who would listen. The development of the transportation system permitted the gospel to spread through, and between, provinces faster than ever before.

3. THE PRESENCE OF **MIRACLES**

As we explored the roots of the House Church revivals, we noted that the Chinese church had a serious lack of Bibles, competent teachers, Christian materials, and other resources traditionally utilized to share the Word. One thing that was not lacking, however, was God's presence. His fingerprints can be found all over the churches in Henan and Anhui, where many people were healed and witnessed miracles.

It is easy to deny rational teachings and moving speeches, or to respond cynically to a religious book, but it is much more difficult to deny the power of God in action. It is also much harder to deny a God who answers desperate prayers when every other option has been exhausted and there is no other hope. Those Chinese who were dying from disease and starvation had no one to turn to for help. The sick had no places to go for treatment. Many of them looked to Jesus as a last resort and found mercy, rest, and supernatural healing through God's power.

Rumors of healings and other miracles spread like wildfire throughout the Chinese countryside. When people were healed, they couldn't help but tell everyone what had happened to them. When other people were sick and had no hope, they looked to the same Jesus whom so many others had turned to, and found hope and relief, as well.

When believers prayed for simple things like Bibles, God would miraculously answer their prayers. When they prayed for safety, God protected them. When they asked for freedom from prison, God sometimes opened the iron gates of the correctional fortresses and let His servants walk out free. The early revivals in Henan and Anhui were fueled by the testimonies of many miracles like these.

4. CHARISMATIC **FAITH AND WORSHIP**

The early movements of the underground House Church were not propelled or supported by academia. Even today, the rough and crude farmers in China who are part of the underground House Church movement are not accepted by theological academics.

The prayers lifted up at an average House Church meeting are not read from a piece of paper prepared in advance, as in some formal Western denominations, but are marked by passionate, impromptu cries and bold proclamations. In addition, the gifts of the Holy Spirit are widely accepted and practiced, but certain activities, like speaking in tongues and prophesying, are not emphasized. Impromptu dancing and singing during prayer and worship times are encouraged and done with great joy, but these are quite natural to the culture and not at all distracting, as they would be in most Western church settings. There is nothing really formal or stuffy about worship in the underground House Church.

What makes the charismatic element unique in China is that it is not disorderly. One of the biggest accusations made by those opposed to charismatic worship is that it can create disorder and chaos, but that is not the case in the Chinese church. Even though such worship is entered into without planning or strategic leading, it is nonetheless done in unity. If one person is singing and dancing in a room full of people praying at an underground meeting, everyone is singing and dancing along with him or her. If one person is on his or her knees, crying and shouting out prayers, the entire room will begin to do the same. The charismatic activities are individual and unique to each person within the church, yet they are also somehow orderly and done as one body.

5. FEMALE **LEADERSHIP**

One of the obvious characteristics of the Chinese House Church is the overwhelming percentage of women in the movement. The vast majority of evangelists and missionaries who are trained and sent to the field are young women. To overlook the dominant role that women have played and how much they have contributed to church growth would be deliberate ignorance.

Although none of the top leaders of the traditional networks is female, many of the movers and shakers in individual churches are. These women have made their mark on the largest revival in history, as well as the largest missionary movement ever.

The women serve in the background and do so swiftly and effectively, accomplishing more in a short period of time than many men are able to who might expect to be rewarded for their efforts. These women don't ask for recognition—in fact, they shun it. Rather, they work as if they are working directly for the heavenly Father.

The women in the underground House Church movement will often set up for a meeting, preach the sermon, feed the attendees, and then clean up after everyone else has departed. They are self-sacrificing warriors and heroes, and, collectively, they are one of the main reasons for the rapid growth of Christianity in China.

6. THE ABSENCE OF **FOREIGN DENOMINATIONS**

Foreign missionaries need to be credited with planting the seeds of the gospel in China. Fruit is still being produced thanks to the past efforts of these missionaries, who labored to till the soil of Chinese hearts. However, the presence of these foreign missionaries, followed by their absence, had more of an impact on the Chinese church than could have been imagined. Their continued presence, coupled with stifling control measures, would undoubtedly have had a negative impact on church growth.

We can understand this issue through the illustration of child rearing. A child needs the care of parents while he or she is growing up. The parents' love, attention, devotion, and sacrifice all contribute to the raising of that child. However, if the parents become overbearing and don't ever teach, or allow, their child to make his or her own decisions, the consequences can be disastrous for the child's maturation process.

Similarly, missionaries and missions organizations often have a hard time with the final phase of missions work, which is to allow the native church to take leadership and to make its own decisions. They often delay recognizing their "offspring" as an equal when it is fully grown.

In the case of the Chinese church, its umbilical cord to foreign funding was severed the hard way. The separation process was difficult for the Chinese, and it was equally challenging for the missionaries. No one would have willingly chosen the road that the underground House Church has had to travel, nor would anyone have willingly accepted the fire that the House Church has had to go through. However, out of the forced separation has come a church that is now independent, self-sustaining, and thriving in an environment that makes it possible for the Chinese and foreign churches to maintain a healthy relationship of mutual respect and support.

7. PATERNAL **LEADERSHIP**

Leaders in China are regarded as parental figures. Their opinions are revered and their commands are obeyed. This leadership style might not work well in Western culture, but the current church growth would never have happened without it.

Being able to give orders and know that they will be followed without question has allowed the leaders to manage an army of believers in China that is ready to march on the gates of hell. This army strongly believes in its cause and completely trusts its leaders. Naturally, there are flaws with this kind of leadership model, as with any, but it has been very advantageous for the Chinese. Whether we agree with it or not, this is the model that the Chinese use and the one that God has chosen to work through mightily.

8. THE BACK TO JERUSALEM **VISION**

The Great Commission compelled the early church to go into unknown lands to share the good news. From Paul and Barnabas's first missionary expedition to today's thriving missionary organizations, the Great Commission has sent missionaries into far-flung regions under less-than-desirable conditions to bring people out of darkness and despair.

As previously stated, the Back to Jerusalem vision of the underground church in China is to take the gospel into the countries between the borders of China and Jerusalem. That swath of land contains the highest level of poverty and the largest number of unreached people groups on earth today. Despite the desperate need in this area, only a small percentage of missions funding from the Western world is used to evangelize it.

This situation is changing due to the Chinese. As the Chinese House Church increases its numbers, the number of its missionaries also increases. Unlike the focus of most of the Western church, its focus is on the hardest-to-reach areas. Its missionaries are being sent to the most difficult countries, and the majority of its resources are being used for this effort.

"Back to Jerusalem" has been the heart cry of the Chinese church for several generations, but only a handful of believers carried this vision through the darkest hours of persecution. Today, the younger generation has caught the vision and is determined to carry out its mission. With a strong unifying vision, the younger generation has a direct passion to funnel its energy and efforts into this task.

In many Christian circles around the world today, the passion for the Great Commission has been lost. At the same time, we see that Western society in general is becoming more secular. The question can be asked, "Is the missions focus in the West not as strong because society has become more secular, or is society more secular because the vision for missions has been lost by the church?" It seems to be the latter. A church without vision lacks the inspiration and direction to make any real impact on society. In contrast, a new day has dawned in China, and a fresh vision has come to life. The vision lay dormant for decades, but it has awakened and is now being passed from person to person with excitement and zeal.

Even for outsiders, the Back to Jerusalem vision of the Chinese House Church is exciting because of what it represents:

+ the rise and global impact of a church once thought to have been wiped out by the Chinese Communist regime
+ the power of God to reach down and breathe life into absolute darkness in open defiance of what everyone thought to be reality
+ a new wave that has been ordained to defy racist statements made by missiologists of past generations who thought the world could be reached by Western missionaries alone

The Back to Jerusalem vision is the unique Chinese version of the Great Commission that God is using to usher in the imminent return of Jesus Christ.

9. THE MOVE OF THE **HOLY SPIRIT**

In many ways, the Holy Spirit trumps all the other elements previously mentioned. If a sterile environment were to be created in which all the elements and characteristics listed above were added, revival still could not be created by human beings. Only the timing and movement of the Holy Spirit could have transformed the church in China in the ways we have seen. For whatever reason, the Spirit has chosen China to be used during this age. This special act of God's sovereign will makes the underground Chinese House Church distinct.

These nine characteristics are by no means exhaustive. They are just a few elements that can help us to understand why the Chinese are experiencing the world's largest revival and why they are focusing on the world's largest missionary movement.

This revival will be hard to stop. In the event that they are imprisoned or killed, leaders throughout the nation have already designated their replacements, who are completely capable of maintaining the present levels of activity. These second-tier leaders are currently involved in training, administration, security, personnel logistics, fund-raising, and the distribution of materials. Generally, they operate with a great deal of autonomy in executing projects, because security issues prevent them from directly communicating with their leadership on a regular basis. They have very little autonomy when choosing direction and vision but much freedom to carry out orders once they have been given.

The underground House Church is mobile and hard for the authorities to follow and observe on a regular basis. Again, this is mainly because the networks and churches don't have "headquarters." There is no large facility that can be monitored, raided, attacked, or razed to the ground. Any facility used for logistical missions, such as Bible deliveries, is rented on a month-to-month basis utilizing fake identification cards and disposable phone numbers that can be quickly discarded.

A WORK OF THE **SOVEREIGN CREATOR**

After examining the underground House Church, one cannot help but be amazed at what God is doing in the world today. It is remarkable that there are no dominant personalities in the movement who lead the charge for their own personal gain. On the contrary, each leader within this movement in China is mostly guaranteed a life of persecution, hardship, imprisonment, and sometimes even martyrdom.

One of the first mysteries we uncovered about the House Church networks was that, most of the time, they were built by people who had sought relief from poverty, sickness, and/or death. They had an illness, or a dear family member was sick, and they saw Christ miraculously move in a way that changed them forever.

It is quite interesting that Chinese Christians who found Jesus in the most desperate of circumstances became passionate about following Him, even to death, despite not knowing much other than His power to save and heal. In the West, where we have access to so much information and Bible knowledge, we can easily live our entire lives absolutely passionless before Christ.

The underground church in China seems to be built on a mixture of ignorance and blind faith, but the believers' blind faith is anchored in their Savior, Jesus Christ. In general, Western churches seem to be built on the confidence of their own understanding of the Word of God and rationalism; they rely more on tangible and reasonably attainable goals.

When the Israelites were at the banks of the Red Sea with a furious Egyptian army at their backs, God commanded Moses to take all the people across: *"Lift up your staff, and stretch out your hand over the sea and divide it, that the people of Israel may go through the sea on dry ground"* (Exodus 14:16). If that command were given to us today, what would be our reaction? Would we rely on our own abilities, or would we trust in the power of God? Would we put a committee together to discuss how to go about obeying the command? Would we try to find some more "practical" way to cross the sea other than by the directions already given by God?

Or would we, with total faith and complete abandonment of our own feeble wisdom, scrap the idea of a committee and any other plans and simply lift our staff and cross the sea as God had commanded, trusting in Him to perform a miracle?

The Chinese House Church didn't have a choice; it had to accept the latter. May we all learn to trust more in the Lord than ever before by seeing what He has done and continues to do in China. May we all stop looking at the teachings of the Word of God through the limited scope of our own culture. May the mysteries that have brought the underground House Church in China through the most turbulent time in China's history teach us to rely on God always for everything. If the sovereign Creator of the universe can use the evil schemes of man to bring about the greatest spiritual harvest in history, surely He can provide for us as we walk in obedience to Him one day at a time.

Notes

Chapter 2: Roots of Chinese Christianity

1. "Middle Kingdom" is the traditional Chinese term for the Chinese Empire.
2. For more information, see Davy Tong and Raymond Petzholt, *The True Spiritual Roots for All Chinese* (Davy Tong and Raymond Petzholt, 2000).
3. Don Richardson, *Eternity in Their Hearts*, rev. ed. (Ventura, CA: Regal Books, 1984), 62–67.
4. An excellent book on this subject is Ethel R. Nelson, Richard E. Broadberry, and Ginger Tong Chock, *God's Promise to the Chinese* (Great Britain: Read Books Publisher, 1997).
5. For more information, see Tong and Petzholt, *True Spiritual Roots for All Chinese*.
6. Paul Hattaway and others, *Back to Jerusalem: Three Chinese House Church Leaders Share Their Vision to Complete the Great Commission* (Carlisle, UK: Piquant Editions, 2003), 4–5.
7. A. J. Broomhall, *The Shaping of Modern China: Hudson Taylor's Life and Legacy*, vol. 1: Early–1867, 2nd ed. (Carlisle, UK: Piquant Editions, 2005), 8–11.
8. Ibid., 38–43.
9. Dr. and Mrs. Howard Taylor, *Hudson Taylor's Spiritual Secret* (Chicago: Moody Press, 1989), 62.
10. Broomhall, *Shaping of Modern China*, vol. 2: 1867–1990, 754.
11. Ibid., 755.

Chapter 3: Clearing Up the Confusion

12. "Report from China," *China News and Church Report*, September 15, 1997.
13. Eugene Bach and Brother Zhu, *The Heavenly People: Going Underground with Brother Yun and the Chinese House Church* (Blountsville, AL: The Fifth Estate, 2011), 82–88. (Brackets in the original quote.)

Chapter 4: Tested by Fire

14. David Aikman, *Jesus in Beijing: How Christianity Is Transforming China and Changing the Global Balance of Power* (Washington, D.C.: Regnery Publishing, Inc., 2006), 213.
15. See Jung Chang and Jon Halliday, *Mao: The Unknown Story* (New York: Anchor Books, 2006).
16. Anna Louise Strong, *Tibetan Interviews* (Peking: New World Press, 1959), 76–78.

Chapter 5: From Goose Feces to Gulags: The Founding of China Gospel Fellowship

17. The excerpts in chapters 5 and 6 are from a translated testimony written by Shen Xiaoming and used with his permission.

Chapter 8: Tanghe (China Gospel Fellowship)

18. Personal interview with Pastor Chen in June 2011.

Chapter 11: Born Again Movement (Peter Xu)

19. Brother Yun and Paul Hattaway, *The Heavenly Man: The Remarkable True Story of Chinese Christian Brother Yun* (London: Monarch Books, 2002), 233.
20. Ibid., 237.
21. Personal conversation with Brother Yun.
22. "Luis Palau Issues Statement After China Comments Disputed," *Baptist Press*, November 30, 2005, http://www.bpnews.net/bpnews.asp?id=22173. (Brackets in the original.) See also "Christians Slam Evangelist's Pro-Beijing Remarks," *Washington Times*, November 27, 2005, http://www.washingtontimes.com/news/2005/nov/27/20051127-115544-7472r/.
23. "China Trip Successful," March 26, 2010, http://legacy.palau.org/news/story/china_trip_successful_344.
24. Tim Funk, "Graham Discourages 'Illegal' Evangelizing in China," *Charlotte (NC) Observer*, May 19, 2008, 1A.

25. "Measures on the Management of the Reincarnation of Living Buddhas in Tibetan Buddhism" (translated by International Campaign for Tibet), Congressional-Executive Commission on China, http://www.cecc.gov/resources/legal-provisions/measures-on-the-management-of-the-reincarnation-of-living-buddhas-in-0.

Chapter 12: The Cave

26. Most of the information for this chapter is from a personal interview with Sister H. in February 2012.
27. Personal interview with Joshua in Shenzhen on February 3, 2012.

Chapter 15: Little Joe's Network

28. Personal interview with Little Joe in Shanghai in June 2011.
29. See also Mats Tunehag, "A Global Overview of the Business as Mission Movement: Needs & Gaps," January 2009, http://www.lausanneworld pulse.com/perspectives.php/1074.
30. Tunehag, "A Global Overview of the Business as Mission Movement."

Chapter 16: Other Networks and Personalities

31. Benjamin and his family are exempt from China's one-child policy for two reasons: (1) he is married to a Taiwanese woman; (2) his second child was born in the U.S. and has a U.S. passport. The one-child policy does not always apply to farmers, parents whose firstborn is handi capped, those who marry foreigners, and children born abroad. There is also a new policy for newlyweds who are both the product of the one-child rule that allows them to have two children. However, it should be understood that, although there are loopholes, the one-child policy is still strictly enforced in China, and huge fines (or infanticide) are imposed on policy offenders.
32. Luke Leung, "Author of 'Canaan Hymns' Xiao Min Gave Touching Testimony of Faith," *Gospel Herald*, December 15, 2008, http://www.gospelherald.com/article/ministries/44870/author-of-canaan-hymns-xiao-min-gave-touching-testimony-of-faith.htm.
33. Paul Hattaway, *Henan: The Galilee of China*, vol. 2 of Fire and Blood: The Story of the Church in China series (Carlisle, UK: Piquant Editions, 2009), 219.

Chapter 17: Wenzhou

34. Nicholas D. Kristof, "Christianity Is Booming in China Despite Rifts," *New York Times*, February 7, 1993, http://www.nytimes.com/1993/02/07/world/christianity-is-booming-in-china-despite-rifts.html.

Chapter 19: The Back to Jerusalem Vision

35. http://data.worldbank.org/indicator/SP.URB.TOTL.IN.ZS.
36. "China's Urban Population to Reach 70 Pct by 2030: World Bank," April 3, 2012, http://news.xinhuanet.com/english/china/2012-04/03/c_131505592.htm; http://www.citymayors.com/statistics/urban-population-intro.html#Anchor-Urbanisation-49575.
37. Faith McDonnell, "Jihad & Genocide," *Touchstone* journal, July/August 2004, http://www.touchstonemag.com/archives/article.php?id=17-06-076-r.
38. "Slave Liberation in Sudan," Christian Solidarity International, http://csi-usa.org/slave_liberation.html.
39. Ricco Villanueva Siasoco, "Modern Slavery: Human bondage in Africa, Asia, and the Dominican Republic," Infoplease.com, April 18, 2001, http://www.infoplease.com/spot/slavery1.html.